European Monographs in Social Psychology
The child's construction of economics

European Monographs in Social Psychology

Executive Editors:
J. RICHARD EISER and KLAUS R. SCHERER
Sponsored by the European Association of Experimental Social Psychology

This series, first published by Academic Press (who will continue to distribute the numbered volumes), appeared under the joint imprint of Cambridge University Press and the Maison des Sciences de l'Homme in 1985 as an amalgamation of the Academic Press series and the European Studies in Social Psychology, published by Cambridge and the Maison in collaboration with the Laboratoire Européen de Psychologie Sociale of the Maison.

The original aims of the two series still very much apply today: to provide a forum for the best European research in different fields of social psychology and to foster the interchange of ideas between different developments and different traditions. The Executive Editors also expect that it will have an important role to play as a European forum for international work.

Other titles in this series:

Unemployment by Peter Kelvin and Joanna E. Jarrett
National characteristics by Dean Peabody
Experiencing emotion by Klaus R. Scherer, Harald G. Wallbott and Angela B. Summerfield
Levels of explanation in social psychology by Willem Doise
Understanding attitudes to the European Community: a social-psychological study in four member states by Miles Hewstone
Arguing and thinking: a rhetorical approach to social psychology by Michael Billig

The child's construction of economics

Anna Emilia Berti and *Anna Silvia Bombi*

Dipartimento di Psicologia dello Suiluppo e della Socializzazione, Università di Padova

Translated from the Italian by Gerard Duveen
University of Sussex

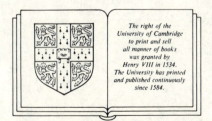

The right of the
University of Cambridge
to print and sell
all manner of books
was granted by
Henry VIII in 1534.
The University has printed
and published continuously
since 1584.

Cambridge University Press

Cambridge
New York   New Rochelle   Melbourne   Sydney

Editions de la Maison des Sciences de l'Homme

Paris

Published by the Press Syndicate of the University of Cambridge
The Pitt Building, Trumpington Street, Cambridge CB2 IRP
32 East 57th Street, New York, NY 10022, USA
10 Stamford Road, Oakleigh, Melbourne 3166, Australia
and Editions de la Maison des Sciences de l'Homme
54 Boulevard Raspail, 75270 Paris Cedex 06

Originally published in Italian as *Il Mondo Economico nel Bambino*
by La Nuova Italia 1981
and © La Nuova Italia Editrice, Florence
Revised edition first published in English by Editions de la Maison
des Sciences de l'Homme and Cambridge University Press 1988 as
The child's construction of economics
English translation © Maison des Sciences de l'Homme and
Cambridge University Press 1988

Printed in Great Britain at the University Press, Cambridge

British Library cataloguing in publication data

Berti, Anna Emilia
The child's construction of economics –
(European monographs in social psychology).
1. Perception in children   2. Economics
I. Title   II. Bombi, Anna Silvia   III. Il
Mondo economico nel bambino. *English*
IV. Series
155.4′13   BF723.E2

Library of Congress cataloguing in publication data

Berti, Anna Emilia, 1950–
The child's construction of economics.
(European monographs in social psychology).
Translation of: Il mondo economico nel bambino.
Bibliography.
Includes index.
1. Saving and thrift.   2. Children – Finance, Personal.
3. Child rearing – Italy.   4. Economics – Study and
teaching (Elementary) – Italy.   I. Bombi, Anna Silvia,
1946– .   II. Title.   III. Series.
HQ784.S4B4813   1988   649′.1   87-25593

ISBN 0 521 33299 0
ISBN 2 7351 0231 9 (France only)

Contents

Translator's foreword   page vii

Preface   ix

Acknowledgements   xii

1 Introduction   1

  1.1 Perspectives on the relations between children and economics   1
  1.2 Reasons for the paucity of research on children's economic
  ideas   3
  1.3 The relevance of studying children's economic conceptions   5
  1.4 The development of ideas about exchanges   7
  1.5 The development of ideas about social stratification   11
  1.6 Piaget's theory as a reference point   14
  1.7 Other theories   18
  1.8 Common trends in the various approaches to economic
  cognition   23
  1.9 The theoretical and methodological background to our research   24

2 Work   28

  2.1 Payment for work   28
  2.2 Access to various work roles   40
  2.3 Genesis of the idea of 'the boss'   54

3 Where does money come from?   59

  3.1 The source of money   59
  3.2 Notions of 'rich' and 'poor'   67
  3.3 The bank   78

4 Money and goods   88

  4.1 The source of goods   88
    4.1.1. The production and distribution of goods   90
    4.1.2. The source of raw materials   94
  4.2 The value and use of money in buying and selling   97

4.3 Differences in price between goods   108
4.4 The formation of prices   114

5 Means of production and their ownership   130

5.1 Previous research about ownership   131
5.2 Previous research about political conceptions   134
5.3 Research outline   138
5.4 The factory and its products: who owns them, and how one
becomes an owner   139
5.5 What use is the factory to the owner?   145
5.6 The ownership and use of farmland   151
5.7 Who owns the bus?   158
5.8 What use is the bus?   164
5.9 The development of the idea of ownership   169

6 Children's conceptions of economics: a developmental
synthesis   174

6.1 Conceptions of the preoperatory period (3–6 years)   175
6.2 Conceptions of the intuitive level (6–7 years)   177
6.3 Conceptions of the concrete operatory period (7–10 years)   179
6.4 Conceptions of the formal operatory period (11–14 years)   183

7 Cultural, social and educational influences on the
development of children's economic conceptions   186

7.1 Cross-cultural validity of developmental sequences of economic
concepts   186
7.2 The source of money according to the children of workers and
merchants   189
7.3 The source of goods according to children able to observe an
entire production cycle   193
7.4 The effect of different environments on children's economic
concepts   195
7.5 Educational research on the acquisition of economic concepts   197
7.6 Developmental transitions in the construction of economic
understanding   207
7.7 Necessary prerequisites for acquiring the notion of profit   208
7.8 Epilogue   215

References   218
Index   224

Translator's foreword

All translations present their own peculiar problems; the particular difficulty of this book was that of finding an adequate way of rendering children's speech. The authors have given many illustrations drawn from their conversations with children which formed the medium for their empirical research. These conversations are always quoted in order to illustrate some feature of the authors' analysis; their primary purpose is never simply that of entertainment. As this is a work of developmental psychology rather than fiction, I have always tried to render the *sense* of the children's ideas, rather than searching for an equivalent 'childish' form in English. It is the ideas which children express rather than the particular linguistic forms employed which are most pertinent to the authors' analyses. If the children do not always speak like English children, I hope that they nevertheless express the ideas expressed in their original conversations. Occasionally I have added footnotes to indicate where children's responses have drawn on peculiarities of Italian. All of these conversations took place in Italy, and often refer to people and institutions which may be unfamiliar to English-speaking readers. Where necessary I have added explanatory footnotes.

The interest shown in this translation by both of the authors, and by James Dashow, has been a great help in its preparation. Their hospitality in Padova and Rome certainly helped to make the task a pleasurable one, and their attentive reading of drafts has clarified many an obscurity. I am most grateful to all of them.

Gerard Duveen

Preface

Recently one of us witnessed a curious little scene while waiting to pay at a self-service restaurant. A child of about 6 years bought himself a piece of pizza and, after paying with a 5,000 Lire note, was preparing to leave when the cashier stopped him and offered him some 1,000 Lire notes. Taking the money the child examined the notes for a moment with a slight amazement before turning to leave again, but the cashier called him back. 'Wait a moment, there's also these!', and gave him a handful of change. The child opened his eyes wide and stretched out his hand; he looked at the cashier, at the money, at his mother who stood nearby, and then again at the money. After a few seconds of immobility, the child finally hurried away, as though he feared that the cashier, having changed his mind, might take back this unexpected treasure.

This young protagonist clearly believed himself to have enjoyed a singular good fortune. A similar stroke of luck nearly happened to the other of us while buying a newspaper. After paying for it with a 500 Lire coin, she saw the son of the paper seller, a child of about 4, hold out a 1,000 Lire note. The paper seller, however, hastened to retrieve such generous 'change' from his son's hand!

Without saying a word, with a look in one case, a gesture in the other, these children made it clear to us that they had ideas about the use of money, and ideas quite different from those of adults. The first child seemed convinced that he had had an unusual stroke of luck, receiving in change for a single banknote the piece of pizza and so much other money, some in paper notes and some in metal coins. The second one appeared to have drawn his own very personal conclusions from observing the activity of his father and seeing him giving change to customers.

It is not unusual for the unexpected actions of children to call the attention of adults to a mode of thought different from their own. Such episodes are not sufficient, however, to illuminate the child's thought entirely; indeed they do not reveal the ideas underlying such actions, nor the level of understanding which accompanies them. With words children offer us another means of access to their thinking, different yet complementary to that offered by their actions. Their questions and assertions indicate which of the events of everyday life claim their attention, which events pose questions for them and which are finally incorporated into their beliefs. Talking with children it is not difficult to hear them expressing their ideas about issues such as work, buying and selling, wages and profits, or other aspects of economic life accessible to them. One of our friends, for example, recorded the following conversation with her own 5-year-old child:

Mummy, who are thieves? – People who steal. – *Why do they steal?* – Because they don't have any money. – *But if they don't have any money, why don't they go to the bank and get some?*

The implicit assumption of the child's question is clear: anyone can restock themselves with money in a bank, and that there is something surprising about some people having recourse to complicated and dangerous methods.

These anecdotes describe nothing unusual. We think, rather, that every adult in contact with children has occasion to collect some examples of children's thinking about economic questions. The observation of children with whom there is direct contact is not, however, sufficient to give us a complete picture of their thought, much less to explain its origins. Episodes such as those described above suggest simply that children do ask themselves questions related to the economic sphere and that the views they form about it are only partly revealed by their discourse and their actions.

The results of our investigations of such thinking form the central part of this book. It is, in fact, a revised version of a book published in Italy in 1981 which presented the results of our own research undertaken between 1977 and 1980. When we began work on this topic there were very few other studies to which we could refer. Today the situation has changed. At about the same time we began our project researchers in various other parts of the world also began to investigate children's economic conceptions. Research has continued to grow and diversify over the past few years. We too have continued to develop our work, trying to analyse the processes which mediate the transition from a primitive to a more sophisticated and correct understanding.

Today, then, there is a much broader range of material to consider, even if the quantity does not match that of research on the development of physical concepts, or logico-mathematical ability, or, within the social field, children's understanding of the psychological characteristics of other persons, interpersonal relations such as friendship or authority, or of moral rules.

The advances which have been made since the publication of the original version of our book have made a thorough reworking of the text necessary in order to take account of more recent research. At first sight this task did not seem easy. How could we connect our research with a body of work which did not exist at the time ours had been undertaken? Fortunately, a notable congruence emerged between our own work and that of other researchers which allowed us to treat all of this material in a coherent way. We decided, therefore, to describe in an introductory chapter a general panorama of the different approaches which have been used to study children's economic conceptions, approaches which have not changed greatly over the past few years. In Chapters 2–5 we present the research through which we have tried to describe the development of children's understanding of diverse aspects of economic reality. These chapters include detailed considerations of the data from other studies which, before or after ours, have examined similar or, in some cases, identical problems. Following, in Chapter 6, we present a synthesis of the developmental lines emerging from these various studies. Finally, in Chapter 7, we have tried to throw some light on the effect which the environment exerts on children's representations of the economic world.

Acknowledgements

The writing of this book, and the diffusion of these results, has been made possible by the assistance of various people. First of all we should like to thank the children who consented to talk to us during the interviews, and the teachers who allowed us to interrupt their school routines. Many of our students also helped us to collect these data, and their names are recorded in the various chapters. Luciano Bettella, a representative for *La Nuova Italia*, was the first to suggest our work to this respected Italian publishing house. Professor Egle Becchi was an attentive and helpful referee. Professor Guido Peter, the then Director of the Institute of Developmental Psychology in which we work, read the original typescript and made many helpful suggestions as well as encouraging us.

The first English-speaking researchers to take an interest in our research were Professor Gustav Jahoda and Maureen Shields. We are particularly indebted to Mrs Shields not only for suggesting an English edition of the book, but also for putting us in contact with Gerard Duveen, who has been a very special translator for us. He combines a deep understanding of the themes of this book with a wide knowledge of the Italian language and its meanderings.

The text which is now appearing in English is a revised and expanded version of the original Italian. We are grateful to Paul Webley and, once again, to Gerard Duveen for their generous help in locating bibliographic material.

Finally, a special acknowledgement to James Dashow, whose status as the spouse of one of us and as an *italiano d'adozione* provided a bridge between us and our translator, helping us to explicate the sense of colloquial and dialectical expressions sometimes used by the children.

1   Introduction

1.1   Perspectives on the relations between children and economics

The relations between children and the world of economics can be considered from two points of view: that of the economically significant actions in which children engage, and that of the understanding which they develop. In our industrialised societies children have a somewhat limited role as economic actors. Child labour is forbidden by law so that children are only marginally active as producers, though there are instances where children do work. They may work illegally in the 'black' economy, for example (see for instance the work of Petrillo and Serino, 1985, on the children of Naples), or in the context of the home or some small, part-time job. At another level the academic work which constitutes the principal 'serious' activity at this age is, in part at least, aimed at preparation for a future working role; so that in the field of occupational guidance there is some interest in the behavioural and cognitive requirements for occupational choice (see Goldstein and Oldham, 1979). More substantial is the role of children as consumers; although they themselves buy only a small fraction of the goods they consume children may exercise a significant influence on their parents' choices, both by their very presence and through specific requests. This explains the existence of a great deal of literature on children and advertising compared to the few studies on working children, inside or outside the home, or on the availability of money and the way in which children spend or save it. Besides market-research studies there is also research inspired by concerns about the possible harmful effects of television on children and, in particular, the effects of advertising which may create conflicts with parents and encourage the development of an overly materialistic attitude toward life. These types of studies have examined the amount of money received by children of different ages and social classes, and the extent to which they save or spend it; how children's choices are influenced by advertising; how children themselves manage to influence their parents' own consumer choices. A brief synthesis of this research is given in reviews by Stacey (1985) and Lea, Tarpy and Webley (1987; see also Ward, Wackman and Wartella, 1977).

It is possible, however, to consider the relations between children and economics from a different point of view. Rather than focusing on the child as

1

economic subject, it is possible to examine the processes through which the child develops the ideas and attitudes regarding economic questions commonly found among adults. This perspective intersects somewhat with the research cited above, but in large measure also goes beyond it. The principal questions which have arisen from this point of view concern, on the one hand, the development of conceptions about the network of exchanges which constitute the economic structure of society and, on the other, how children of various ages understand social stratifications determined by income. As we shall see in the following sections, studies of children's economic understanding have been rather scarce, particularly when compared with the quantity of research concerning other aspects of social development.

It is not easy to explain this lack of research interest. As regards the study of children's *economic behaviour*, Lea, Tarpy and Webley (1987) point out that until recently economic psychology has been subordinated to economics and that, consequently, it has construed its object of study in terms of subjects able to make economic choices. As we have already observed, in our society the economic activities of children, whether in the guise of consumers, savers or producers, are of negligible importance when compared to those of adults, with the result that they have received very little attention in studies of economic psychology.

One explanation for the scarcity of studies of *economic understanding* within the field of social sciences has been suggested by two neo-Marxist researchers, Scott Cummings and Del Taebel (1978). These authors assert that in American society there is a widespread conviction that economic activity is a consequence of the action of laws analogous to laws of nature, having an autonomous existence independent of individual beliefs or comprehension. It is this conviction, with its assimilation of economic laws to natural laws, which underlies the lack of interest in the development of beliefs and attitudes about economics, since these beliefs and attitudes are thought to be the product simply of observations about the way in which reality functions. Such beliefs and attitudes would, in any event, be of little consequence in explicating economic dynamics. For these Marxist-oriented researchers, however, the idea that economic laws are similar to natural laws is itself an effect of the intellectual dominance exercised by the class holding economic power which has every reason for presenting capitalist relations of production as a natural fact. From a Marxist point of view, therefore, studying the acquisition of economic ideas and attitudes takes on a fundamental importance since it affords the analysis of the process through which the ideas of the dominant class become also the dominant ideas. Cummings and Taebel (1978) describe this process as a form of economic socialisation which progressively inculcates in the minds of children ideas and value orientations favourable to the capitalist system. To verify this hypothesis the authors asked a sample of

American children aged 8–17 years to explain what communism and social-ism might be, and to express their agreement or disagreement with a series of institutions such as trade unions or private property, and policies such as state intervention in the economy. As anticipated, the results showed that with age children's orientation became increasingly more favourable to capitalist values:

> The data suggest the progressive development, in individual
> consciousness, of political ideals endorsing and legitimating some
> of the more important features of capitalistic economic thinking:
> private ownership of the means of production, individual striving
> and meritocratic explanation of inequality, and limited state
> intrusion into business affairs. Conversely, children appear to
> develop explicitly anti-collective, anti-union and anti-socialist
> sentiments. (Cummings and Taebel, 1978, p. 209)

The reasons given by Cummings and Taebel do not seem to be entirely sufficient to explain the scarce attention of psychologists to the development of economic conceptions in children, especially given the resurgence of interest over the past 15 years among students of cognitive development in the analysis of social cognition (see, for example, Flavell and Ross, 1981; Pryor and Day, 1985; Shantz, 1983). Psychologists as much as other social scientists may be ruled by the 'dominant ideas' which form the basis for consent to the capitalist system. There must also, then, have been other reasons why so little attention was given to children's economic ideas, reasons which are more intrinsic to the history of psychology.

1.2   Reasons for the paucity of research on children's economic ideas

In order to understand clearly the reasons why so little attention has been devoted to children's economic ideas it is necessary to cast a brief glance at developmental research on social cognition. Two approaches have tradition-ally been contrasted in the study of socialisation processes (Turiel, 1983). One view, widely held in sociology though also found in some psychological currents, including some influenced by psychoanalytic and behaviourist views, considers socialisation as a process of moulding in which the environ-ment has the function of providing models for individual conduct. Accounts influenced by psychoanalytic or behaviourist views rely on different mechan-isms and mediating processes to explain how this happens. A common and characteristic theme of these perspectives, however, is their lack of interest in the contribution of processes of rational judgement. The other approach construes social development as the fruit of an interaction with the environ-ment in which individuals have a truly active role because of their ability to analyse and evaluate the data at their disposal, whether these are the behaviour of other people, conversation or rules.

> In coming to understand social systems, people act like social scientists, attempting to observe regularities and explain their existence. Correspondingly, individuals attempt to understand and critically evaluate the sources, functions and justifications for the rules they are expected to obey. In other words, social life is not detached from thought processes. (Turiel, 1983, p. 4)

As Turiel observes, in the past 50 years the cognitive approach to social development has benefited from an ample series of supporters, from the Gestalt school (Asch, 1952; Heider, 1958; Lewin, 1935) to the Soviet school (Vygotsky, 1934/1986), from George Herbert Mead (1934) to Heinz Werner (1948) and, above all, Jean Piaget (1932). Until the 1960s, however, it was the behaviourist paradigm, in its various forms, which dominated the field. In that perspective the focus of attention for research lay primarily in analysing the circumstances in which children acquired various types of social behaviour, and the influences through which these behaviours were learned, rather than the way in which the child understood the social world. Only in the mid 1960s, with the decline of behaviourism, was there a flowering of research on the development of social cognition as the approach which Kohlberg (1969) labelled *cognitive-developmental* came to dominate developmental research.

Studies in this field, however, have shown a marked preference for some themes to the detriment of others. One major area of research emerged from Kohlberg's (1963, 1969) rereading of Piaget's (1932) account of the development of moral judgement and his own substantial contributions to this theme (cf. Lickona, 1976; Damon, 1977; Rest, 1983). A second group of studies consists of a series of works on interpersonal perception (e.g. Livesley and Bromley, 1973; Shantz 1975, 1983); some of these studies take up Heider's (1958) theory of 'naive psychology', others focus on the notion of 'role-taking' (Mead, 1934) or, alternatively, the Piagetian concepts of 'egocentrism' and 'decentration'. Recently interest has shifted from children's conceptions of other people as individuals towards their understanding of such relations between people as friendship or the power dynamics of group relations (Shantz, 1983). Such studies remain focused on children's conceptions of face-to-face relationships. However, there are still fewer studies of the 'impersonal' aspects of society (not only economic, but also political and juridical etc.). An examination of recent reviews of the development of social cognition leaves the impression that the child's social world does not extend beyond the family, friends and school (Emiliani and Carugati, 1985; Overton, 1983; Pryor and Day, 1985; Shantz, 1983).

One reason for this concentration of research on face-to-face relationships is that 'macro-social' events (economic, political, etc.) enter in only a sporadic and fragmentary way the range of social reality which it is possible for children to experience directly. Indeed, the greater part of the information available to children about work, the means of production, or buying and selling comes through adults' conversations or the mass media. One of the characteristics of the 'cognitive-developmental' approach to socialisation is precisely a focus on direct experience. Indeed in this perspective cognitive structures are elaborated through the interactions between individual and environment, such interactions being effected through either material (exteriorised) or mental (interiorised) actions. Until the onset of formal thinking in adolescence the child's thinking remains strongly tied to material action, whether it pertains to things or relationships between people.

This assumption seems to have channelled the interests of cognitive-developmental theorists towards the study of ideas which refer to those aspects of reality with which the child is in direct contact, which lie within the grasp of the child's action. In other words, these theorists have given a privileged place to the study of what Piaget termed *real thought* as opposed to *verbal thought*, which is exercised in the solution of verbally formulated problems or in the formation of ideas derived from listening to verbal discourse rather than direct practical experience.[1] Piaget himself only considered verbal thought in his early work (1926, 1928, 1929), returning to this theme in only one brief study of some political ideas (Piaget and Weil, 1951). Some authors (e.g. Selman, 1980) have taken Piaget's point of view as implying that an ability to operate at a 'societal' level of analysis is a characteristic of formal thinking; the child's thinking may become gradually more decentred but, essentially, it is only concerned with interpersonal relations. From such a perspective it is simply premature to enquire about children's economic or political ideas.

1.3 The relevance of studying children's economic conceptions

A different perspective on social cognition has emerged with the theoretical work of Turiel (1983) who considers it necessary to identify distinct categories of social knowledge from early childhood.

> On the basis of the assumption that the individual's social world includes other persons, and institutionalised systems of social interaction, it is proposed that the child's structuring of the social

---

[1] Piaget has briefly described the reasons which led him to shift his interst from *verbal thought* to *real thought* in his preface to the third (French) edition of *Le Jugement et la Raisonnement chez l'enfant* (Neuchatel: Delachaux et Niestle, 1947). [Translator's note: A similar brief description in English may be found in Piaget's preface to *Causal Thinking in the Child* by M. Laurendeau and A. Pinard, New York: International Universities Press, 1962.]

> world revolves around three general categories. These are (1), concepts of persons or psychological systems (the psychological domain) (2), concepts of systems of social relations and organisations (the societal domain) (3), prescriptive judgements of justice, rights and welfare (the moral domain). (Turiel, 1983, p. 4)

The one aspect of the societal domain which Turiel examines is the genesis and development of ideas about social conventions, and he too considers as crucial those situations in which the child's participation in social life provides the opportunity for direct experience. Thus he points to children's interactions with their peers in nursery or school in which norms of various types are upheld or violated. He also considers information and instructions given verbally by adults as relevant social experience, though he stresses that children are not the passive recipients of such data but, rather, elaborate them according to their existing cognitive structures.

In our view, for a complete description of the development of social understanding it is necessary to consider with particular care just those experiences which are verbally mediated. If studies of verbal thought are insufficient for exploring the mind of the child, studies of real thought will not suffice either. In point of fact children do not live in a universe composed entirely of manipulable objects and 'brute facts' (Searle, 1969); they also inhabit a social world which extends beyond their immediate field of action. Through observation, conversations with adults and the mass media children receive information about the various institutions in which our society is articulated and about the diverse activities which they encompass. It may be that in making sense of all this children are not in a position to use the most advanced instruments of their intelligence, but this does not at all imply a need to eschew studying how they manage to cope with this task. On the contrary, it seems to us of great importance to study children's knowledge of areas distinct from those which they can apprehend through direct action. Some of the nodal aspects of society are to be found in precisely those sectors least accessible to the child's thought, yet which are, from a developmental point of view, intrinsically interesting. If one accepts that the task of psychology is not only to study those activities in which the highest levels of intelligence are expressed but also to sketch a more complete profile of mental development, then it becomes important to examine the development of children's thinking about less accessible areas of knowledge. Considerations of this kind have led a growing number of researchers to investigate children's ideas about society in general and economic relations in particular.

Most studies of the development of economic ideas have examined children of different ages with the aim of describing a developmental sequence. Research methods have included questionnaires (Strauss, 1952, 1954),

attitude scales (Furnham, 1982) or, more frequently, Piagetian-type interviews (Danziger, 1958; Furth, Baur and Smith, 1976; Connell, 1977; Furby,
1979; Jahoda, 1979; Leahy, 1981, 1983), sometimes linked to concrete tasks
such as seriation, classification, paired comparisons, etc. (Mookherjee and
Hogan, 1983; Duveen and Shields, 1984; Siegal, 1981; Emler and Dickinson,
1985).

A second and more recent group of studies has tried to test the cross-
cultural validity of developmental sequences (Hong Kwan and Stacey, 1982;
Jahoda and Woerdenbagch, 1982; Jahoda, 1983), as well as examining the
relations between economic concepts and other notions, both social and
nonsocial (Jahoda, 1984b; Wong, 1985) and clarifying the processes of
transition between one stage and another (Berti and Bombi, 1981; Berti,
Bombi and De Beni, 1986a, 1986b; Berti and De Beni, 1986; Echeita, 1985;
Ng, 1982; Wong 1985).

In this chapter we shall consider only the first group of studies, subdivided
into two groups: those which examine children's conceptions of the network
of relations determined by the exchange of goods, money and work, and those
which consider the problem of economic stratification. At the end of the book,
after having enriched the description of children's economic ideas with data
from our own research, we shall consider those studies concerned with
problems of cross-cultural validity and transitions between stages.

1.4 The development of ideas about exchanges

Our exposition begins with the research on the development and transformation of monetary meaning in the child which Anselm Strauss undertook in
the 1950s (Strauss, 1952, 1954). It is not only for reasons of historical
accuracy that we have chosen to begin with Strauss's work, though this
author was the first to investigate children's economic understanding, but
also because it provides a convenient point of departure. Strauss in fact
considered the problem from a very broad perspective and the results which
he obtained provide a framework within which to present the work of other
authors who have examined more specific aspects of children's economic
understanding, or who have not integrated their own results into such a
complete and coherent account.

Strauss considered the development of children's understanding of money,
of various economic roles (such as shopkeeper, customer, shop assistant,
factory owner) and of the network of exchanges through which these roles
are inter-related. These themes were explored in wide-ranging questionnaires
with American children aged 4:6–11:6 years.[2] Using scale analysis he

---

[2] Translator's note: Throughout the text ages are given in years and months, written with the
numbers separated by a colon.

grouped the responses into a sequence of nine stages preceded by a sub-stage. The sub-stage was identified from interviews with about 10 children aged 3–4:6 years, though they were not part of the formal investigation.

During the *sub-stage (3–4:6 years)* children distinguish between money and other objects but are unable to differentiate various types of coins, and they have only a very limited grasp of the fact that money is used in buying and selling. In fact they are not aware that one needs to pay for the things one wants from a shop, or they believe that one only needs to give pennies, ignoring the fact that other coins could serve the same purpose.

Stage 1 (4:8–5:11) children are still unable to distinguish and name every type of coin, but they understand that money has to do with buying. This does not, however, indicate that they understand the function of money in buying and selling. They are unable to give any other justification for the rule imposing payment except that one must do it. They believe that the shopkeeper also gives money to the customer and that every type of coin is equally suitable for the purchase of every kind of thing. The only relationships of which children form some kind of representation at this stage are, in fact, transactions between shopkeeper and customer. They still do not distinguish the shop assistant from the shop owner, and believe that to obtain the goods which they sell the shopkeeper goes to another shop which gives them the goods without asking for any money in exchange. Children at this stage do not yet understand that the shopkeeper may also be a customer.

Children at *stage 2 (6:0–6:8)* have a clearer understanding of money; they can distinguish and name the various denominations of coins and know which of them will purchase more sweets. They understand that there is a correspondence between money and objects, though they are convinced that each coin can only buy its exact equivalent. A nickel, for instance, can buy an object costing five pennies, but not something which costs any more or less. The conception of buying and selling at this stage remains very similar to that of stage 1. Children still do not understand why it is necessary to pay, and continue to believe that the shopkeeper always gives money to customers. On the other hand there is some progress regarding the way in which the shopkeeper obtains goods for sale; at this stage the idea appears that there is a manufacturer who the shopkeeper has to pay.

At *stage 3 (5:9–7:2)* children no longer say that one needs to pay for an object with the exact money; only if there is not sufficient money is an exchange impossible. At this stage, too, the role of the shop assistant is distinguished as someone who helps the shopkeeper and receives money. However, the essentials of employer-employee relations are still far from clear. Indeed, children are convinced that the shop assistant receives money directly from the customers, and when asked how the manufacturer spends the money he receives it is only his personal spending which children describe, rather than any payment for materials or employees.

In *stage 4* (*6:0–6:11*) there is a notable improvement in children's understanding of the function of money in buying and selling and payment for services. For the first time children recognise that shopkeepers need money because they also need to pay; some children even understand that manufacturers give money to employees.

Stage 5 (*6:9–8:9*) is marked by progress in the comprehension of the value of money. Children are now able to compare all coins and say correctly which are worth more and which are worth less. In addition more and more persons and acts are being drawn into the monetary net, since children now understand that manufacturers need to pay not only their employees but also for raw materials.

In *stage 6* (*7:5–8:9*) the conception of payment becomes more abstract with the first appearance of the idea of credit. However credit is only seen as a feature of the relationship between shopkeeper and customer, and not yet extended to include the manufacturer. Nevertheless the appearance of an idea of credit marks the first step in stripping concrete and temporal aspects from economic relationships and in understanding their logical and monetary aspect.

At *stage 7* (*6:8–10:6*) the role of shop owners becomes more abstract; shopkeepers are no longer seen only as figures working alongside their employees, they may also control the shop without being physically present, or even delegate to others the task of management. In this way there is also a broadening in children's comprehension of the ways in which people obtain money. Not only is money available through selling goods or working but also through the possession of goods; there is now an understanding that money begets money.

In *stage 8* (*8:4–11:0*) children understand for the first time that shopkeepers realise a profit by selling goods at a higher price than they bought them. This increase in price is also considered to be justified by the service which shopkeepers perform for their clients. At earlier stages children could not consider such a possibility, or if they did it was opposed on moral grounds, with such an increase in price considered to be either theft or fraud.

Finally at *stage 9* (*8:4–11:0*) children are aware that shopkeepers may sometimes cheat, showing that they also recognise the possibility of conflicts between individual interests and the welfare of the community.

One observation needs to be added to this sequence. In none of the stages described by Strauss is there any mention of an intermediate figure between the shopkeeper and the manufacturer; on the contrary even at stage 9 children deny both the existence and utility of any such role. In this sense the network of commercial relationships constructed by children through the sequence described by Strauss appears rather limited.

The developmental sequence through which children construct relations between economic roles and exchanges has been investigated by other researchers who have used interviews on specific issues considered to be emblematic in some way. Rachel Sutton (1962) studied how children aged 6–12 years understand savings and banks. Gustav Jahoda examined the notion of buying and selling among 6–12-year-old children (Jahoda, 1979), and ideas about the bank among 11–16 year olds (Jahoda, 1981). Other authors have undertaken more wide-ranging research, interviewing the same group of children about issues of economic relations or about a variety of aspects of the adult world. Danziger (1958) examined ideas about the shop, the boss, wealth and poverty in children aged 5–8 years. Hans Furth and his collaborators studied 5–11-year-old children's conceptions of the 'world of grown-ups', including buying and selling, the bank, the acquisition of certain social roles, and those things and people important to the life of a town (Furth, Baur and Smith, 1976; Furth, 1979, 1980). Val Burris (1983) interviewed 4–12 year olds about notions of commodity, value, buying and selling, stealing, work and income. David Leiser (1983) presented children with questions about the formation of prices, payment for work, the bank and inflation.

In some cases these authors did not know of Strauss's work, though they obtained the same type of responses about buying and selling as he had. For some notions, such as that of the boss, they found the same conceptions as those described by Strauss, but via a different route.

The more primitive conceptions about retail buying and selling first described by Strauss have also been found in children younger than 7–8 years by Danziger (1958), Furth (1976, 1980), Jahoda (1979) and Burris (1983). These studies have also confirmed that up till 10 or 11 years children do not understand that shopkeepers make money only if they charge higher prices than those they pay.

The late appearance of the idea of work as paid employment, which Strauss found by asking children about the relations between shopkeepers and their assistants, has been confirmed on other grounds. Danziger (1958) was the first to investigate this theme directly, interviewing 5–8-year-old children about the functions of the boss and how people come to take on such a role. He found that younger children construed the boss as a kind of helper or advisor for the workers. Progressively, towards 7 years, they began to see the boss as an economic figure who took on the role by inheriting or buying a factory and had the function of paying the workers, the money for such payments coming from the bank or the government or previous savings. The older children, though, said that the boss paid the workers with money received from the sale of the factory's products.

One theme which Strauss did not examine was that of the bank. From the work of other authors, however, it seems that children frequently speak spontaneously about it, describing it as a distributor of money to which not only the boss could turn, but also shopkeepers who had difficulty in balancing their books when selling goods without raising prices (Furth, 1980; Jahoda, 1979). Sutton (1962) noted that children think that people deposit money in a bank so as not to lose it, or to ensure that it is not stolen from them, or so as to receive interest on it. Many different ideas emerged about what happens to the money once it has been deposited, ranging from the most fantastic (Father Christmas took it) to the erroneous, though less absurd (that is was locked in bags with the owner's name on it). After this somewhat superficial study the theme of the bank has been more thoroughly investigated in recent work by Gustav Jahoda (1981) who examined 11–16 year-old children's understanding of interest and of the way in which banks make profits. The levels which he describes go from a complete ignorance of the existence of interest, typical of 11 year olds, to a comprehension, present in a few 13–16 years olds, that the bank makes a profit by charging higher interest on loans than it pays on deposits. These data, confirmed in a later study by Leiser (1983), show how difficult it is to understand the idea of profit. Children first encounter this difficulty when they try to explain how the shopkeeper makes money, and again when they begin to think about economic transactions which take place beyond the field of their immediate experience, such as those which take place in the bank.

1.5 The development of ideas about social stratification

A second area of research on economic concepts consists of those studies concerned with the problem of economic inequalities. In this field too, apart from a few early studies (Stendler, 1949; Jahoda, 1959), it was only from 1970 on that psychologists took a more consistent interest in these issues.

One theme examined in various studies (Baldus and Tribe, 1978; Jahoda, 1959; Stendler, 1949) is children's ability to determine social class on the basis of a person's visible attributes. A recent study by Harsha Mookherjee and H. Wayne Hogan (1981) illustrates the research technique. They showed 5–17-year-old subjects a set of drawings depicting 3 men, 3 women, 3 boys and 3 girls dressed so as to suggest that they belonged to different social categories: the poor, the middle-class and the wealthy. Subjects were asked to group these figures into three families of different social classes. They were then asked to select the appropriate car and house for each family, again from a set of 3. Subjects were then asked if the wealthy 'father' or the poor one had the greater education. They were also asked whether the wealthy child would prefer to play with the middle-class or poor child. Only the 5-year-old children made chance choices in constructing families and saying which parent had a better education. However, even at this age children assigned the wealthy child a middle-class playmate rather than a poor one. Between 6 and 10 years there was an increase in children's ability to group the figures and make choices which took account of the social class. From 10 years on there were no errors on these tasks.

Other researchers have investigated the discrimination between social classes by asking children to seriate various work activities on the basis of income as perceived from drawings, photographs or in verbal descriptions (Duveen and Shields, 1984; Dickinson, 1984; Emler and Dickinson, 1985; Siegal 1981; Goldstein and Oldham, 1979).

Using paired comparisons of photographs of people at work Gerard Duveen and Maureen Shields (1984) have shown that even by 3:6 children recognise that not every activity receives the same payment, even if they mistakenly assign the highest income to the police rather than doctors or shopkeepers. Michael Siegal (1981), too, in a study of 6–13 year olds, has shown that although younger children are able to differentiate some jobs by pay (such as doctor, shopkeeper, driver, waiter) they are not able to order them correctly. Correct seriation appears only around 8 years, a result confirmed in analogous data reported by Nicholas Emler and Julie Dickinson (1985).

It is possible to integrate these data on the recognition of differences with research in which other authors asked children to describe wealth and poverty (Leahy, 1981; Connell, 1977; Danziger, 1958). Only Danziger (1958) reports finding subjects who had no idea of what 'rich' and 'poor' meant, though he did not specify how frequent this kind of response was, or whether it was typical of a particular age group. Leahy and Connell, on the other hand, both found a precocious recognition of differences, even if expressed in more generic and superficial terms than those typical of later ages. Robert Leahy (1981) asked children of four ages (6, 11, 14 and 17 years) to describe rich people and poor people, how they are similar and how they are different. The responses were classified on the basis of the type of characteristics used to represent the rich and the poor, and on the basis of the use of general conceptions about social classes. The analysis showed that, with age, descriptions based on 'peripheral' characteristics (that is referring to external characteristics of people, cf. Livesley and Bromley, 1973) were replaced by descriptions containing 'central' aspects (that is referring to psychological characteristics of people), and by 'sociocentric' characteristics (Selman, 1976) including the differences in life-chances for rich and poor, people's political orientation and their personal prestige. Children younger than 11 found it easier to say how the rich and poor differed, rather than the ways in which they were alike. Robert Connell, a neo-Marxist sociologist, has also shown that the younger children (5–8 years) interviewed in his study of the Australian 'ruling class' construed wealth and poverty in terms of a 'dramatic contrast'. 'The people who are rich, well they can buy everything but the people who are poor, well, they can't buy anything'. Other children described the poor as 'nearly dead broke', or as people who 'sleep in the cold' (Connell, 1977, pp. 136–7). However the condition of being rich or poor was represented as a transitory state depending on the 'availability of money'. What characterised the following level (8–12 years, described by Connell as the 'stage of concrete realism') was the overcoming of this dichotomy with the emergence of an intermediate group between rich and poor, and the connection between well-being and position in the occupational scale. Finally, Connell found, as other authors have also reported, that the oldest subjects (12–16 years) were able to use more precise and detailed politico-economic concepts (the 'stage of true class schemes').

Even if this type of information is useful in showing that young children are aware of economic differences, it has nothing to say about the way in which children explain and justify these differences. This aspect, central to the analysis of children's economic thinking, is examined in some of the studies already described as well as some others dedicated specifically to explanations and evaluations of retributive differences. Leahy (1983) has also presented data on the reasons and justifications given for wealth and poverty, on the possibility for individuals to improve their economic circumstances and, more generally, on the elimination of poverty. In this analysis, too, children's ideas changed with age. The explanations for these social phenomena given by the youngest subjects were concrete and personalised: the rich are rich 'because they have money', to become rich you have to 'ask rich people to give money'. To solve the problem of poverty all you would have to do with the poor is to 'send them away' (Leahy, 1983, pp. 114–15). Adolescents, on the other hand, took into consideration not simply 'the elements making up the system' but also 'the factors that regulate the system' (Leahy, 1983, p. 121).

Both Burris (1983) and Danziger (1958) report similar results, at least as far as the earlier stages are concerned. The youngest children interviewed by Danziger (5–6 years) said that to become rich it was necessary to steal the money, or to mine gold, or to get it from God. Around 7 years the idea of getting money by working appeared, and that the more one worked the richer one would become. Finally among his eldest subjects (8 years) there were some who mentioned other ways of getting rich such as saving, inheriting money or selling goods or possessions. Siegal (1981) investigated the issue of economic differences by asking children to judge the adequacy of the remuneration received by four occupations. The youngest children (6–7 years) justified the differences solely in terms of factual criteria, while older children also spoke about the different abilities and strengths of each worker. In a study of personal possessions undertaken in Israel, Lita Furby (1979) also found that older children (11 years) tended to relate differences in wealth to differences in merit more frequently than did younger children (6 years).

1.6   Piaget's theory as a reference point

The majority of the studies of economic concepts described so far have been undertaken in the context of a cognitive-developmental framework. Generally they have referred explicitly to Piaget's theory, either accepting it as a valid paradigm for the investigation of social concepts in general and economic ones in particular, or, more rarely, questioning the possibility of applying the theory to this field.

Strauss (1952, 1954) refers to Piaget's theory of logical development to interpret changes in children's representations of various economic roles and their interconnections through an increasingly broad network of relations. Strauss argues that a capacity for classificatory operations is necessary to be able to differentiate roles. Distinguishing between shopkeepers, customers, shop assistants and manufacturers amounts to classifying individuals according to the activity they perform. Progressively children become able to define classes ever more precisely (including those corresponding to economic roles), gradually approaching the definitions given by adults. The activity of classification becomes ever more flexible; classes which were initially seen as being mutually exclusive come successively to be seen as being related in various ways. The development of role-taking allows every economic subject to be considered from the perspective of the others to whom they are connected, and for the organisation of these different perspectives in an increasingly abstract and generalised fashion.

Strauss, then, refers to Piaget in very general terms without trying to establish any precise correspondence between the developmental stages of intelligence described by Piaget and the stages through which children's understanding of economics progresses. Burris (1983), too, takes a similar approach and, commenting on her own research, emphasises the qualitative differences which allow distinctions to be drawn between the responses given by children of different ages. She also notes the presence of some general features of children's thinking similar to those described by Piaget. Both of these authors, therefore, draw the same general conclusion from their research: children progressively construct their own understanding of the economic world rather than being limited to the passive reception of information provided by adults.

For Furth and Jahoda, on the other hand, relations with Piaget's theory are more complex. A crucial issue concerns the attempt to describe the development of economic understanding in terms of the development of representational intelligence from the preoperatory stage to the stage of formal operations. The use of this sequence does not, in itself, carry any expectation that economic concepts or, more generally, conceptions of social institutions, will develop at the same rhythm as that found by Piaget in his studies of the development of physical concepts. In fact Furth and Jahoda have supported opposing arguments on this point.

According to the first thesis, proposed by Furth (Furth, Baur and Smith 1976), the understanding of social institutions presents a much greater difficulty than the understanding of physical objects; social institutions are not manipulable as are physical objects, being abstract entities which can only be grasped in all their complexity through thought. The fragmentary and predominantly verbal way in which children receive this kind of information makes the task of comprehending social institutions a difficult one. A disjunction is likely, therefore, between physical knowing and 'societal' knowing. One needs to wait until children reach the age of 11–12 years before being able to identify in 'societal' knowing ideas which have the coherence and systematic quality which Piaget describes for the stage of concrete operations.

The second point of view, proposed by Jahoda (1979), suggests that social institutions, particularly economic ones, constitute systems. The level of difficulty which they present to the child trying to comprehend them is not, therefore, any greater than that presented by the physical systems examined in some of Piaget's work (Inhelder and Piaget, 1958) and for this reason there should be a synchrony as well as a parallelism between the development of physical and economic notions.

Although holding widely divergent points of view Furth and Jahoda present very similar data; differences appear only in their interpretations of these data. From amongst all the data he collected for his research on the world of grown-ups Furth is most reliant on that concerning buying and selling, the only theme for which the children he interviewed gave clearly distinct responses which could be ordered in a sequence of stages. According to Furth it is only at about 11 years, when they understand that wholesale prices are lower than retail prices, that children present a coherent and logical societal knowledge. The conceptions of earlier stages, with their fantastic elements and only fragmentary and incoherent agreement with reality, may be closer to preoperational thinking.

Jahoda in his research on buying and selling (1979) reaches the opposite conclusion because he considers the shop as an institution constituted by two distinct systems, and he takes children's understanding of the existence of these systems as evidence of concrete operational thinking, even if children are not yet able to relate them in a single inclusive system. The first system, that of *profit*, is constituted by the relations between shopkeeper and customer; the second, *work*, is constituted by the relations between the shopkeeper and the shop assistants. Integrating the two systems enables the child to realise that shopkeepers pay their assistants with money received from sales. On this basis Jahoda identified three response levels in his subjects. At the first level (6–8 years) children have no idea about either of the systems implicated in buying and selling since they believe that the shopkeeper receives goods without paying for them, redistributing money obtained from customers when giving them change, and do not understand that it is the shopkeeper who pays the shop assistants. Some recognition of the existence of the two systems emerges at the next level (8–10 years) when children understand that the shopkeeper has to buy goods and also pay the shop assistants. The two systems remain unrelated, however, as children do not understand that shop assistants are paid with the money received from the sale of goods. Limited as it may be, such an understanding of the two systems allows Jahoda to compare this level with the stage of concrete operations. Connections between the two systems begin to emerge around 10 years when children assert that the shopkeeper pays the assistants with money received from sales, and children at this age also begin to recognise that the shopkeepers pay less for goods than the price for which they sell them. Jahoda considers such conceptions to be a manifestation of formal operational thinking, since the integration of the two systems into a single inclusive system depends on the child being able to relate propositions through hypothetico-deductive reasoning. As we noted above, Furth considers these same conceptions to be an indication of concrete operational thinking.

Both Furth and Jahoda have subsequently modified their positions. In their more recent publications each of them has considered which characteristics actually distinguish the 'societal' field from the interpersonal and the physical. In doing so they have focused on a different aspect of Piaget's theory; attention has now shifted from questions of stage and sequence to the issue of equilibration.

> Societal refers to the life of the community as an interrelated
> whole with its institutions, rules and customs, its services and
> products, its roles and symbols. This societal world 'out there' is
> experienced by adults as distinct from what may be called the
> personal life or the self in relation to other people. (Furth, 1980,
> p. 3)

According to Furth (1980) the distinction between societal and interpersonal domains is not given for children, but arises through a process of differentiation and is only finally realised in adolescence. Jahoda (1984a) has recently provided further clarification of the same issue. The point of departure for his reflections is that for the development of an understanding of social systems children need to acquire both general information, such as information about factories, for example, or the distinction between work and leisure, as well as information about the rules which govern relations within the socio-economic domain. The first type of information is easily accessible to children, through the conversations of adults and the mass media. On the other hand a characteristic of rules is that they tend to remain implicit, making it unlikely that children will hear them being discussed. They thus interpret information about economic systems in terms of the rules governing relations of which they have personal and direct experience through their family, school or peers. This is what happens, for instance, when children come to understand that everything has a price and believe that this price remains unchanged across the various commercial transactions regarding the object. The shopkeeper who, according to the child, sells something at the same price he paid for it is applying the principal of strict reciprocity which regulates relations among friends. Jahoda concludes that it is only by liberating themselves from the interference of interpersonal norms that children can understand how economic systems function. Since there is no comparable obstacle to understanding in the physical domain, it makes little sense to look for any parallelism in the operations through which children come to understand these two diverse domains (Jahoda, 1984a) or to label children's responses in terms of Piagetian 'stages' (Jahoda, 1984b). The most useful Piagetian concepts for this field of research appear to be conflict and equilibration.

Jahoda (1979, 1981) has tried several times to interpret the development of economic concepts in terms of conflict and equilibration. However it is Furth (1980) who has given the most general and systematic account of this interpretation, incorporating not only data about buying and selling but also from the heterogeneous complex of responses he obtained across all the themes of his study. He suggests the following sequence of stages:

Stage 1 (5–6 years): Personalistic elaborations and absence of interpretative system. Children do not have a systematic interpretive framework for the events which they observe, and therefore conflicts are hardly possible. They accept every new bit of information which comes their way without feeling any need to link it with what they already know. An example of this kind of attitude is the idea that the shopkeeper also has to give money to customers.

Stage 2 (7–9 years): Understanding of first-order societal functions. Children begin to understand some isolated economic relations of which they have direct experience, differentiating between apparently similar actions. They distinguish between various ways of 'giving money' such as giving money as a gift, giving money in payment or giving money as change. These distinctions enable children to understand the relations between shopkeeper and customer. They retain, however, a childish and playful image of all those economic relations of which they lack direct experience. As they also feel no necessity for logic or integration of these ideas they seldom experience any conflicts.

Stage 3 (10–11 years): Part-systems in conflict. The playful attitude gradually gives way to a search for logical coherence and systematisation. Children become able to infer relations which they have no means of observing; having understood that one must pay to acquire goods they reach the conclusion that shopkeepers must also buy the things they sell. In this way children construct systems of relations which, in the absence of a more general integrating framework, come into conflict with one another. Children at this level have two ways of resolving these conflicts – reluctant thinking and compromise solutions. The first of these procedures consists of avoiding the conflict by refusing to examine a problem thoroughly, while the second consists of shifting the grounds which cause the problem. An example of the first strategy is the answer given by a child who is convinced that books in libraries are paid for by fines for overdue books, and who, in reply to the interviewer's doubts, says that it must be like this since otherwise he couldn't understand how the libraries come to have all these books. An example of a compromise solution is the idea that a headmaster obtains the money for a school by working in another school.

Stage 4: A concrete-systematic framework. Only very few of the children interviewed by Furth had reached this stage which ought to be regarded as typical of preadolescence. It is characterised by correct solutions to conflicts between partial systems through the construction of a unified and integrating system. This is made possible by formal logical thinking. It is at this stage that children understand that the shop owner buys for less and sells for more, and appreciate differences in scale between personal and societal events.

Stage 5: Analytic-systematic understanding. A full understanding of political functions and a more abstract conception of economic relations belongs to a later stage typical of adolescents and adults.

1.7   Other theories

Danziger (1958) was the first to distance himself from Piaget. He criticised Piaget for having elaborated a general theory of the development of thought on the basis of research undertaken predominantly on the development of physical concepts. In this way, according to Danziger, physical concepts became the model for the whole of children's thinking without any alternative hypotheses being explicitly formulated or tested. It was precisely in order to test whether the development of social concepts followed the same development course as that described by Piaget for physical concepts that Danziger examined children's ideas about economic topics such as buying and selling, the boss, wealth and poverty. From responses to these questions, and extrapolating from them to suggest developments after the age of 8, Danziger outlined the following developmental sequence:

> (a) an initial pre-categorical stage occurs when the child lacks economic categories of thought altogether. There is no special realm of economic concepts differentiated from social concepts in general. (b) At the second, or categorical stage, the child becomes able to represent reality in terms of isolated acts which are explained by a moral or voluntaristic imperative. (c) At the third stage the child becomes able to conceptualise relationships as such, by virtue of the fact that reciprocity is established between previously isolated acts. But these relations are in their turn isolated and cannot be explained in terms of other relationships. (d) Finally, the isolated relationships become linked to each other so as to form a system of relations. We then have a conceptualisation of a totality wherein each part derives its significance from its position in the whole. At this point a purely rational explanation becomes possible. (Danziger, 1958, pp. 239–40)

Comparison with an earlier study of kinship relations (Danziger, 1957) in which children gave responses following a similar course, enabled Danziger to suggest tentatively that this sequence might generalise to the whole domain of social understanding.

Leiser (1983) has recently tried to abandon every reference to Piaget's theory altogether by using ideas from more recent cognitive theories, such as 'scripts' and 'metacognition', to reformulate the sequence proposed by Furth. According to Leiser the economic conceptions of the earliest level constitute scripts or 'scenarios', that is, 'cognitive structures which define the role of a participant in an extended interaction, and specify the actions that are to take place successively' (Leiser, 1983, p. 298). These scripts then develop into conceptions which make sense of the actions of the individual actors, although often in a distorted and one-sided way. In this way children reach a second level which corresponds, according to Leiser, to the second stage described by Furth. In a similar way Leiser also redefines the other two levels described by Furth, noting that it is progress in reasoning and meta-cognitive awareness which makes possible the discovery and elimination of contradictions, the characteristic of the fourth level. Leiser does, in fact, move away from Furth somewhat in his conception of the later stages in the development of economic ideas. He emphasises that the whole system characterising the fourth level is composed of vignettes which group together various roles in a series of transactions. At this level it is still impossible to understand the functioning of real economic systems which are constituted by the cumulative effects of multiple actions of various economic subjects and impersonal economic forces.

As with the other authors considered in Section 1.4, Leiser and Danziger only considered age as an independent variable, restricting themselves to a cognitive-developmental perspective. The understanding of socio-economic stratification, on the other hand, has seemed to many authors inseparably tied to children's own social class; consequently many of the studies described in Section 1.5 examined children who differed not only in age but also in social class. Indeed, the study of the idea of social differences has, for some authors, been prompted by a desire to escape from a narrowly defined developmental logic which remains insensitive to environmental influences on children's economic conceptions (Emler and Dickinson, 1985; Dickinson, 1984). Not every author, however, has found such differences, and those which have been reported have not always been easily interpretable as a coherent trend. Leahy (1981), for instance, reports data which seemed to him could be better understood in either a functionalist (Parsons, 1960) or Marxist (Marx, 1844/1966) sociological perspective. Supporting a functionalist view, for instance, was the increase among adolescents of fatalistic conceptions of the social order (the impossibility of eliminating poverty) and the tendency of subjects from the more advantaged social classes to assert satisfaction with their condition. On the other hand some of the differences which emerged between subjects from different social classes and ethnic groups could be construed as supporting a Marxist perspective. The tendency to justify wealth and poverty on the basis of a principle of equity (those who have more are better, more intelligent, work harder, etc.), for example, was predominant among middle-class subjects, and some of these subjects also believed in the immutability of social stratification. These findings suggest a tendency for the members of more advantaged classes to justify their own position of privilege in order to maintain it.

These data do not, however, agree with those reported by other authors such as Furnham (1982) or Goldstein and Oldham (1977). Adrian Furnham examined rich and poor 15-year-olds' agreements or disagreements with a series of statements about the causes of wealth and poverty. He observed a tendency for rich subjects to agree with individualistic explanations of the type, 'The poor don't try to improve their condition', while poor subjects were more likely to accept 'societal' explanations of the type, 'It is the industrialists who don't give enough work to the poor' or, 'There is prejudice and discrimination against the poor'; though no differences were found for fatalistic explanations such as, 'The poor are less talented'. Bernard Goldstein and Jack

Oldham (1977) did not find any differences in the ability of middle- or lower-class children to recognise that social differences exist, or the criteria used to differentiate rich and poor, or the ability to identify the better paid occupations. These authors also reported no differences in the explanations which children gave for these facts. The only difference which they did find was the tendency for lower-class children to explain inequalities in payment in terms of hours worked; but since this is a common explanation among young children the effect for social class appeared in this study as developmental retardation.

Emler and Dickinson (1985) and Dickinson (1984) have tried to reformulate the problem in terms of Moscovici's notion of 'social representations' (cf. Moscovici, 1976, 1984). These authors express a dissatisfaction with the cognitive-developmental approach as this perspective reduces social knowledge to an 'individual cognitive accomplishment and one to which specific social influences contribute nothing of substance' (Emler and Dickinson, 1985, p. 192). Following Moscovici they argue that knowledge is socially generated and sustained, created and disseminated through processes of social influence and interaction. In addition, these authors also argue that the most commonly used index of social class, parental occupation, does not provide a clear identification of the 'social world' in which children are immersed. In the absence of a more reliable index, results from this research can only be confusing. Social class, in fact, influences beliefs and judgements in so far as it contributes to determining environmental characteristics. For instance, children who come from different classes according to income or culture but who attend the same school may share the same social environment for a considerable part of their everyday life, so that clear differences in social representations should not be expected.

Emler and Dickinson, therefore, compared two groups of children who differed in both the socio-economic status and the residential locality of their families as well as in the types of school they attended. There were differences both in the payments which the two groups attributed to various occupations and professions (with middle-class subjects showing a clearer capacity for making distinctions), and in their reactions to a proposal to eliminate inequalities in payment (more strongly supported by lower-class subjects). As regards the effect of age, however, these authors found that the responses of older and younger children differed only in respect of a few questions (for instance in the reasons given to justify inequalities in income, or the connection between income and property). There were no differences in the estimates of income given by children of different ages.

Emler and Dickinson's attempt at theoretical redefinition has resulted in clearer identification of the groups to be compared and thus enabled them to record more clearly differentiated results than those reported by other researchers (e.g. Leahy, 1983). However, their own explanation of their results in terms of 'social representation' appears somewhat vague. Some of the differences found between children from different social classes (for example the tendency of lower-class children to support egalitarianism in payment for work) are also typical of younger children, so that again one could think of the effect for social class as a retarding influence on the development of such knowledge (as Goldstein and Oldham, 1979, also showed). On the other hand the absence of differences between age groups in their pay estimates could be a consequence of the age range considered (7–12 years) which did not produce any discrimination on this particular task. The authors themselves add a note of caution when they conclude that

> Cognitive-developmental principles can tell us something about the sequence in which children acquire knowledge but not everything about the particular knowledge they will acquire. This also depends on its currency and availability in their various social milieux. (Emler and Dickinson, 1985, p. 197)

This clarification would be almost superfluous from a correctly understood interactionist perspective, but the problem remains of identifying the processes through which children assimilate the information which is dominant, widespread and important within their community.

More convincing is the approach adopted by Robert Connell (1977), who examined the development of the understanding of class through clinical interviews with 5–16 year olds on the themes of wealth, poverty and their causes. To interpret the responses Connell used a Piagetian framework to order them in a developmental sequence. He construed the different types of response as the product of the interweaving of the various traditions of thought to be found in Australia, and the child's cognitive level which, at different times, made them more receptive to one or another cultural idea. Thus, for example, the conceptions of 5–8-year-old children which, as we have seen, Connell characterises by their dramatic contrast between wealth and poverty, and the idea that the poor should be helped, reflect both the limited cognitive ability of the preoperatory period as well as echoing fables and the Christian charitable tradition. Adolescents, on the other hand, describe a more articulated image of social stratification and one which is closer to reality. The explanations and evaluations which they give for this image reflect more complex traditions of thought to which they have differential access according to their social origins. While the children of working-class parents articulate ideas originating in the labour movement, the majority of other children assert that there are no dramatic differences in the economic conditions of the Australian population, reflecting a tradition of thought which construes Australia as 'classless'. Connell (1971) has also demonstrated a similar interweaving between intellectual development and traditions of thought in the emergence of ideas about the functioning of political institutions.

1.8   Common trends in the various approaches to economic cognition

The theories considered in Section 1.6, and some of those considered in Section 1.7, share some basic assumptions notwithstanding the variety of expressions used to distinguish the different developmental levels in children's economic understanding, and the various ways in which these authors regard Piagetian theory. Firstly, all of these authors assert that children's understanding becomes more complex from a structural point of view. Conceptions of exchanges, for instance, develop from a level in which no economic relations can be identified to one in which relations are integrated in a single framework of exchanges, with intermediate levels in which only partial and isolated systems of relations are constructed. The understanding of social stratification also undergoes a development toward more complex structures. At the earliest level only the most striking characteristics for distinguishing rich and poor are identified, while older children reach a level in which social classes are construed in abstract and general terms, with intermediate levels in which only some elements are defined (for instance, the existence of a middle class).

Secondly, all the authors who refer to Piaget do so in substantially the same way. They are interested in asking whether societal knowledge or economic knowledge develops according to the rhythms and modality of the general stages of intellectual development described by Piaget, particularly as these relate to 'physical knowledge'. Even when other concepts such as equilibration take precedence over Piaget's stage theory the latter is necessarily assumed as an explanatory basis. How else could the child, as described in Furth's (1980) third and fourth stages, become sensitive to contradiction and feel a need for logical coherence? What allows children to make intelligent inferences? In fact all of these authors have related the child's economic knowledge to the development of operations and cognitive abilities analogous to those proposed by Piaget; or they have limited themselves to saying that Piaget's theory does not explain everything, without proposing any convincing alternative.

Thus we can see that the majority of those authors who have studied the development of economic concepts adopted a Piagetian approach; authors who wished to formulate a different theory (e.g. Danziger and Leiser) proposed concepts which are in fact Piagetian; while others such as Emler and Dickinson admit that a cognitive-developmental approach is necessary to explain at least some, if not all, aspects of children's understanding of economic reality. These variations reflect, in fact, a state of affairs which is typical of the whole field of research on children's social cognition. The structural approach initiated by Piaget has, over the past few years, proved to be the most successful means of characterising the understanding of children at different ages, and in permitting an explanation for the parallelisms between different cognitive areas, such as the social and the physical, or the linguistic and the non-linguistic. The reasons for this success are succinctly described by Robbie Case:

> One of the strengths of Piaget's theory was that it offered a method and a conceptual framework for distinguishing children's cognition across broad periods of time. Moreover, it did so, in effect, by postulating that there was a natural grain to human cognition, that is, children at different stages of life operated at different epistemic levels, and that their approaches to tasks had to be analysed in light of this fact. That some sort of structural analysis might be necessary in order to introduce order into the newly emerging data bases, therefore, was not really surprising. In effect, structural analysis was best suited for describing the forest of cognitive development, while process analysis was suited for describing the trees. (Case, 1985, p. 55)

Lastly, another characteristic shared by these writers on children's economic conceptions is the failure to distinguish different types of economic thinking; though dealing with only some notions, they have nevertheless claimed, implicitly or explicitly, to be concerned with economic or societal thinking *tout court*. This is one point at which these authors stand at some distance from Piaget and others who have studied physical notions.

Piaget in fact never claimed to have explored the problem of physical cognition through a single study, seeking instead to identify the operations underlying such diverse notions as velocity, time, distance (Piaget, 1969, 1970), or causality (Piaget, 1930). He later even introduced distinctions between notions of the same type, such as the conservations of substance, of weight and of volume (Piaget and Inhelder, 1974). More recently other researchers interested in physical problems have also tried to identify distinct sequences, only later drawing out indications of developmental processes of a more general character (Case, 1985; Siegler, 1981). This is also the approach we adopted to the study of the development of children's economic understanding.

1.9   The theoretical and methodological background to our research

We share Turiel's opinion (see Section 1.3 above) that social understanding is articulated in distinct domains. To identify these domains it is not sufficient merely to compare the various types of experience available to the child (such as direct or verbal experience, for example, or the manipulation of objects as against interpersonal interactions, etc.). One must also refer to the conceptual fields established by the various social sciences and to the themes and arguments which they have considered. Our research, however, is concerned with the ideas of young children, so we have generally taken the common sense of adults rather than scientific economics as our reference point. We propose to demonstrate how the child comes to possess the ideas which nonspecialist adults hold about various facts relevant to economics (such as the price of goods), or about those aspects of social organisations which it is necessary to understand in order at least to 'place' economic phenomena (the existence of different means of production, for instance).

Our first objective was to further the analysis of the themes already examined by other authors so as to add more detail to the picture which they had begun to sketch; we also wanted to take up some aspects of economic reality not yet considered in other studies. A group of studies are, therefore, presented in the following four chapters which seek to describe developmental sequences regarding various economic notions. Following these studies we have attempted to reconstruct a unified sequence through a comparison and synthesis of the various results. For this work we have made use of Piaget's theory, particularly the notion that in the ideas which children of different ages express about particular themes it is possible to identify qualitatively distinct levels which can be ordered hierarchically (cf. Turiel, 1983). Since the conceptions which characterise these levels depend on the interaction between evolving mental structures and experiential information concretely available to children it is not possible to construe this unified sequence as universal without some consideration of the cultural influences. Can the same sequence be identified in different cultures? Some cross-cultural data relevant to this issue are considered in the final chapter.

A second objective which we have explored more recently has been to study the mechanisms of transition between one level and another, and the possibility of facilitating these transitions through appropriate educational interventions. In the final chapter, after considering the question of the universality of developments about economic notions, we consider the results of our own recent work and that of other authors about mechanisms for the acquisition of these ideas.

As regards our choice of themes we have followed the same basic approach to questions of 'economics' adopted by other authors which seem to us to be correct. We, too, have therefore considered elementary aspects of economic activity, selecting them so as to be able to reconstruct the representations which children form of the principal economic roles in our society and the exchanges through which these roles are linked in a complex system. In terms of method, however, we have distanced ourselves both from those authors who considered a wide range of economic concepts in a single study (such as Furth, 1980), and those who selected certain notions as emblematic in order to be able to generalise their conclusions across the field (such as Jahoda, 1979). It might instead be opportune to reconsider in an organic and extensive manner the description of these beliefs so as to provide a more solid basis for further studies (such as those aimed at identifying the modality of the transition from one developmental level to another). Our approach has been to conduct a wide variety of in-depth interviews, each of which was dedicated to a single issue. We interviewed children about the passage of goods from production to consumption and the circulation of money which accompanies it, the distribution of services, payment for work in various economic sectors, and the productive structures of industry and agriculture. This choice of themes allowed us to collect various images held by children about the system of relations determined by the division of labour. Each theme considered the issues from a different perspective, and a consideration of these different points of view served several purposes. Firstly, it contributed significant details to the observations we were able to make of children's representations of economic life. Secondly, it helped to overcome some of the difficulties associated with the clinical interview method, such as the contingent influence of this method of interviewing on children's thinking, or misunderstandings by the experimenters of unusual conceptions expressed by the subjects.

Taken as a whole, then, the results of these studies should enable us to reconstruct a complex picture of the representation of economic reality according to the different phases of development. We have taken the opportunity of extending the range of themes previously studied, of furthering the analysis of some points which had not been adequately covered before, and also of giving fresh interpretations of data which were unclear or contradictory. After examining the development of various economic ideas through a series of studies, the problem of the relation between economic understanding and intellectual development is redefined in more detailed terms. We have sought to identify the lines of developments of each economic notion, and to interpret this development in relation to the development of logical abilities. In this respect we have been guided by the hypothesis that for some particular aspects of economic reality a concordance might emerge with the lines of development specified by Piaget.

All of the studies presented in Chapters 2–5 have a cross-sectional design; that is, a comparison of the responses of groups of subjects of differing ages to the same problem or groups of problems. The data were gathered through Piagetian clinical interviews, though the procedure was somewhat more structured than that described by Piaget (1929) himself. Children from nursery through to senior schools were interviewed individually (usually 10 boys and 10 girls at each age level). Each interview lasted between 10 and 30 minutes according to how the subjects responded, and all were tape-recorded. The interviews were structured by a schedule which not only gave the standardised questions but also the directions the interviews could take on the basis of the children's responses. In keeping with the exploratory aim of the research and the spirit of a Piagetian interview the possibility was always left open for following the child's line of thought whenever unexpected responses emerged.

The complete interviews were transcribed and a preliminary review of all or some of the protocols allowed the specification of various categories of response and their ordering into a sequence of levels. The reader will see that the criteria adopted to define and order the categories varied from study to study. Where the aim of the study was to test a specific hypothesis formulated on the basis of existing research or from material which we ourselves had previously collected, then the response levels have been ordered according to the provisions of that hypothesis. In the exploratory studies, however, criteria of a general order were used which derived from a consideration of Piagetian studies of cognitive development.

The protocols were then read by two independent judges who knew neither the age nor the sex of the subject.[3] The inter-judge reliability was always very high, confirming the validity of the category systems used. On this basis it was possible to examine the correlation between the response level and the age of subjects using Spearman rank order coefficients (r_s). The coefficients, always strongly positive and significant, are reported at the foot of each table.

The ordering of Chapters 2–5 represents a compromise solution between an arrangement of the material according to the economic questions examined and a grouping of the beliefs which emerged in psychological terms. The empirical presentation begins in Chapter 2 with a wide-ranging study organised around the themes of *work* and *payment for work*; the aims of this first study were avowedly introductory and chronologically it preceded the other studies. In Chapter 3 the dominant theme is the *source of money* in which we examine how children think people obtain the money they live on, how the conditions of wealth and poverty are determined, and about the functions of the bank. The third empirical study concerns *the source of goods and commercial exchanges* (Chapter 4) beginning with retail selling, then moving on to consider those transactions which lie behind them. We also consider various aspects of the problem of prices. Lastly, Chapter 5 concerns the function and ownership of the *means of production*, both industrial and agricultural. The organisation of public transport is also examined as an example of the distribution of services.

[3] The protocols were given randomly assigned numbers and the personal details of the subjects were recorded separately.

2 Work

The theme of work and its remuneration has, somewhat strangely, only been a marginal concern in research on the development of economic concepts. Some of the authors who have considered children's ideas about economic exchanges have taken the theme of buying and selling as their point of departure and then used this theme to examine such wider issues as production, the formation of profit, or monetary exchanges between various types of figures. On the other hand those authors who have been concerned with the question of social stratification have generally been more interested in differences between rates of pay for different jobs than in the way in which the child comes to connect the activity of work with payment for it. Furthermore, such research has generally not considered other issues related to the understanding of work (the aim of work, for instance, or the source and reason for its remuneration, or the range of work activities known to the child), though the studies by Goldstein and Oldham (1979) and Duveen and Shields (1984) are both exceptions in this respect. Goldstein and Oldham were specifically concerned with the analysis of different aspects of the idea of work as it develops between the ages of 6 to 11 years; their work is more descriptive than interpretive, aiming to document the existence in this age group of conceptions structured according to considerations relevant to later occupational choice, rather than explaining how these ideas are formed and how they develop. Duveen and Shields did consider various crucial aspects of the development of the idea of work, though they only considered young children aged 3–5 years in their research.

The first study described in this chapter is also the one with which we began our series of investigations into the child's construction of economic reality, and for this reason we decided to tackle as general a theme as possible. The choice fell on the theme of work and the relations which it sustains with social organisation. Data from this study of the conceptions of the relationships involving payment for work are extended in the two following studies, the first on ideas about access to work roles, and the second about the idea of the *boss*.

2.1 Payment for work

Danziger (1958), Strauss (1952) and Jahoda (1979) all concur in indicating 7–8 years as the age at which children recognise the existence of employment as a form of work and of the payment associated with it. While Strauss and Jahoda limit themselves to giving data about shopworkers, Danziger addresses the issue in wider terms. In the part of his investigation dedicated to the idea of the 'boss' he showed that the oldest subjects he interviewed (about 7–8 years) attributed to the boss of a business the function of paying workers, without, however, understanding that the money required for this came from the sale of the goods produced. Danziger suggested that such an idea must be grasped by older subjects and hypothesised a higher level of response in which the circulation of money would be fully understood. His own research however did not produce any empirical data regarding this hypothesis. Goldstein and Oldham (1979) asked children of first, third and fifth grades for definitions of work and found that only a few subjects from the youngest age group could not say anything about work, or defined it simply as 'a place where people go'. The commonest definition, and the one which became more frequent with age, proposed that work was 'a way of getting money'.

This, briefly, was the state of existing research regarding children's conceptions of work and payment for it which we took as our point of departure in designing this study. We set the lower end of the age range for our study at 6 years, because it is more or less at this age that children might be expected to recognise the existence of employment and payment for work, and we extended the upper limit to 14 years, in order to test Danziger's hypothesis. The interview[1] began with some questions about the reasons why people work, followed where necessary by others aimed at recalling the child's attention to the fact that generally people are paid for work. We then ascertained which work roles the children knew, and what their ideas were about payment. To do this we asked them to give the names of some jobs (a list which usually began with their father's or mother's work); where necessary we integrated the list of jobs spontaneously introduced by the child with other jobs representing various public and private economic sectors. Thus we ensured that the list of jobs discussed by each child included the following: factory worker, bus driver, teacher, farmworker and doctor. For each of these occupations we asked the child who paid for it, and where that money had been obtained.

The examination of the data showed that on the first point of the inquiry children's responses did not differ except in their linguistic formulation; in one way or another they all asserted that one works to earn money. However, the type and range of work relations mentioned by our subjects allowed us to determine a developmental sequence comprising four levels. At the first level the child recognises a very limited range of occupations and argues, rightly or

---

[1] The subjects were 60 children, 15 in each of the following age groups: 6–7 years, 8–9 years, 10–11 years and 13–14 years. The number of males and females were approximately the same in each group. Most of the subjects came from middle-class families, though the sample included a few children from upper-class families. All these children attended a private school, though it should be noted that the vast majority of Italian children attend state schools.

wrongly, that they are paid directly by consumers. At the second level the range of known activities widens and for some of them the existence of a 'boss' is also recognised. The idea of the 'boss' is consolidated at the third level, being extended, sometimes at the expense of the truth, to every type of work named by the child. At both the second and third levels, however, the child could not say how the 'boss' obtained the money to pay wages. Only at the fourth level do the sale of goods or services produced and the payment of work come to be connected.

Level 1: Monetary exchanges within pairs.

The most primitive image of economic relations is characterised by the absence of ideas about production and the child's inability to represent the circulation of money. The range of activities spontaneously listed by the children is very narrow and not representative of the different economic sectors; usually it includes the parents' occupations together with a few other jobs accessible to children living in a city, such as teacher, doctor or hairdresser. The terms *farmworker* and *factory worker*, once introduced by the experimenter, call to the child's mind only a vague and imprecise meaning. The former is associated with fragmentary images of life in the country, while the latter is either given a very restricted meaning in which the *worker* is identified with the *bricklayer*, *plumber*, or the *electrician*, or remains wholly unknown.

Payment for these activities is described in two ways. For some children the person who performs a job is paid directly by whoever benefits from such services; and the customers often receive money in their turn, such *change* frequently amounting to more than the sum they had originally paid. According to other children money could also come from bilateral exchanges between pairs of workers who are 'friends' (we might say 'partners'); though in reality it is sometimes a case of employer and employee. When they are unable to specify a 'customer' or a 'partner' the child is also unable to say who pays the worker, or denies immediately that there is any payment at all, asserting that there are other ways in which the workers could find the money they need to live on, such as getting it from a bank (who will give money to anyone who asks for it) or by going into a shop (and getting 'change' by buying something).

Nearly all these elements can be seen in the protocol which is given below as an example. In other children one or other of the tendencies described was particularly prominent.

PATRIZIA (6:5) begins by stating her father's work, saying that – *He types.* – Where does he type? – *In an office near here. Close to some shops. You go over a bridge.* – And does your mother work? – *Yes.* – What does she do? – *She gets … paper, writes on it, on a machine, like my daddy.* – (…) – Could you tell me the names of other jobs that people do? – *Some … are teachers, then also some*

... *also do ... are in a bank. Then there's also the baby-sitter who brings me to school ... Then there's the mummies who have to go to the office and stay out at night, then the baby-sitter looks after you. Then that's all.* – Do you know what a farmworker does? – *Works with a rake ... takes out, no, plants the seeds and ... then, see, the grass comes up; you put some more seeds in and lettuce comes up.* – And workers, what do they do? *Operations.*[2] – The workers, those who work in the factories? – *Don't know.* – People who work as teachers, do you know who pays them? – *The mummies.* – Your mother works in a bank, who pays her? – *It's ... not the bank ... she makes it, the money.* – Your mother makes money when she's in the bank and then brings it home? – *Yes, there's also another friend of hers in the bank, she makes it.* – They make it? – *Yes.* – And then take it home? – *Yes.* – As much as they want? – *They only take a little, they don't want to be rich.* – If they wanted to be rich could they take a lot home? – *If they wanted to, but I don't know if they want to.* – Who gives money to the bricklayer? – *The same, Mummy.* – And to the shopkeeper? – *Oh, Mummy.* – And to the pilot of an aeroplane? – *Those who go up, those who get in it. Children, though, don't pay.* – And someone who drives the bus here in Padova, who is it who pays them? – *No one ... because there's something, there are ... you put the money in and there's a box, the driver opens it, takes the money out and puts it in the bag.* – The money for the tickets is for the driver? – *Yes.* – And who pays the farmworker? – *The one who grows, who helps him to grow ... the one who does that.* – I don't understand. – *The one who helps him to grow ... helps the farmworker; or the farmworker.*

While Patrizia's replies are dominated by the idea that it is the 'customer' who pays, Emilia's responses show a conception according to which payment is not associated with the work or service rendered, but with the passage of goods from one hand to another.

EMILIA (6:3) – Do you know what a farmworker does? – *Harvests the grapes.* – Do you know if they also do anything else? – *No.* – The road sweeper? – *Cleans.* – What? – *The street* – The bricklayer? – *Builds.* – What? – *Houses.* – Can you tell me the names of some other jobs? – *I don't know any.* – Do you know what a factory worker does? – *No.* – Wait a minute, the road sweeper who cleans the street, how does he get the money he needs? – *Because after he's swept away those things, if he finds anything useful he sells it, and so he makes money.* – Do you know what a farmworker does? – *Makes flour, and then goes to the shops, and in the shops he puts it in bags and then someone gives him money.* – Does a teacher get money? – *Yes.* – Who gives it to them? – *Mummy.* – And who is it who gives money to the bus driver? – *Don't know.*

CHIARA (6:0) is an example where 'change' is considered as an alternative to work for earning money – *Some daddies don't work.* – Really, how come? –

---

[2] Translator's note: The Italian for workers is *operai*; Patrizia's response is derived from the assonance of this word with *operazioni*, meaning operations.

Because he himself also . . . even if he doesn't work, then he goes out and then he always gets money. – So you think that it's possible to get money without working? – *Yes.* – How? – *. . . Go to another chemist* (Chiara's father is a chemist). – Go to? *. . .* – *When you go to get medicine, then the money they give you for the medicine you keep for getting someting to eat.* – I don't really understand. – *. . . When a man goes into the chemist's and . . . and he doesn't work, he goes in the chemist's and they give him money, and then if he gets medicine, he goes out and takes the money . . . from Daddy!* – You mean that your daddy gives money to people who come into the chemist's – *Yes.* – How come? – *Well . . . because they take things.* – Let's see if I've understood. People come into the chemist's to buy medicine? – *Yes.* – When they buy medicine they give your daddy money? – *Yes.* – And what does your daddy do? – *He gives them money.* – The money which your daddy gives them, is it more or less or the same amount as the money they gave him? – *My daddy gives them different amounts.* – But the money which your daddy gives them, is it more or less than what they gave him? – *My daddy gives more than they gave.* – And your daddy, where does he get the money to give to these people? – *He goes to get it in the bank.* – And when the bank gives your daddy money, can he keep it forever . . . (Interrupting) – *Yes.* – . . . or after a bit does he have to give some money back to the bank? – *No, he keeps it.* – Do you know what a farmworker does? – *Yes, keeps his field in order.* – How does he keep it in order? – *He puts things on the ground.* – Why? – *So that the flowers will have a good earth.* – Do you know who pays for what the farmworker does? – *The people who go to look after the house . . . or the . . . um . . . for instance, the gardener pays money at the end of the week. My daddy, too, gives money to the girls in the chemist's at the end of the week. And also at home we give the gardener money at the end of the week.* – You (emphasised) give money to the gardener? – *And then he gives us back the change.*

In these last exchanges with Chiara one can see bilateral payments between employer and employee. In the following example this idea is presented in a more systematic form, together with the idea that the pair constitute a couple of 'friends'.

ANDREA (6:6) – Can you tell me the names of some jobs which people do for money? – *The names?* – Yes. – *Car mechanic, notary, bicycle repairman, motor bikes, aeroplanes . . . houses.* – Do you know what farmworkers do? – *Yes.* – What do they do? – *They . . . put, in the field, they put fertiliser to make the corn and everything grow.* – Do you know what the workers in the factories do? – *Um . . . no.* – Do you know what factories are? – *Yes.* – What are they? – *They're houses made a bit longer.* – You've never asked yourself what they do inside those houses? – *No.* – What work does your daddy do? – *A notary.* What does it mean, to work as a notary? – *To work.* – When your daddy goes to work what do you think he does? – *Works, puts things down, does things, studies things, oh, does jobs, tells the ladies that he won't make a contract.* – Who is it who gives money to your daddy when he works? – *It is, it is his notary.* – And who gives money to the bicycle repairman? – *His friend, who works there.* – And his friend, who gives money to him? – *He does . . . he gives it to him . . . his friend gives the money to the other one, he gives him his money.* – And people who sell things in shops, who gives them money? – *He gives it first, then the other who buy things.* – I don't understand, let's take the greengrocer for example, who is it who gives him money? – *Mummy . . . and him.* – Him too? – *Yes.* – And the person who drives the bus, who gives him money? – *Nobodies (sic).* – How does he manage to live? – *Maybe he has a lot of friends.* – What do his friends do? – *Drive buses.* – What about someone who's a farmworker? – *No money, because they're a farmworker.* – He doesn't get any money? – *No.* – Well then, why does he work if he doesn't get any money? – *To make the corn grow and he can't get any money because he's all alone.* – But then how does he manage to live, him and his wife and his children? – *Oh, they get things, maybe he gets it from his friends, and that's how they have money.*

Level 2: Hierarchical relations between those who work and those who pay.

At this level the image of economic relations begins to become more complete as the range of working activities which the child knows broadens. All the same, the factory worker is rarely mentioned, and very few children have any idea about what happens inside a factory. The children speak more frequently about the bricklayer. As well as being more complete, the child's image of society is also more articulated; indeed, in addition to payment for services by customers or consumers the child now includes examples of payments by the 'boss'. Nevertheless, the image of economic relations remains incomplete in one important respect. The child does not know how the 'boss' obtains the money to pay the employees, or they explain it by reference to various types of external sources: the bank, the government or the council; savings accumulated by the 'boss' through previous or present business activities; the payment of a kind of enrolment tax by the workers when they are taken on. The idea that a 'boss' could obtain money by selling the goods or services produced by the workers is not one which occurs to children at this level.

The relationships between the 'boss' who pays and the workers who perform the required activity are hierarchical, and it is the capacity to represent such relations which constitutes the novel acquisition of this level. Other conceptions of Level 2, however, represent more complex translations of modes of thought characteristic of Level 1. The form of bilateral exchanges returns in the idea that the bank gets money from the council who in turn get it from the bank; or in the idea that the 'boss' pays the workers with money from the 'enrolment' payments; in some children the idea of 'change' also persists.

MASSIMO (6:4) – Can you tell me who it is who pays the bus driver? – *He goes ... where there's ... where he's ... where he takes the bus back ... he goes ... in a room where there's a man who pays him.* – And someone who's a teacher, who pays them? – *Um, when they go to buy something outside.* – And the workers, who pays them? – *The engineer or the architect ... maybe the one who organises the work, who could be the engineer, the electrician ... and that's all, he could be the architect.* – The engineer and the architect, how do they come to have the money to pay the workers? – *Sometimes they get it from home, maybe they ask their wife for it and ... sometimes they find it in their wallet, if they don't have much they go and get if from those who have.* – And the man who pays the bus driver, how does he come to have the money? – *He could go to the bank and get it.* – What is the bank? – *Where they go and put money, and when they need it they go and take it.* – So the man who pays the bus driver goes to get money in the bank? – *Yes, but I think he needs to know how much to pay him.* – How does he know how much? – *I don't know, I think he counts how many trips they make.* – To get the money does this man have to have put some in the bank already or does the bank give him some all the same? – *The bank gives it to him.* – If someone needs money, they go to the bank and the bank gives them some? – *I think so.* – And how does the bank come to have money? – *I think the men who go there put money in the bank who take it and put it somewhere, I don't know where.* – Why do these men take money to the bank? – *They take it there because ... because they want to ... they take it ... because ... I don't remember why ... because they want to take it there, I don't know, they don't like to have it in their wallet.*

CRISTINA (8:3), after having said that the farmworker *ploughs the earth to make the plants grow* and that workers in a factory *make things*, is asked about her parents' work – What job does your father do? – *A clerk.* – And your mother? – *She's a hairdresser.* – Who is it who pays your father? – *A man, a man who tells him what to do.* – And who is it who pays the hairdresser? – *The people who come.* – And the teacher? – *Here at the school there's a teacher who tells the others what to do and he pays everybody.* – And this teacher pays with his own money, or someone else gives it to him? – *The bank gives him the money.* – And someone who works in a factory, who are they paid by? – *Don't know.* – And a farmworker? – *By nobody.* – Nobody? – *No.* – But even a farmworker needs money for himself and his children. Where does he go to get this money? – *The bank gives it to him, and the bank also gives it to those who clean the streets and to those who sweep the pavements.* – And the money the bank gives them, is it the bank's or ... (Interrupting) – *It's the bank's.* – And where do they get it from? – *They have lots of it, lots, lots.* – But if they keep giving it away they might use it all up! – *Another bank would give them some.* – And this bank . . . – (Interrupting) – *And then stop . . . they close the bank for a while, and they go and do another job to get some money and when they have a lot they open again.* – The owner of the bank? – *Yes*. But why does the bank pay the farmworkers, the teachers, the road-sweepers? – *Because they are men who have lots of money and they don't know what to do with it, so they give it to these people. And the bank keeps money for people, too. And then along comes someone who needs it, perhaps someone who's poor, and they give it to them.* – If the rich people decided that they'd had enough of giving away their money like this, and decided to keep it all for themselves, what would happen? – *They wouldn't clean the streets, they wouldn't teach, they'd go and do something else.*

Level 3: Generalisation of hierarchical relations.

In the responses of Massimo and Christina there were 'bosses' with authority who pay their employees as well as banks which distribute money without security for loans, and residues of varying degrees from earlier ideas about 'change'. The idea that the 'boss' pays the workers with money which they must first give to the 'boss' when they are taken on for a job is to be found in the following protocol, MAURO (6:7). This payment to the boss is, however, generalised by Mauro to every activity considered in the interview. This kind of generalisation constitutes a characteristic of level 3.

– Who is it who gives money to someone who is an architect? (A job which Mauro had named) – *I think that first he works and does a job, maybe a doctor and then . . . he doesn't want to do that anymore, and he asks the chief doctor, he doesn't want to do it anymore, so he doesn't go anymore. With his money he goes and buys things, he takes up . . . saving the change, and then he has enough money to become an architect, he goes to the chief architect and gives him the right money, and he's an architect.* – But when he's an architect who is it who gives him money? – *The chief architect.* – And this chief, how does he come to have the money to pay the architect? – *Well, first they give it to him, an architect gives him money, and then it increases with the money from the others, and then he gives them money again, and in the morning he doesn't have any money, but then when he returns the architects come back too and they give him money again.* – (. . .) – And who is it who pays the farmworker? – *The chief farmworker.* – And how does the chief farmworker come to have the money to pay him? – *Like the architects, first there was a farmworker, he was poor, and they gave him money, he bought himself the job, the old chief went away . . . and he became the chief, and then all the other farmworkers gave him money . . . and . . .* – And then he gives it back to them? – *No, he gives them a little less, so that little by little the money . . . the amount he has increases.* The idea that in working one is paid less money than the sum one spent in buying oneself the job does not at all disturb the child – But if the chief farmworker gives him less money than he gave him, wouldn't it be better for him to stay at home and not go to work? – *No, because after he's used up all the money on food, after he's spent all the money on food, and he's become poor, he takes some blankets and lies down by the column of an arcade and begs for charity.*

As can be seen, generalising the hierarchical model leads to some incorrect responses, but it also allows the child to explain the manner of remuneration for the most varied occupations, thereby constructing a wider vision of economic reality.

Many children identify this 'boss' who pays employees who work as the 'council', or the 'state' or the 'government'. Such an idea was already apparent at Level 2, and it frequently reappears at successive levels, each time a little more precisely. At first these terms do not specifically designate any particular body, and nor are they used with a sense which distinguishes them very clearly from a private employer. The 'state' or 'the council' are 'important persons', who are attributed the functions of authority and of paying people who work.

ROBERTO (8:8) begins by saying (wrongly) that the 'council' pays his father, an insurance agent: – Can you explain to me what work an insurance agent actually does? – *For instance, he has to reassure[3] a person, for example, someone dies, assure, assure ... now I don't really know why.* – What does it mean to 'insure yourself'? – *... for instance, someone has an accident, they're insured ... but if they're not insured ... they can't ...* – What use is insurance? – *... When someone gets hurt ... then ... at least they're insured.* – What do you mean? Someone gets hurt and what does the insurance do? – *... He told me about it when I was little but now I can't remember it.* – Who is it who pays your daddy? – *The council.* – The doctor? – *Him, too, I think.* – And the farmworker? – *I don't think so.* – You don't think what? – *That he gets paid by the council.* – Who do you think pays him? – *No, maybe he is paid by the council, because there's no one else who could give him money.* – Someone who works in a factory? – *The council.* – What is the council? – *It's a ... how do you say ... it's like a room like this one, and there's a man that ... then there are chairs too ... and he decides ... people go there, people who want to work, and ... then he decides with his friends.* – How do you get to be this man at the council who gives people jobs and pays them? – *I think that it's like ... maybe he goes to a ... someone who has lots of money, and, and he for example gives him the money he has, and he gives him his money, so then he becomes ... so he's got lots of money to give to those who work.*

ALESSANDRA (8:0) also makes generalisations which seem to originate from her more or less exact knowledge of her father's work: – *Someone who*

---

[3] Translator's note: The Italian verb *assicurare* can mean both *to assure* and *to insure* in the commercial sense as well as *to assure* in a personal sense. Roberto's answers draw on all these meanings.

works in a factory, how do they come to have money? – *My daddy (an industrialist) gives money to those workers who work a lot. My daddy, though, goes to the bank to get it.* – Someone who's a doctor? – *There's someone in charge of the hospital, and they see that they work well, and they give it to them.* – And where do they get it from? – *From the bank again.* – And what about someone who's a farmworker? – *A farmworker? Someone wants a job, and they look for the head of this, this* . . . – Farmworker? – *No, he's the head of the house, the dogs, the cows, so, and someone wants a job and he takes him on, and he works for so many days, and the one who's in charge of the house and the other things that are there, sees that he works a lot, the farmworker who wanted . . . and he gives him money.* – And the one who's in charge? – *Oh, he has it in the house, he keeps it in the house, or in the bank.* – Someone who's a shopkeeper? – *Oh, the shopkeeper . . . there's someone in charge of the shop . . . there are lots . . . lots of men and women, I don't know, who want a job, and he gives them a job, and every day he sees that they are busy with the people . . . and he gives them money.* – And someone who drives a bus? – *There could be a boss of all the buses, and he lets other men drive, and sees that they take people here and there, and then he gives them the money that he finds in the bank, or in the house if he has it.*

Level 4: Coordinations of various economic exchanges.
A more complete and articulated image of economic relations is constructed by subjects at the fourth level, due to the recognition that the 'boss' of a business gets the money to pay their employees by selling the goods or services which are produced. In this way children generate a representation of the circulation of money. At the preceding levels money is exchanged only within the pairs worker-'customer', or employee-'boss', although the pairs remain unconnected with each other. Now, however, money is seen to move from the consumer to the 'boss' who uses it to pay the employees.

MICHELA (10:8) is the daughter of an industrialist. The interviewer asks her – Who is it who gives money to the doctor? – *The guests.*[4] – You mean the patients? – *Yes.* – And someone who's a farmworker, who gives them money? – *No one . . . oh, the boss of that land . . . if he gets him working.* – What do you mean 'if he gets him working'? – *. . . Well . . . I don't know.* – How does your father come to have the money to pay the workers? – *By selling, trading with others, and he gets money.* – How would it be, then, for the farmworker? – *The farmworker works, then, like sowing the seed, or growing some fruit, for example. He markets the fruit, then with the money for the fruit that he sold to other bosses, the boss that had this fruit gives the farmworker money.* – And who is it who pays the teacher? – *The boss of the school, the head teacher.* – And

---

[4] Translator's note: Michela's answer is *'gli ospiti'* which means *the guests*, but which is also a slip of the tongue, a misconstruction from the word *ospedale* which means *hospital*.

who is it who gives the head teacher money? – *The people who come to school
... oh ... yes, they have to pay something and ... they bring money, then they
give this money and go to the head teacher.*

The responses of Level 4 are also distinguished from those of preceding
levels by the differentiation between privately paid employment and that
paid by public institutions such as the council or the state. These organisations are now represented as associations charged with generating activities of public interest.

GIOVANNI (10:5): – Who is it who pays factory workers? – *The owner of the
factory.* – And how does he get the money? – *Because while the others work to
produce various objects, the owner sells them at a higher price, then he gives a
small percentage to the workers, and he himself keeps the greater part of the
money he's made.* – Who explained that to you? – *No, I heard it like that ... and
... you see it on the news sometimes.* – Who does the farmworker get money
from? – *From the person who buys what he sells.* Your mother and father
(both nurses), who do they get money from? – *From ... from ... from the
owner of the hospital.* – And someone who cleans the streets? – *From the
public services.* – What are the public services? – *It's an association that there is
in every city and that ... and ... in the morning, during the day, works to keep the
roads in order, the streets of the city, the roads of the countryside.* – And this
association, where does it go to get the money to give to the street cleaner? –
I wouldn't know. – And bus drivers, how do they come to be paid? – *By the
council.* – What is the council? – *The council? It's another association that ...
that people who live there have to pay taxes to ... and ... other things and with
what they get from these taxes they ... buy other buses for the inhabitants.* – You
said that the council is an association, what do you mean? – *Association?
People who meet together to discuss a problem.* – If someone wants to be a
member of Padova council, of that association, what do they have to do? –
*... First become an employee who writes some letters ... so ... and then civilise
themselves ...* – Civilise themselves? – *Civilise themselves in that job and
manage to become a councillor of the council.* – How do you become a
councillor of the council? – *Civilise yourself more and more in your job.* –
When they're really good at it you mean? – *Yes.*

The developmental trend which emerges from this study may be defined
according to three parameters: the number of economic figures recognised by
the child; the type of relationships through which all or some of these figures
are connected; and the whole system constructed through these relations.
The image of social relations which mediates payment for work develops,
therefore, in both a quantitative and a qualitative sense. There is a gradual
increase in the number of economic figures identified by the child, and of the
relations which connect them, which is finally translated into a broader

Table 2.1 *Payment for work*

Response level	Age groups				Total
	6–7	8–9	10–11	13–14	
1. Monetary exchanges between pairs	8	1	0	0	9
2. Hierarchical relations between payer and paid	7	5	1	0	13
3. Generalisation of hierarchical relations	0	6	5	0	11
4. Coordination of various economic exchanges	0	3	9	15	27
Total	15	15	15	15	60

$r_s = 0.86$, $p < .001$

vision of the world of work. There is also a modification with age in the relations called upon to explain the source of the money with which people are paid.

At the first level the picture is composed of only two figures standing in a symmetrical relationship; one who provides goods or services, and one who consumes them and 'pays' for them. We enclose 'pays' within quotation marks because the direction in which the movement of money occurs is not yet included in the child's representation, and 'to pay' means a reciprocal exchange of money. The relationships between employer and employee are also considered as if they were symmetrical; both are assimilated to a pair of 'friends' who 'pay' one another. Not many children gave such primitive responses, and nearly all who did were in the 6–7-year age group. Such responses seem, therefore, to be the last residues of conceptions characteristic of an earlier age. When the child becomes able to represent hierarchical relations (that is, at both Levels 2 and 3, which included most of the 8–9-year-old children) this pair of friends become differentiated due to the appearance of the figure of the 'boss'. The 'boss' appears on the one hand as the private owner of a business or, on the other, as the council, state of government considered as a kind of private owner, although much richer. Moreover, children at this level begin to distinguish a correct notion of payment, as is indicated by the progressive disappearance of allusions to reciprocal exchanges of money. Nevertheless it is still not clear if the boss who pays the employees is also paid, or how the 'boss' obtains the money to pay the employees. Only from 10–11 years (Level 4) does the child assert a relatively complete and articulated vision of economic reality. The various private or public 'bosses' are related to tradesmen or customers who buy the goods or services supplied by the business.

This sequence confirms, in its general outline, the data given by Danziger (1958) on younger children and offers empirical support for the developments he hypothesised in older children. It also shows the generality of some ideas reported by Strauss (1952) and Jahoda (1979) regarding a single occupation, that of salesman. Indeed, by 6–7 years the idea that one works for money is well consolidated. The data collected by Duveen and Shields (1984) show that from at least the age of 3 years the great majority of children recognise that shopworkers and factory workers are paid. The youngest children are divided approximately in half between those who recognise payment for such familiar jobs as doctor, police, farmer and teacher, and those who do not; by the age of 5 the proportion of children who do recognise that these jobs are paid rises to about 70–80 per cent. In our sample, too, some children had difficulty in admitting that certain activities (such as the farmworker) are paid, notwithstanding the initial assertion shared by all that 'one works for money'. Moreover, in the youngest children such ideas are often accompanied by the conviction that there also exist other ways of obtaining money, such as being given it by the bank, or receiving it from a shopkeeper, or directly from an employee by way of tax. Duveen and Shields's data and the emergence of these primitive beliefs about how people obtain money suggest that the relation between work and money is only gradually constructed (see also Burris, 1983). To observe its origin it would be necessary to extend the inquiry to children younger than those interviewed in this study. This is a problem which is considered from a different point of view in the next chapter. For the present it is sufficient to note the particular prominence of ideas about 'change', understood by the youngest children as a means for obtaining money. As will be recalled, conceptions of this type were also found by Strauss, Danziger, Furth and Jahoda in interviews about buying and selling. In those cases one could suspect that it was a question of beliefs formulated by the child on the spur of the moment to explain the fact that the shopkeepers in their turn gave money to the customers, a point to which the interviewers themselves drew attention. The fact that children also mentioned this strange way of obtaining money in a study which began from a quite different theme leads one to think that there are spontaneous beliefs in this respect. Such beliefs are not limited to trying to explain an aspect of buying and selling but are included within a wider vision of economic processes. We shall seek to demonstrate as much in the following chapter.

2.2   Access to various work roles

In this section the theme of how children represent relationships determined by the division of labour is approached from another point of view, that of access to work roles. This issue emerged spontaneously in some of the protocols of the preceding study (see, for instance, that of Mauro) when the children asserted that workers were paid with the money that they themselves had paid on taking up a job. The question of access to various work roles has also been examined by Furth (1980) who asked children to describe various jobs, including doctor, teacher and bus driver, and to explain how people obtained these jobs (that is, children were asked, 'How does someone become a doctor?'). He reports four types of response: (1) it is enough to grow up or to want a particular job to get it; (2) one must ask the permission of some authority; (3) someone else needs to have left a vacancy for that particular job; and (4) it is necessary to possess or to acquire an expertise in the relevant activity. Furth, however, did not describe a developmental sequence for these ideas. After recording some examples of responses of 5 year olds he limits himself to observing that the same type of responses which appear in 'childish' or 'fanciful' forms in preschoolers, appear in more well-adjusted forms in older children. In our view this result should not be imputed to the nature of the theme, but rather to the way in which it was approached. The examples reported by Furth indicate that in fact the issue was dealt with in very few questions. A more extensive interview could probably have solicited a clearer explication of children's ideas and allowed a better discrimination between the younger and older subjects.

Goldstein and Oldham (1979) asked 6- to 13-year-old children a similar question (How do you get a job?). They found a clear age-related trend in the responses. Answers which emphasised the necessity of getting into contact with whoever was offering a job (responses which could be described as 'realistic' in Piagetian terms) faded in favour of responses which stressed introspection and an evaluation of the goodness of fit between the job and one's own interests, capacities and qualifications. These authors also stressed that however incomplete the responses of the younger children were, they were rarely based on fantasy alone. The younger children were able to give reasonably accurate accounts of job-hunting.

The little information which was available from existing research, therefore, was not at all congruent and we decided to approach the issue afresh. In a preliminary study children were asked about a wide range of work activities, both manual and intellectual, undertaken as self-employment or as employment by others.[5] This very broad approach proved, however, to be of little value since the children, especially the younger ones, did not clearly differentiate between the various roles and described the means of access to them in a

[5] The subjects were 60 middle-class children living in a city, divided in three age groups (6–7 years, 8–9 years and 10–11 years) with 10 boys and 10 girls in each group. The occupations considered represented various economic sectors: industrial production (worker, manager); agricultural production (farmworker); retail selling (shop owner, shop worker); the distribution of services (doctor, plumber bus driver); political activity (mayor). The data were collected by Daniela Beolchi.

rather generic manner. For instance, the response 'study' frequently recurred as a means of becoming a doctor, a plumber, a factory worker, etc., without the children being able to trace any distinction between the various scholastic curricula. We decided, therefore, to focus the interviews on the activities of factory workers, managers and farmworkers, thereby limiting the inquiry to the way in which children understood access to a few occupations represent- ative of both employed and self-employed work roles. Moreover, to avoid the vagueness resulting from the child's lack of knowledge of the occupations considered, this time we interviewed the children of factory workers living in the province of Modena, an area which is characterised by the presence of numerous factories producing ceramic tiles and with strong residues of an agricultural economy.[6] Each interview began with questions designed to ascertain that the child knew at least in general outline the occupations under consideration; there followed the question 'Do you know how someone becomes a ... (factory worker, farmworker, factory owner)?' and numerous requests for clarification of the initial response, which was generally rather vague.

The three parts of the interview, corresponding respectively to the factory worker, the farmworker and the factory owner, were classified separately in three sequences of 4 or 5 levels. As the more primitive responses were rather similar in all three cases we shall begin by describing these levels for all three occupations.

Levels o and 1: 'Don't know' or 'They just want to do it'.
   Children at level o have no idea of what the worker, farmworker or factory owner actually does, or they know nothing of how someone might take up these occupations.
MARIO (4:8) – Do you know what a worker does?[7] – ... – Do you know what the workers do in the ceramics factory? – ... *make tiles?* – Yes. Do you know how someone becomes a worker? – ... – What do you think they have to do? – ...
ANGELA (6:3) when asked 'What does the farmworker do?' replies – *I don't know, I only know that farmworkers have a dog.* – Do they have other things besides a dog? – ... *I don't know.* – Do you know how someone becomes a farmworker? – ... – What would you say? – *I don't know, don't know at all.* Regarding the factory owner, Angela, like many other children at Level o, does not have anything to say, since she does not even suspect his

---

[6] 80 children divided into four age groups (4–5 years, 6–7 years, 8–9 years and 10–11 years), each group comprising 10 boys and 10 girls. The data were collected by Carla Balestrazzi.
[7] Translator's note: The Italian verb *fare* means both *to do* and *to make*. In these conversations, therefore, it is only in the English translation that any explicit distinction has been made between what these work figures make and what they do.

existence, asserting: – *The factory doesn't belong to anybody ... it's everybody's, everybody who works there.*

FILIPPO (6:0) believes, on the other hand, that the factory belongs to the stoker – What does the stoker do? – *Makes the fire.* And anything else? – *Yes, writes on a machine in the office.* – Do you know how someone becomes the owner of a factory? – ...

Children who have some idea, however vague, of the occupations named are classified at Level 1. They believe that to gain access to these roles it is sufficient that someone wants to do it, or that they possess some very general requirement such as being old enough, or wearing certain types of clothes.

ANTONIETTA (6:2) – Do you know what the factory worker makes? – *Tiles.* – What do they do to make them? – ... – Do you know how someone becomes a factory worker? – *They eat.* – And then what happens? – *Then they grow up.* – And when they're grown up? – *They work.* (The owner of the factory also *makes tiles.*) – Do you know how someone becomes a factory owner? – *They grow up.* – And then? – *Then they are factory owners.* – And the farmworker? – *Hoes the ground.* (To become a farmworker it is the same story.) *They eat, they grow up and then they are farmworkers.*

FAUSTA (8:10) – *The farmworker sells cheese, makes hay, goes to cut the grass.* – How do they become a farmworker? – *They have to be old.* – And when they're old? – *Oh, they can be a farmworker.* – Do they just have to be old to be a farmworker? – *They have to be old but ... they have to be a bit strong because they live by the sweat of their brow.* – Does everyone who wants to be a farmworker manage to become one? – *If they're a little old, yes.*

Finally, for LUIGI (5:9) someone who wants to become a factory worker – *Puts on worker's clothes.* – Do they just have to put on those clothes to become a worker? – *No, they also have to have the other ordinary clothes, trousers.*

From the succeeding level the responses tend to differentiate between the occupations, either according to the descriptions of the duties to be performed, or according to the means of access to the role. We shall, therefore, describe each sequence separately, beginning with the factory worker.

Later development of ideas about factory workers. At Level 2 this occupation begins to be described with a certain precision.

ENRICO (8:3) – *There are some workers who go to the mills, some who make bricks, some who put them in a carton, then they transport them with those special trucks that there are in the factory, then there are some who glaze them.*

Moreover, the idea now emerges that it is necessary to apply to someone (boss, owner, employment office or council) to get a job in a factory.

And then? – *Then you try it out.* – How? – *In the ceramics factory.* – They go there and try it out? – *They have to ask the boss of the factory for it.* – Do you think the boss of the factory takes on everybody who goes there? – *He only takes a few, because if there are others inside . . .* – How does he know which ones to take? – *He takes the ones he likes best.* – Who are they? – *Those who the owner likes best.*

To be able effectively to carry out a job it is no longer sufficient, therefore, just to wish subjectively to do it, nor to possess some more or less generic requirement. The recognition of the need to take account of the decisions of other people is not accompanied, however, by any clear vision of the difficulties and objective limits which someone who wanted to work might meet. *Everybody works* says LORENZO (8:1); other children identify the unemployed as idlers.

For FLORA (10:4), however, the unemployed are *Those who don't work, who stay at home without doing anything.* – Someone who is unemployed is someone who doesn't want to work? – *No, because to be unemployed means they can't find work, or they don't need to work, on the other hand, someone who doesn't want to work . . .* – Why do you think there are people who don't find work? – *Because they've lost a leg, or they're ill, they can't work if they're ill.* – But are there healthy people who don't find work?. – *No, those who are healthy, who can work, look to find work, and they find it.*

The idea that to get a job it is necessary to pay the boss, which has already been noted in the previous study on payment for work, reappears here at this level, giving rise to a particular conception of unemployment.

PAOLO (8:8) – How does someone become a worker? – *They have to take money.* – And then? – *They give it to the boss of the ceramics factory and he lets them work.* – It's enough just to do that to become a worker? – *Yes, then they work.* – But does the boss of the factory take on everybody who wants to work there? – *Yes.* – But if he already has plenty of workers? – *Then if other people arrive and give him money, then the boss says that he already has enough.* – Enough what? – *Workers.* – How does the boss choose who to take on? – *Those he doesn't want he sends to another ceramics factory.* – And how does he know which ones to send away to another ceramics factory? – *. . . Oh, he sends them to another factory.* – Do you know what the unemployed are? – (. . .) – Do you think there are people who don't work? – *Yes.* – Yes. – Why? – *Because they don't have enough money to pay the boss so that he could let them work.*

Only at Level 3 do the children recognise that a request for a job depends on many factors which go beyond individual volition, both for the worker and the employer.

GUIDO (11:1) – How does someone become a worker? – *My mother, for example, had to go to the employment office to look for a job, and then find out.* –

And what do they do at the employment office? – *I don't know, ask the people in the office if there are any jobs.* – And then what do they do? – *From the office they send them to the ceramics factory. There they take them on for a three-month trial, and if they're good they keep them on.* – (. . .) – Do you think the boss of the factory takes on everybody who asks to work there? – *No, I don't think so.* – Why not? – *Because according to him there are only some people who can work, since there are some pregnant mothers and old men who he can't take on there.* Those who have asked for a job, Guido says, are taken on permanently after a period of trial and training. The experimenter then asked – Have you heard people talk about the unemployed? – *Those who don't work, who don't manage to find a job.* – Why not? – *Because of the immigration.*[8] – What do you mean? – *Because there are too many people looking to find work here and they don't all manage to find it.*

Later development of ideas about the farmworker. For this job we found different types of conceptions at Level 2 according to how the child considered the activity of the farmworker. If they thought of it as a form of self-employment they spoke of the farmworker obtaining land, tools or animals; if they thought of it as an employed occupation it was necessary, instead, for them to find work, more or less as in the case of the factory worker.

For instance, PAOLO (8:8), whom we have already quoted above, believes that to become a farmworker it is again necessary to pay a kind of tax – *They must have money to work.* – What do they use the money for? – *To become a farmworker. They give it to the head farmworker and he lets them work.* – Is that all they have to do to become a farmworker? – *Yes, and those who haven't got enough money can't work, and they have to look for another job.*

Other children spoke of the 'head farmworker'[9] without mentioning this 'enrolment' tax. The most frequent replies, however, were those in which the farmworker appeared as an autonomous worker, which corresponded to the type of situation actually prevalent in the area where the inquiry was conducted. The importance children accorded to hierarchical relations likewise appeared in a few cases, when the acquisition of the means of work is subordinated to the scrutiny of an authority.

For example, SILVIA (8:6) says that to become a farmworker it is necessary to – *Get some bits of land and cultivate it, make themselves a house.* – How can someone get some bits of land? – *The bits of land belong to the council, so they have to go to the council, and they tell them if they will give them a bit of*

---

[8] Translator's note: Guido is referring to immigrants from the Southern regions of Italy, the Mezzogiorno.

[9] Translator's note: The Italian word *capo* may mean either *boss* or *head*. Thus one can speak about *il capo della fabbrica*, the boss of the factory, and *il capo della scuola*, the head of the school. While there is some distinction between these terms in English it is important to bear in mind that the Italian word *capo* is used for all these circumstances, a point which is particularly relevant for the following section on the genesis of the idea of the boss.

land, or they could go to a hill which isn't anybody's, which doesn't belong to anybody, they can build a home for themselves there and be a farmworker there.

After having specified one way of becoming a farmworker children at the second level were unable to understand that there are other ways: working as a day labourer if they did not possess the means to work for themselves, or buying land and tools if they had the means to do so and did not want to work for someone else. A comprehension that these diverse possibilities existed (at least on a theoretical level) is what distinguishes Level 3, which is clearly shown in the following protocol.

OSCAR (10:10): – *A farmworker works the land, the countryside; but now there aren't so many of them because they all go to the factory which is less tiring to work in. However, some of them organise themselves into agricultural cooperatives and together they buy modern implements, and instead of each one working on a small piece of land on their own with old-fashioned methods, they have some capital available and all together they can buy modern tools to produce more and also make money.* – How does someone become a farm worker? – *Well, I think it's a tradition; a father teaches a son to work the land, though it also depends if they want to work on the land; if they don't want to they go on a course and become a worker.* – But if someone wasn't born in the country, could they become a farmworker? – *If they want to, yes; they get someone who is a farmworker to teach them how to work the land and then they can do it.* – And when they've learnt what do they do to become a farmworker? – *Oh, they buy some land, a house in the country and then begin, and then teach their children. Then they can do what they want to, work the land not only for grain, but also for vegetables.* (. . .) If someone isn't able to buy themselves some land and a house . . . (Interrupting) *Well, then they must do some other job to make money, then buy some land.* – But if they wanted to do it straightaway, could they do it all the same? – *No.* – Isn't there any way? – *Well, they could go and help a farmworker who needed them.*

The farmworker would then choose the stronger and more able, who would be able to practice the craft only after they had learnt from him what was necessary.

Later development of ideas about the factory owner. The examination of the ideas about the factory owner revealed the existence of more varied conceptions than those concerning the factory worker or the farmworker, both as regards the functions undertaken by the owner and the way in which they gained access to this role. Following the two earlier levels already described, we found, in fact, three types of responses, some of which bore no comparison with those already seen in relation to the factory worker or farmworker.

In the first place, children classified at Level 2 asserted that to be an owner one must build one's own factory oneself, eventually with the help of some 'friends'. This 'owner-builder' has no other specific function in the daily life of the factory; either he is a worker like all the others, or he comes to be identified as a figure like a caretaker or a clerk, a little different from the men in blue overalls, but actually just as much an employee as they are.

MARCO (6:7) gives us an example of the first type of response – *The owner of the factory works too.* – How did he become the owner? – *With tiles.* – How's that? – *With tiles, one on top of the other.* – When he's the owner the factory is his? – *Yes.* – Why? – *Because he made it.* – What did he do to make it? – *The bricklayers helped him.* And then what did he do? – *Then he put in everything that was needed.* – What use is building the factory to the owner? – *Because he must work in it.*

MARIANGELA (8:0) on the other hand, identifies the owner as a porter – Do you think there is an owner of the ceramics factory? – *The owner is still him.* – Who? – *The doorman.* – What did he do to become the owner? – *He grew up and then he became the owner.* – Does everyone who grows up become a factory owner? – *No.* – Why not? – *Because the others, they can't all be owners, they have to work.* – But then why is it that some can and some can't? – *Because ... because they can't all become owners.* – Why did he become the owner? – *He has to decide with his friends.* – Who is it who decides? – *The one who has to become the owner.* – Yes, and how does he do that? – *Oh, he says 'I want to be it' and he is it.* – When he becomes the owner the factory is his, or not? – *Yes, it became all of theirs, everybody who works there.* – But in the factory is there or isn't there an owner? – *Yes, but it's always him.* – And the factory is his? – *No, it became his, though the bricklayers made the factory, it's always owned by the bricklayers.*

This child can be seen oscillating between the primitive idea that to be able to do something it is sufficient to want to do it, or to grow up, and the idea of the 'owner-builder' (the bricklayers).

At Level 3 the role of the owner acquires its own specific identity; he is a 'boss' who supervises and gives orders to the workers. He becomes the 'boss' by election or by promotion, or he comes to take on the role by actually exercising that function. The majority of children think that by becoming the 'boss' he also becomes the owner of the factory.

TOMMASO (8:11) – *The owner sees if the people work.* – What did he do to become the owner of the factory? – *They taught him.* – And after they had taught him? – *He goes to the council.* – And what does he do at the council? – *Oh, he has to put his name down to go to the factory.* – After he's put his name down what does he do? – *He can begin to work as the owner.* – When someone has become the owner of a factory, does the factory become his or not? – *I think so because, he's the boss.*

For others such as Stefano and Marinella, however, the factory does not belong to the owner but to the council.

STEFANO (8:10): – *The owner of the factory also does what the workers do, though he also goes around to see who's making mistakes.* – What does someone do to become the owner of a factory? – *If they're very good, and everybody thinks they are, they become the owner.* – When they become the owner, the factory is theirs or not? – *No, because the factory belongs to the council.*

MARINELLA (8:4): – *The owner controls the whole factory, the women, the men, he has to pay for the kilns, also for the tiles and the lime for the ceramics.* – What does someone do to become the owner of a factory? – *If there's an owner who has to leave, the council doesn't want him any more, I think there's another worker who works well and who asks the council if he can become the owner.* – When this worker becomes the owner, does the factory become his or not? – *No, not all his, it's still a bit of the council's.*

In these examples the owner is just a boss, becoming such either by appointment or by election. In other cases children oscillate between the idea of the 'owner-boss' and the 'owner-builder'.

FRANCA (6:0) – *The owner of the factory sees if the work people are doing is going well and then gives them the envelopes of money which they get.*[10] – What did he do to become the owner of a factory? – *I think he had to become good at working.* – And when he became good at it? – *Well, if he keeps on being so good all the time they appoint him boss.* – When he is the boss, does the factory become his or not? – *I think so . . . no, no, not his, because he didn't build it, he only tells the workers what to do.* – Then who does the factory belong to? – *Oh, it must be the person who built the factory.* – And this man, what must he do to become the owner? – *He has to build the factory, and then he has to say to the owner 'Look, I'll become the boss of the factory, and you will tell the workers what to do; then if something breaks you pay for it'.* – This man who built the factory, what does he do after he's built it? – *Looks for another job because he really can't stay without work when he's finished building it.*

Only the children at Level 4 have clearly recognised that to become the owner of a factory it is necessary to have the money to pay for the builders and the machinery.

EMMA (10:8) – *To become the owner he needs to have capital.* – What's that? – *The money to build the factory.*

A clear recognition that to be the owner of a factory it is necessary to be the proprietor of it (and not only the 'boss' or the builder) distinguishes the subjects of Level 4. However, as regards the tasks of the owner we find both responses similar to those of the preceding level and, more rarely, the idea that he is limited to overseeing the business and to directing the intermediate bosses.

[10] Translator's note: *Busta-paga* is an Italian expression for salary or wage. Literally it means *pay envelope*, and Franca has taken this meaning of the expression from the interviewer's question in constructing her response.

In the protocol of PIERPAOLO (9:1) we find an example of the most common type of response – *I wouldn't know what the owner does, but I think he stays there to look after it, to see, also to help a little, because sometimes the owner also does some work if someone's missing, but he doesn't really work like one of the workers who's always there.* – How does someone become the owner of a factory? – *First of all they have to be taught, then they have to have the money to set up a ceramics factory, the bulldozers, the tractors, the mills, and then they have to teach themselves a lot too.* How does someone set up a ceramics factory? – *They ask the builders if they will build a ceramics factory, though with a very big wage because to build a factory is a very big job and they need a very big wage (...) when they've built it they set up those machines, because the first people who go inside make them explain how the machines work, then they explain to them and others and so it comes to be a ceramics factory. And then they have to begin to get used to having factory meetings, and deciding about strikes with the others ... the other guys, that is.*

Looking at the distributions of these various types of responses, shown in Tables 2.2, 2.3 and 2.4, one can see that for all three work activities considered there is a high proportion of children who know nothing or very little; this proportion includes practically all the 4–5 year olds and the majority of 6–7 year olds. This result does not agree with Goldstein and Oldham's (1979) assertion of a precocity in the understanding of access to work roles. However, this difference may be the consequence of interview technique rather than developmental variations between the samples. The question posed in the American study (How do you get a job?) was much more of a generic question than the ones used in our study (How do you become a farmworker?, for instance). Hence, the American subjects could respond on the basis of those occupations with which they were familiar, while our Italian subjects were forced to think about jobs which may have been unfamiliar. The results of the present study confirm those of our earlier study on payment for work, where the youngest children (6–7 years) only rarely named the factory worker or the farmworker or, when asked by the interviewer, could say little enough about them. In that study, however, the subjects were middle-class urban children, with little opportunity to see farms or factories, or of hearing them being spoken about. The scant knowledge of such subjects could have been considered to be a characteristic of that particular sample. The data obtained from this study with the children of factory workers living in a region where factories and fields lie on their doorstep leads one to think that the difficulty of representing these occupations derives from reasons of a more general order than a lack of familiarity. Indeed, both industrial and agricultural production include a variety of tasks, which are, in many cases, extremely specialised, and which are undertaken at

Table 2.2 *How one becomes a factory worker*

Response level	Age groups				Total
	4–5	6–7	8–9	10–11	
0. Don't know	14	9	1	0	24
1. Just want to do it	6	5	0	0	11
2. Just ask the boss	0	6	9	5	20
3. Don't always find work	0	0	10	15	25
Total	20	20	20	20	80

$r_s = 0.81$, $p < .001$

Table 2.3 *How one becomes a farmworker*

Response level	Age groups				Total
	4–5	6–7	8–9	10–11	
0. Don't know	13	11	1	0	25
1. Just want to do it	7	6	3	0	16
2. Just ask to do it or have the tools	0	3	13	4	20
3. There are different ways	0	0	3	16	19
Total	20	20	20	20	80

$r_s = 0.85$, $p < .001$

Table 2.4 *How one becomes a factory owner*

Response level	Age groups				Total
	4–5	6–7	8–9	10–11	
0. Don't know	12	7	1	1	21
1. Just want to do it	5	4	1	0	10
2. Necessary to build the factory	3	6	1	0	10
3. Necessary to become the boss	0	2	9	1	12
4. Need to buy a factory	0	1	8	18	27
Total	20	20	20	20	80

$r_s = 0.79$, $p < .001$

different times and frequently by different people. To embrace the whole of these activities calls for co-ordinations on the part of the child which are not possible at the level of pre-operatory thinking. Actually, the younger children found it easier to characterise the different occupations on the basis of a single task (the farmworker 'hoes') or a syncretic vision of multiple tasks (the factory worker 'makes tiles'). Only towards 8–9 years (Level 2) do they list different activities or groups of operations which need to be undertaken to realise any industrial production or to further any agricultural enterprise. In parallel with their scant knowledge of the task or group of tasks characterising these work roles, the younger children also showed a certain realism (cf. Piaget, 1929) in their conceptions of the way in which a person gets a job. The idea that it is sufficient to satisfy some generic requirements (to become grown up) or, more specifically, the accessories for a certain role (the possession of suitable clothing, considered as a kind of uniform, or the instruments which accompany a certain activity) indicates how the child's thinking is only able to encompass the most superficial aspects of social roles. From this point of view, it is indeed the cowl which makes the monk! The other idea frequently expressed by the younger children is that it is sufficient to want to be a farmworker, factory worker, or owner to become one *ipso facto*. This shows another feature of infantile realism, the inability to differentiate between the subjective aspects and the objective aspects of reality; the expression of a desire is, consequently, confused with its realisation.

It is around 8–9 years that children's conceptions about these three occupations become more precise and articulated, differentiating the means of access appropriate to each of them. Among the dominant ideas of this period is the notion that one must be appointed by a 'boss' to go to work in a factory and, in some cases, also to become a farmworker. On this point there is a close agreement with the data from the study on payment for work, in which it was also at 8–9 years that children articulated their conceptions of payment within asymmetric pairs, in which one member was the 'boss' of the other. At this age the majority of children manage to grasp only some aspects of the problems posed by entrance into the world of work. They highlight selection by the 'boss' or, for farmworkers, the acquisition of the means necessary for pursuing that activity. These conditions are, however, considered in an exclusive way, either because difficulties which might arise are insufficiently appreciated (as, for example, when the supply of labour exceeds the demand for it in a particular area), or because alternative opportunities are not considered (as, for instance, the day-labourers or tenants who work for others rather than cultivating their own land). The vision of the roles of factory worker and farmworker which appears at 8–9 years, while being more correct than that of younger children, remains simplified. At this age children lack a capacity to take into account simultaneously the multiple aspects of the problem, a capacity which is only apparent at the third level, to which most of the 10–11 year olds belong.

A different analysis needs to be presented for the factory owner. In this case there is an intermediate level between the primitive and generic conceptions of Level 1 (in which the owner is not attributed with any specific functions, and for which it is sufficient either to grow up or to wish to be an owner to become one) and the higher levels characterised by an understanding of hierarchical relations or by the idea that to be an owner means to possess a business. Around 6 years children assert that one becomes an owner by building a factory with one's own hands; they do not distinguish the owner from the factory worker, or else they limit themselves to identifying him on the basis of characteristics which, though they are visible, are not in fact pertinent (such as the doorman's uniform, or the clerk's tasks). One may say, then, that at this level the role of an owner is not yet recognised, given that their activity and position in the factory are described in the same terms as those used for the factory worker. Why, then, do children attribute to the owner a special career which distinguishes him from other workers by asserting that he has built the factory? This assertion that the owner of a factory is also its builder, as it appears at Level 2, seems to us to be associated with the tendency towards artificialism in children's thinking, which is particularly pronounced at this age. Indeed it is precisely at this age that, according to Piaget, the child manifests an 'integral artificialism' (Piaget 1929, p.372). From asking themselves about the origins of the things around them, children, Piaget argues, come to formulate myths in which human beings (parents, adults, or a rather special man called 'God') are the ones who have made the lakes, the sky and the mountains, and who have produced the various meteorological phenomena. The brief outline given by Piaget of a study on the idea of 'country' allows us to glimpse how such artificialism may be coupled with the idea that the builder of something is also its owner: 'A country is really a group of houses and a piece of land which have been built and had their boundaries fixed by a "man" and to which the "man" has given a name so as to distinguish them from other territories.' (Piaget 1928, pp. 128–9). In one of the three extracts from protocols reported by Piaget to illustrate this study we find the following assertion about the 'owner of a country':

> SCHLA (7:11) considers that *France belongs to another man* (than Switzerland). – And does Switzerland belong to a man? – *No, yes to the man who wanted to give us passports.* (Piaget 1928, p. 129)

It may well be that our subjects already understand the fact that the factory must have had a beginning at an age when they are not yet able to understand the activities which take place there, nor the various roles of the people who work there. To the 'owner', therefore, is attributed only the specific function of building the factory, a 'role', or rather an activity, situated in the past. Once he has built the factory the 'owner' has completed his particular task and then begins to engage in the same generic activities which the child attributes to the workers.

Going from the second to the third level we find a qualitatively different conception; the owner comes to be described as a 'boss' who achieved this status following an election, or as the crowning achievement of a career. He is thus characterised on the basis of specific functions which, according to the child, he performs in the factory. The capacity for discriminating social roles with a certain degree of accuracy seems to be typical of the 8–9 year olds; it was also at just this age that children began to describe fairly adequately the job of the factory worker and the farmworker. Nevertheless the figure of the owner, like those of the other workers, is sketched in a rather naive way at Level 3. To be in authority means to have the function of directly supervising people and of telling the workers face to face what they have to do. Children at this age do not seem to suspect that authority might also be exercised in more mediated ways, just as at the preceding level they did not believe that the owner could entrust to others the material execution of the work of building the factory. The advance from level 2 to Level 3 is constituted by the greater specificity of the role. The children no longer believe that the owner might also perform the same activities as the workers.

A particular interest is to be found in some protocols where the conceptions of Level 2 and Level 3 exist side by side in a contradictory way. There were a few children who (like Franca) asserted the existence of two owners, one who managed the factory and one who had built it. These responses make apparent the difficulty of synthesising in a single role both the function of originating the factory and that of managing it. The builder is in fact represented as a bricklayer, or in any case as someone whose principal activity consists precisely of building factories; such a person cannot also undertake the task of managing industrial activity. The synthesis of these two functions is only effected around 10–11 years, through a capacity to represent the origin of the factory in more abstract terms. The owner is again identified as the 'builder', but in a less restricted and concrete sense. Here it is a question of someone who has taken the initiative for building the factory and has paid for that work, rather than having done it with his own hands. Only a few children also managed to construct an idea as abstract as this for the concept of authority, saying that the owner could delegate to others the supervision of the workers. A distinction between the figure of the owner and that of the manager may be hypothesised as a characteristic of a later level which is probably to be found among subjects older than those interviewed in this study. On this point we shall present some data in the following study, and in those of Chapter 5.

2.3   Genesis of the idea of 'the boss'

The idea of the 'boss' came, as we have just seen, to predominate in children from 8 years on in the interviews about how one becomes an owner. Such an idea is certainly a crucial element in children's social conceptions. The study of payment for work showed that an articulated image of economic relations begins to be formed at the point when children become able to represent, in different working situations, a 'boss' who has authority and who pays. Danziger (1958) found that the youngest children he interviewed (5 years) were not able to understand the asymmetry in the relation between worker and boss, though older children (7 years) recognised both the function of authority and of paying the workers. Goldstein and Oldham (1979), on the other hand, did not find a similar developmental progression when they asked their 6- to 13-year-old subjects to explain what is a boss. Children at every age described the boss above all as an *instrumental leader* who told the workers what to do and who controlled their work, while the function of paying the workers was only rarely mentioned. Goldstein and Oldham also found a growing tendency among 6- to 11-year-old children to identify the boss with the owner.

We have taken up this topic in the following study which investigates the origin of children's notions about the 'boss' and how these ideas relate to notions about the owner. Specifically the study examined children's ideas about the boss of the factory and of the school (head teacher).[11] The subjects,[12] all working-class children, had the opportunity to be acquainted with both institutions, the one indirectly through their parents' conversation, and the other through direct experience.[13] The interviews began by seeking to ascertain if the children knew the word 'boss', and if so what meaning they attributed to it. If the word was not known we nonetheless sought to ascertain if they could represent these authority roles by asking: 'Do you know what it means to give orders?'; 'In this school (or nursery) is there someone who gives orders?'; 'Who is it who gives orders?'; 'In the factory where your father works is there someone who gives orders?'. For both the school and the factory the subsequent questioning focused on three points: who is the 'boss', how did they become the 'boss', and if this 'boss' was or was not also the owner.

[11] Translator's note: In Italy the director of the school does not have an active teaching role. The position is therefore closer to that of the principal in U.S. schools than the head teacher of a British school.

[12] There were 56 subjects, 7 boys and 7 girls at each of the following age levels: 4–5 years, 6–7 years, 8–9 years and 10–11 years. They all lived in a small town in the Province of Padova. The data were collected by Rita Benetton.

[13] Burris has recently reported that the teacher is cited by the great majority of primary-school children as an example of a boss, so frequently in fact as to make her suggest that 'school-aged children's explanations of what bosses do and why we need bosses seem to derive largely from the model of the teacher-student relation.' (Burris, 1983, p. 806).

Some children had never heard the word 'boss', nor did they know what it means to give orders. For instance, ELSA (5:1) – Do you know what it means to give orders? – *No.* – Doesn't the Mother (this term was used to refer to the nuns who taught in the school) ever tell you to do something? – *Yes.* – What does she ask you to do? – *To go and dry the spoons, to look after a child's bag, to bring in the trolley.* – Do you think a child can tell a Mother what to do? – *Yes.* – What could a child tell a Mother to do? – *Mother, I have to pee.* – Is that an order? – *Yes.*

With children who, like Elsa, did not know what a 'boss' was and who confused the 'giving of orders' with simply making requests, it was not possible to enter upon the subject of the later questions. These children were classified at Level 0.

The other children gave three types of responses regarding both the school and the factory. At Level 1 they asserted that there is a 'boss', or someone in authority, but did not understand the specificity of this role. Indeed, the 'boss' of the nursery was identified with the bus driver, that of the school with the caretaker, while the 'boss' of the factory undertook the same activities as the workers.

NIVES (6:10) – Where your father works, is there someone who gives orders? – *Yes.* – Why do they give orders? – *Because they're the boss of that factory.* – What does the boss do? – *My father makes the bars, his boss makes the bricks.* – Does the boss work too? – *Yes, a little, sometimes he doesn't work, sometimes he does.* – What does he do? – *Works with the bars, he takes the bars the other men make and puts them together.* – And what does the boss say to the workers? – *Tells them to work on the bricks, to work on the bars because they need a lot of things.* – (...) – Is the factory somebody's? – *The boss.* – And he's the owner? – *Yes.* – How did he come to be the boss? – *Because he's very big and he knows what to do.*

The 'boss', then, is an owner, and for the majority of children he acquired both roles at the same time either through a simple act of will, or by growing up, or by dressing himself as the boss. These are the same ideas which emerged in the preceding study and which were classified at Level 1. Other children, however, said that the boss is the owner of the factory because he built it or the builders had given it to him (as in Level 2 of the preceding study).

ANTONIO (6:8) – Is there a head in this school? – *Yes, Gino* (the caretaker), *the teachers.* – How did Gino become the head? – *He grew up.* – He grew up and then he became the head? – *Yes, because he made the school.* – He made the school? – *Yes, but not on his own, also with some helpers.* – The school belongs to Gino? – *Yes, but also to the teachers.* – Did the teachers also make the school? – *No, they waited till Gino and the others had finished.* – And how did the teachers become the head? – *They bought all the things, the books, and also the felt-tip pens(. . . .)* – How did your father's boss become the boss? – *Because he made a house, then other men wanted to go and work there, then they helped him.*

At Level 2 the 'boss' exercises the role of authority. At school it is the head teacher, in the factory someone who supervises the workers and gives them orders. The 'boss' is always the 'owner', and to become such it is necessary to build the factory or the school (usually having others build it, or buying it), or – but more rarely – to be appointed by the builder to run it.

ANNA (8:2) – Do you know what 'boss' means? – *Yes, the one who governs the work.* – What do you mean, they govern? – *That he tells the others what they have to do.* – Is there a head in this school? – *Yes, the one who runs the school.* – Who's that? – *The head teacher.* Returning to this discourse later the interviewer asked: – Does this school belong to someone? – *Yes, the head teacher.* – And he's the owner? – *Yes.*

LUCA (8:4) – Is there a boss where your father works? – *Yes.* – What does he do? – *He says what they have to do, how to make the bottoms for the tank.* He just tells people what to do, or does he also do something else? – *Sees if they do it well, if they do it right.* – Who owns the factory? – *The boss, he made the factory and bought all the machines.*

At Level 3, finally, the 'boss' and the 'owner' become differentiated. The 'boss' of the factory supervises the workers, and the 'owner' in his turn gives directives to the 'boss' and controls his work. In the school the 'owner' is the council or the state, which delegates to the head teacher the functions which are its duty as 'owner' but which it does not have time to carry out itself. To become a 'boss' calls, therefore, for a different procedure and requirements from those necessary to become an 'owner'. For the former it is a question of undertaking the necessary studies and being appointed; for the latter it is a question of having the factory or school built, or of buying it.

WALDIMIRO (8:4) says that in his father's factory there is a boss who – *Orders the sacks, then to load the lorry, and many other things.* – Whose is the factory? – *Mr Matteazzi's.* – And he's the owner? – *Yes.* – Is he the boss you told me about before? – *No, the boss is the one the owner tells what to do and he tells the workers(. . . .)* – Does this school belong to someone? – *Yes, the council.* – Why then isn't it in charge? – *Because its got other things to think about and so it put the head in charge of the school.*

Tables 2.5 and 2.6 present the distribution of responses for the head of the school and the boss of the factory. They show that for both concepts children's ideas develop at the same pace, even though they are two distinct institutions

Table 2.5 *Who is the head of the school?*

Response level	Age groups				Total
	4–5	6–7	8–9	10–11	
0. Doesn't understand the questions	8	0	0	0	8
1. There's an owner-boss with general functions	6	12	3	0	21
2. There's an owner-boss with specific functions	0	2	7	4	13
3. The boss works for the owner	0	0	4	10	14
Total	14	14	14	14	56

$r_s = 0.89$, $p < .001$

Table 2.6 *Who is the boss of the factory?*

Response level	Age groups				Total
	4–5	6–7	8–9	10–11	
0. Doesn't understand the questions	8	0	0	0	8
1. There's an owner-boss with general functions	6	13	4	0	23
2. There's an owner-boss with specific functions	0	1	7	9	17
3. The boss works for the owner	0	0	3	5	8
Total	14	14	14	14	56

$r_s = 0.87$, $p < .001$

with which the child also has differing experiences, personal and direct in one case, only verbal reports in the other. The very high correlation ($r_s = 0.87$) between the response levels given by each child for the two institutions allows us to speak of the development of the idea of the 'boss' in general. These results, which agree with those reported by Danziger (1958), show that these notions only become clearly delineated around 8 years. At younger ages either the difference between orders and other types of requests is not understood, or there is no conception of a role uniquely characterised by this function. This is true not only for the reality which the child experiences indirectly, such as the factory or the world of work in general, but also for extremely familiar situations such as the school. Moreover, in their domestic life children also very frequently have the opportunity to verify the existence of hierarchical roles superior to their own, receiving orders or having their own wishes contradicted. In a study of the development of the concept of authority, Damon (1977) found that the youngest children he interviewed (4 years) were not able to distinguish between orders they had been given and their own desires. Only around 8–9 years did authority come to be not only recognised but also legitimised as the basis of a real training for authority, which represents the assumption of a stable role. In the intermediate levels, Damon traced the passage from the simple recognition of the physical characteristics of those who exercise authority, to a legitimisation founded on requirements which were progressively more 'psychological' and adequate. It seems, then, that young children cannot initially even pose themselves questions about roles such as that of the 'boss'.

The data just described clarify the relations between the notions of boss and of owner. We have, in fact, been able to see that for a long period these two notions are not differentiated. Both the word 'boss' and the word 'owner' (which, moreover, remain closely associated even in adult language) signify initially the same concept in which the notions of authority and of possession are syncretically included. Around 10–11 years, however (which differs from the age given by Goldstein and Oldham) children come to differentiate these two notions. Owners do not cease to be represented as bosses; they become, in fact, 'bosses of the second order', from whom the 'boss of the first order', who is in direct contact with the employees – workers or teachers – takes direction. To construct this 'pyramid of authority', the child uses the operations of seriation, ordering social roles according to the power relations which run between them. This task, apparently banal, carries cognitive difficulties which are not unimportant. Piaget has shown that it is not until 7–8 years that the child is able to construct a series of concrete objects (wooden sticks of varying lengths, for instance). If it is then a case of ordering a series of elements which are only verbally described one must wait till the child is 11 years or more (Piaget 1928). In our case too, only a few of the oldest children were able to differentiate the 'boss' and the 'owner' and to connect them in a hierarchy composed of three figures.

3   Where does money come from?

In the research on payment for work discussed in the previous chapter, various hints arose of themes which it was neither possible nor opportune to pursue in that context. There were, for example, some 6–7 year olds who expressed quite fanciful ideas about the source of money, ideas which, however, moderated and rapidly disappeared at successive age levels. Indeed, from about 8–9 years children are convinced that work is the only legitimate way of acquiring money. Some children also then went on to describe criteria which might regulate remuneration: for example, that people are paid according to the number of hours they have worked, or in consideration of how difficult or tiring a particular activity might be; some children resorted to more objective measures such as counting the number of things a worker produced, or the number of journeys made by a bus driver. Such responses indicate an awareness of the fact that there are differing levels of income, and that the child is attempting to explain this by relating varying levels of income to varying characteristics of the work undertaken. Finally, at various ages, many children described the bank as a principal source from which money flows, either for everyone who needs it, or for the 'boss' who thus becomes able to pay the workers.

In this chapter we take up and pursue these points, and the results of our own research will be compared with those of other authors. The first study examines ideas about the source of money among 3–8-year-old children, the more primitive ideas on money and work thus completing the picture which was traced in the previous chapter. Differences of income and the reasons for them are reconsidered in the light of a second study in which children were asked about wealth and poverty. The chapter concludes with a study of an institution so often spontaneously mentioned by the children: the bank.

3.1   The source of money

In this study we wished to examine the more primitive conceptions about the source of money, and to see how, beginning from these ideas, the child comes to understand that one earns money through work. We have seen in the previous chapter that all the children we interviewed asserted that 'one works to earn money', even if the younger children (6–7 years) did not seem to apply this principle to every job. These young children suggested the possibility of living on money donated by the bank or from money obtained as 'change' in shops. Probably for these younger children the affirmation that 'one works for money' constituted only a repetition of phrases or discussions overheard from adults, and which had not yet been effectively understood. In fact since the notion of remunerated working activity could not have been acquired by children through their own personal experiences, it clearly must have been reconstructed from information furnished by adults, above all their parents, on those occasions when they have told their children that they are off to work, or that they go to work to bring money into the house. Younger children appeared incapable of precisely this process of reconstruction. Their spontaneous (and quite erroneous) ideas about the source of money go hand in hand with an inability to comprehend information about work and payment for it, these ideas gradually disappearing as such comprehension is achieved.

It seemed opportune, therefore, to organise the interview around two distinct points. Firstly the source of money and, secondly, the father's occupation, together with that of other figures readily visible to a child. Since this study was also undertaken with quite young children[1] for whom a comprehension of money and its functions could not be assumed, the interview began with a short trial in which the children were shown some money and asked to say what it was and what it was used for. Performance on this trial determined how the interview continued. If the children recognised the money and also that it served to buy things, they were asked how adults came to obtain it; if the reply to this question was that they received money for working they were asked if there were also other ways of obtaining money, and the interview than went on to examine how the child represented payment for their father: 'What work does your father do?'; 'Who gives him the money he earns?'; 'Why do they give it to him?'; 'What would happen if they didn't give it to him?' etc. Subjects were then asked about three occupations easily recognisable for children (dustman, fireman, and bus or train driver). For each occupation they were asked if the person who did it was paid, and, if so, by whom.

The theme of work (and eventually of payment for it) was presented in different terms to the children who did not recognise money, or who did not mention work among the ways in which it could be obtained. These subjects were asked where their parents were at the moment, what they were doing and why; they were also asked in a similar way about the same list of

[1] There were 100 subjects, 10 boys and 10 girls at each of the following age levels: 3–4 years, 4–5 years, 5–6 years, 6–7 years and 7–8 years. The interviews took place in a nursery and a primary school in Padova frequented by middle-class children.

occupations noted above. If in response to these questions children mentioned payment for work, then this theme was pursued through the same questions described above.

The responses to these questions were arranged in a sequence characterised by the progressive consolidation of the relations between work and payment for it. At the first level are those children who have no idea of the necessity of obtaining money, and who do not consider earning money as one of the reasons inducing people to work. At the second and third levels, however, children understand that money is consumed through being spent, and that it could be obtained by working, or from other sources. At the second level the activities which allow someone to earn money are reduced solely to their father's activity, while at the third level only a few other activities are also recognised as paid jobs. Finally, at the fourth level, work comes to be considered as the only way in which people can earn money.

Level 1: No relation between work and earning money.

Children do not maintain any connection between work and earning money and, in the majority of cases, do not even set themselves the problem of the source of money. Some of them have absolutely no understanding of money, others have nothing to say about how adults obtained it or, like the girl whose responses are given below, do not seem to be aware that money could be used up by being spent.

ESTER (3:5) – How do daddies come to have the money they need? – *They take money.* – How do they take it? – *They take it in their pocket.* – The money they have in their pocket, was it also there yesterday? – *Yes.* – And before then? – *It was in their pockets.* – When it's finished what does Daddy do? – *He takes it from his other pocket.* – And when that one's also empty what does he do? – *He takes some more.* – Where from? – *From wallets.*

For the most part these children know that their parents regularly leave home to do something which is called 'work', but they have no idea of the reasons they go out to work, or they give as a reason the fact that 'they have to do it', or 'they want to do it'. If their attention is drawn to the activity of the dustman, bus driver, etc., they show no comprehension of them, or say that they do it to provide people with a useful service, without relating this fact to the possibility that such employees draw a wage from their work. Here, for example, is how the interview with ESTER continues:

– Where is your daddy now? – *At the Institute.* – Why does he go to the Institute? – *Because … my daddy brings me to school and then goes to the Institute.* – And where do the daddies of the other children go? – *They go to the Institute too.* – What does your daddy do in the Institute? – *I don't know.* – Have you ever been in a bus? – *Yes, when I went to Venice.* – Why do the people who drive the busses stay there driving them? – *Because otherwise then they would stop. – Could they stop driving if they wanted to? – No, because when someone has to get on a bus . . . they couldn't and so they'd have to get off.*

In a limited number of cases we do find some ideas, however wrong they might be, about the source of money.

ROBERTO (5:0) says that money is obtained by – *going to buy it.* – Where? – *Where you buy things.* – Can you explain to me what you do? Let's pretend that I'm a shopkeeper and that you've come to buy. – *Can you give me some money? –* What do you want? *– Some paper money. –* Is this one alright? *– Yes.* – What do you have to give me in exchange? *– Nothing . . . what do you want?* – What you want. What can you give me? – *One thing, a sweet.* – To go and buy money, are sweets what you need? Or do you need other money? – *Sweets.* – Are there other ways of getting money? – *Yes.* – What? ... Mummy and Daddy, for instance, what do they do? – *Go and ask for it in a shop.* – The other mummies and daddies as well? – *Yes.* – Where are your mummy and daddy now? – *Mummy's at home, Daddy's at work.* – Why does Daddy go to work? – *Because he has to write.* – What job does he do? – *Looks, writes, and then he looks at the books and reads.* – Could he stay at home? – *No.* – Why not? – *Because he always wants to go out.* If he didn't want to any more, could he stay at home? – *He could go for a walk.* – And the other daddies? ... Do they all do the same as your daddy? – *They also work.* – A daddy who is a road sweeper, if he didn't want to clean the streets could he stay at home? – *Yes.* – Why does he have to clean them? – *Because the streets are dirty.*

Level 2: Only their father's work is paid.

Level 2 consists of a small but interesting group of children who are beginning to connect payment with the performance of a work activity, but who recognise as 'work' only that of their own father. In fact they deny that other activities could be defined as work, affirming that they are not paid. To obtain money people who drive trains, or clean the streets, or perform some other activity must also undertake that 'work' which the child maintains is the only one to be paid; so they must go to the office, or be a lawyer, or whatever. Alternatively they must go to the bank to get money, or get the shopkeeper to give them some.

DAVIDE (4:10) says that to have money grown-ups – *have to go to work.* – Give me the name of a job. – *What my daddy does?* – Yes. – *He's a lawyer.* – The money he gets for being a lawyer, who gives it to him? – *There's someone else who's also a lawyer, my grandad.* – The money your daddy gets for being a lawyer, who gives it to him? – *My grandad.* – And your grandad, how does he come to have it? – *Another lawyer gave it to him.* – Is driving a train work? – *No.* – Why not? – *Because not.* – The men who drive trains, do they get money? – *Oh yes! Because if someone doesn't get money they can't drive a train, because to buy the train they need lots of money, thousands, because ... haven't you ever been to a station?* – Yes, I live right in front of it. – *Well, there, when you go to look at the trains haven't you ever seen long, long, long trains?* – Yes. – *And to buy those trains you need to have lots and lots of money.* – But after spending so much money to buy the train, how do they get the money they need for shopping? – *Those who drive trains, you know, also go to work.* – What work do they do? – *Lawyer, like my daddy, lawyers.* – All the mummies and daddies are lawyers? – *No-oh! Only the daddies are lawyers, not the mummies.*

SILVIA (4:8) – How do grown-ups come to have money? – *The daddy has to go to work, otherwise how do you get money?* – Otherwise? – *Nothing.* – Can you tell me the name of a job that grown-ups do to get money? – *Where my daddy goes?* – Yes. – *To the office, no?* – And at the office, what does he do to get money? – *No, he only goes to work ... or else by buying, no, people in the shops also give it to him.* – When he works, who is it who gives him money? – *The head of the office (...)* The men who take away the dustbins, do they get money? – *No-oh!* – Is it a job? – *No.* – And driving a train, is that a job? – *Yes, it's a bit of a job, because ...* – They get money? – *Perhaps not, perhaps yes or no.* – Do you know what a farmworker does? – *Grows wheat.* Do they get paid? – *No.* – Why not? – *Oh, because there's no one to pay them, no! The wheat grows by itself.* – People who drive a bus, do they get money for driving it? – *No, because no one gives it to them, they just put a ticket in.* – But listen, the farmworker, the bus driver, the train driver or the dustman, how do they get the money they need to buy things to eat, clothes, and all the rest? – *They go to work like normal men.* – And what work do normal men do? – *They go to the office and write.*

Level 3: *Other jobs are also paid.* At level 3 children recognise that other jobs, as well as their father's, are also paid, though they persist in maintaining that one can also obtain money in other ways, either through change or from the money given by the bank, without conditions, to whoever asks for it.

SILVIA (7:7) – Is a fireman paid? – *Yes.* – Who pays the fireman? – *... to find a job, they work, and they give money where they work in that ... that house ...* – Where they put out the fire, or the fire station? – *... the fire station, yes.* – They give money in the fire station? – *Yes.* – Does the plumber get money? – *Yes.* Who gives it to him? – *Mummy.* – The one who called the plumber? – *Yes.* – Could she not pay him? – *If not he'd call the police.* – And where do farmworkers get the money to buy the things they need? ... Are they paid? – *They have money.* Where do you think they might have got the money from? – *From the work they do.* – How come? – *Because he goes to buy tomatoes, they give him change and he can get money.* – Are the road sweepers paid? – *Yes, because they bought the lorry, they give change and they too get money.*

Apart from the confusions about 'change', there is also in this protocol the idea, already familiar to the reader, that one must pay to go to work. However, since our main interest is in work as a source of money, we note that the reasons given to justify remuneration remain imprecise. In the case of the plumber, for instance, if he is not paid the worker will call the police. That is to say that payment is an obligation, with the threat of sanctions, but without any reason being given. More generally for children at this level, payment for work, in those cases where it is recognised, occurs for reasons which may be termed 'non-retributive' since the child only affirms that payment actually happens. Sometimes the payment is justified by the existence of a law or a moral obligation; at other times there are finalistic criteria (such as the necessity that those who work do not remain without money) to justify payment. What never emerges at this level is the affirmation that one is paid because one has worked.

Level 4: Money comes only from working. Finally, at the fourth level, children clearly and univocally connect work and the receipt of money. To obtain money it is necessary to work, and there is no other way. Some children think that not every activity they consider is paid, since they are unable to imagine in what form the payment occurs. Nevertheless, contrary to the ideas of the preceding level, these children deny that there are other sources of money apart from work, and the way in which some workers are paid remains an unresolved problem for them.

STEFANO (5:9) – What do grown-ups do to have money? – *They go to work.* – Is that the only way, or are there also other ways? – *Only that way.* – Tell me some jobs that people do to get money? – *A worker, an accountant.* – What do you mean a 'worker'? – *Builds houses.* – And an accountant? – *Studies.* – The money a worker gets for his work, does he get it by himself, or does someone give it to him? – *Someone gives it to him.* Who? – *The person who wants the worker to build a house.* – And if he doesn't give him any money? – *The worker won't go to build a house for him any more.* – Have you ever seen the men who take the rubbish away in lorries? – *Yes.* – Do they get money? – *... I don't think so.* – Why not? – *I don't know.* – Nobody gives them any money? – *No.* – What do they do to get money? – *They work.* Isn't taking the rubbish away work? – *Yes.*

As regards the reasons for payment and the way in which it is made, these can now be defined as 'retributive' since the money is given in proportion to the work done and actually because someone has worked.

MICHELE (7:1) says that his father repairs scales. – Does he do it in a factory or a shop? – *He's never told me.* – The money your daddy gets for repairing scales, is there someone who gives it to him, or does he go to get it from somewhere? – *There's someone who gives it to him because he's worked.* – Who? – ... *I don't remember.* – How would he know how much money to give him? – ... *Because he works, and then he gives him money because he works.* – But how would he know how much to give him? – *If he sees him working a bit more he gives him as much as he thinks ... if, instead, he works a little less he gives him a little less.* – Could he not give him any? – *No.* – What would happen if he didn't? – *Then he wouldn't go to work any more, because if he didn't give him any money he wouldn't get any.*

MILENA (7:7) says that her father, a council employee, is paid by the boss. – Who is he? – ... – What does the boss do? – *Sees that they do things properly and when ... every week he gives him his pay ... for the work he's done.* – What would happen if the boss didn't give him the money? – *All the workers would go on strike.*

As Table 3.1 shows, the responses of Level 1 are predominant only among the 3 and 4 year olds. These responses indicate not only the absence of any connection between money and work, but also of any curiosity about the source of money.

Duveen and Shields (1983) have also reported such responses, but only among their youngest subjects (3 years) were they at all frequent (23 per cent). From 4 years on, the idea that money comes from handbags or pockets was much rarer among their sample (5 per cent). These authors suggest that, at least in part, such erroneous identifications of the source of money is a consequence of a linguistic constraint in the discourse of the interview. The child may not recognise that the question 'how do people get money' is intended to refer to the *social* process through which people gain access to money; in this case the 'local' responses reported by Duveen and Shields (that is, responses referring to the *place* in which money is found) may be a pertinent response. However it is also possible to suggest a different explanation.

The attitude of these young children, who do not know where their parents get money from, or who imagine that when they have used up all the money in their wallet there is always some more in their pocket or in a drawer, corresponds to that described by Piaget from interviews on other themes with children of about the same age as those interviewed here (cf. Piaget, 1929, pp. 369–71). Younger than 5 years, in fact, children do not ask themselves questions about the origins of various natural things and phenomena, since they tend to explain everything by connecting it not with the cause which produced it, but with the ends for which it provides a means. For children at this age the explanation of why things exist and function is only that they satisfy human needs. Progressively the finalism which is implicit in this type of conception becomes explicit giving rise to beliefs that the inanimate world,

Table 3.1 *Where does money come from?*

Response level	Age groups					Total
	3–4	4–5	5–6	6–7	7–8	
1. No connection between work and money	17	9	1	1	0	28
2. Only their father's work is paid	1	5	4	0	1	11
3. Other work is also paid	2	3	6	8	5	24
4. Work is the only way to earn money	0	3	9	11	14	37
Total	20	20	20	20	20	100

$r_s = 0.72$, $p < .001$

as much as the human one, obeys moral rules, and that humans are not only the end, but also the initiators of objects and natural events, which they produce through their own activity.

An analogous passage from an implicit to an explicit finalism occurs at the second level of our sequence. Children from 5 to 7 years no longer limit themselves, as the younger ones did, to taking it for granted that money is there because it is actually necessary, they also try to explain the various ways in which people come into possession of it, and they identify sources such as the bank, shops and work. These are the same sources as those mentioned by preschoolers in research by both Burris (1983) and Duveen and Shields (1983). It seems clear to us why these rather than other sources are the most frequently cited. Children are in a position to ascertain that people have money and that it has something to do with shops or the bank; they also have occasion to hear 'work' spoken of as a place where their parents go, bringing money back with them to the house. What effectively occurs in shops or banks or at 'work' remains unknown to the child for a long time, as, equally, do the reasons for which, on different occasions, grown-ups receive money. Whether money comes from the bank, from change, from rich people, or whether it is earned through work, until 7–8 years (Level 4) its distribution is motivated finalistically; it would be disastrous for people not to get any.

We shall see later the development of concepts about the bank and the shop. As regards work, this is first of all (Level 2) identified with that of their father, which appears to constitute a *script* (see Nelson, 1981) more or less articulated according to the type of activity and the possibilities available to the child for observing its characteristics. There is a progression in such scripts from the idea of leaving the house and going somewhere else (which may be called 'the Institute' or 'the office'), to the representation of the actions undertaken (writing, reading, etc), to the identification of the appropriate social relations (the presence of clients, colleagues and, eventually, the boss). Payment, however, does not form a part of these scripts. Indeed the affirmation that going to work allows Daddy to get money signifies nothing more than that the job is a source of money which functions in the same way as banks or shops.

In this study we did not seek to examine developments in children's comprehension of their father's job. This information is available from the work of Goldstein and Oldham (1979) who describe the increasing detail reported by children about their fathers' activity as they move from primary- to secondary-school age. What interested us was, rather, the development of the concept of work as an activity for which one is paid. The essential point is the generalisation of the distinguishing characteristics of a job (particularly the idea of payment) to activities other than that of the father; this emerges at Levels 3 and 4.

The generalisation of the idea of work and the parallel disappearance of finalistic conceptions, which are replaced, in the end, by an understanding that payment is a remuneration, is associated with various strands in the child's intellectual development. The broadening of the concept of work indicates the overcoming of an egocentric vision in which their own situation (in this case their father's job) is not differentiated from that of others. The idea of payment given in exchange for service and, for some children, also in proportion to what has been done, indicates an ability to perform operations of compensation, relating different quantities of work to different amounts of money (even if there is only an approximate quantification). The age at which this occurs is the same as that at which the child begins to conceive, and to put into effect, a distribution of rewards among peers according to criteria of retributive justice in which each receives in proportion to what they have given. Damon's (1977) research, which produced these data, also revealed the relationships between the development of the notion of 'retributive justice' and that of the operations of classification and compensation. The comparison of these results with our own suggests that the logical development of the child, the formation of concepts realised through peer interaction (such as that of a 'just distribution'), and a progressively more adequate vision of the relations which organise the adult world proceed in a parallel and, at least in the case under consideration, synchronous way.

3.2   Notions of 'rich' and 'poor'

As we saw in Chapter 1 the question of social stratification has been one of the major themes in research on children's economic understanding. However when our own research was undertaken much of this other work had not yet been published, and indeed very little information was available to us about the theme of the following study, children's ideas of wealth and poverty (what was available was the research of Danziger 1958; Connell 1977; Goldstein and Oldham 1979). From these studies a clear relationship emerges: as children get older they make an ever-closer connection between wealth and work. Our own investigation was intended, in part, to see if Italian children showed a similar progression. We also undertook an inquiry with working-class children to see if the connection between wealth and work was also apparent when the head of the household's income was insufficient for the family to be well-off.

The interview[2] began with questions intended to ascertain what the child understood by rich and poor: 'Do you know what it means to be rich (or poor)?'; 'Is your family rich or poor?'. We then continued by asking how one becomes rich or poor, and by examining how far children thought changes in economic conditions possible. Examination of the data revealed five types of response. In the most primitive type (Level 0) children do not even know what the words rich and poor mean. At the next level (Level 1) rich and poor come to be identified with the availability and the lack of money respectively; children believe, however, that anybody could obtain money from the bank or the shop, and that therefore poverty is an exceptional condition. At Level 2 children think that money could only be obtained by working, and that therefore those who work are rich while the poor are those who are unable or unwilling to work. For the most part these children also characterise their own family as being rich. At Level 3 the children add to the distinction between rich and poor a third term, those who are 'normal' (neither rich nor poor). This is exactly what they believe their own families to be. Various degrees of richness are also derived from the varying intensity or quantity of work. Lastly, at Level 4, the children asserted that payment for work did not depend only on the effort expended or the time spent working, and also denied that it was enough to work hard to become rich.

Level 0: 'Don't know'.

We shall begin with an example of a child for whom the words 'rich' and 'poor' are without significance.

ALBERTO (4:8) – Do you know what it means to be rich? – *Yes.* – Who are the rich? – *Children.* – The children are rich? – . . . – Do you know what it means to be poor? – *No.* – Do you think your family is rich or poor? – *Yes.* – Yes what? – *Poor.* – Do you have lots of money, or only a little? – *Lots of money.* – Could you buy everything? – *Yes.* – How come there are poor people and rich people? – *Because they're good.* – Who is it who's good? – *The family.*

---

[2]   100 children from 4 to 13 were interviewed; 10 boys and 10 girls at each of the following age levels: 4–5 years, 6–7 years, 8–9 years, 10–11 years and 12–13 years. The data were collected by Chiara Chatel.

Level 1: Almost everybody is rich.

Responses such as Alberto's are in fact rather rare; already by 4–5 years the majority of children belong to Level 1, having some idea of what is meant by the words 'rich' and 'poor'. The rich are *those who have lots of money; those who have bracelets and watches.* The poor are *those who don't have money, are without money, who have nothing;* very often the poor are identified with the old.

The totality of the responses given in the course of the interview indicates, however, that while for 'poor' the child intends those who are completely without money or goods, or who have less of them than other people, the word 'rich' does not at all mean those who possess an abundance of money and goods, nor even more than an average amount; rather it refers to those who are able to satisfy their most elementary needs. This is evident both in their descriptions of 'rich' and from the fact that the children, who come from working-class families, nearly always assert that their family is rich. In the few cases where this was not so it was because richness was defined as the actual possession of money; if the money is deposited in a bank, or if it has just been spent, then one is no longer rich.

ELSA (4:5) – What does it mean to be poor? – *That you don't have anything, don't have money, can't eat, like that.* – Can the rich and poor do the same things, or not? – *No.* – Why not? – *Because the rich have lots of money and can eat, the poor don't have any money and can't eat.* – What about your family? – *Rich.* – Are there people richer than you, or are you the richest in the world? – *Mummy's rich, my brother's rich, my daddy's rich.* – Apart from your family, are there people richer than you, or not? – *Only a neighbour who's poor.*

The idea that their own family (and the great majority of other people) are rich goes with the idea of an unconditional accessibility of money, which is obtained by drawing it from the bank, or through the change given by shopkeepers.

MARIO (5:2) – If a man wants to become rich what does he have to do? – *He has to go to lots of shops and then they give him money.* – Who is it who gives him money? – *Those in charge who say 'do you want bread? here, 50 lire' and they give it to him and he comes back and then becomes rich. (. . .)* Is it easy or difficult to become rich? – *Easy.* – Can everybody become rich or not? – *Of course not.* – Who is it who can't become rich? – *My neighbour who's called Mrs Gemma isn't rich.* – Why not? – *Because she never goes out.* – Could a rich man become poor? – *Yes, if he gives it back where he got it he'll be poor again.* – Who does he have to give it back to? – *For instance, he went to a shop, got lots of money and took it back to them and so became poor again.* Asked about his father's work Mario says – *He goes to the factory at night and comes back at midday.* – Why does your father go to work? – *Because he's used to going to work and also he wants to go to work.*

How is the existence of the poor to be explained if it is so easy to obtain money? In the responses of these children poverty appears as a transitory condition, in which the poor are those who have just spent their money, though when they get some more they will be rich again; or else poverty is a product of obstacles which limit the possibility of accessing sources of money (as is the case for Mrs Gemma, who does not go out of the house nor go to the shops).

CLAUDIA (5:5) – Can the rich become poor? – *Yes, because they buy lots of things to eat.* – And they can't get any more money? – *Yes they can, they go to the bank.* – Is it easy or difficult to become rich? – *Easy.*

More rarely the identification of the 'poor' with the 'old' leads to the identification of the conditions which determine wealth or poverty with those which, according to the child, regulate the life cycle.

IRIS (4:8) – How come there are rich people and poor people? – *Because the poor people are old and the young ones are rich.* – Are all the young people rich, or not? – *Yes, all of them.* – If a man wants to become rich what does he have to do? – *Doesn't have to do anything, because if he's old he can't become young.* – How did the young people become rich? – *Because they are born from the tummy of a woman and then become rich.* – Can a man who is poor become rich, or not? – *No.* – Why not? – *Because he's already been young and rich and then become old and poor.* – And can a rich man become poor? – *Yes, because he's already been young and rich and then become old.* – If a man wants to become really rich what does he have to do? – *He has to stay young forever and never become old.* – How could he stay young forever – *Only eat one time.*

Level 2: Everyone who works is rich.

At Level 2 children continue to think of their own family as rich, identifying wealth with a modest well-being. However, they no longer believe that it is sufficient to go to the shop or the bank to have money, but argue instead that the only way to get money is to go to work. When the interviewer persists in asking if there are also other ways apart from work, the children mention exceptional events such as winning a lottery or gifts from some benefactor, or illegal activities such as theft or fraud.

MARCO (6:8) – How come there are rich people and poor people? – *Because the poor don't have any money.* – And why don't they have any money? – *Because they don't work.* – And the rich, on the other hand? – *They go to work.*

If the poor don't work it is because they are unwilling to do so or are prevented from doing so for various reasons.

GRAZIELLA (8:4) – How come there are people who have lots of money and people who have only a little? – *Because the ones who have lots of money go to work.* – And those who have only a little? – *They don't go to work.* – Why not?

– If a man who is poor goes to work he doesn't have the money to get a job. – You need money to get a job? *– Yes. –* How come? *– ...*

For EMILIO (6:4) the poor are *'old'* – What does it mean to be poor? *– That they're old like that, usually they don't have any money, they don't have anything. –* Who are the people who have lots of money? *– Young people.*

MARCO (6:8) asserts that the poor do not work *because they don't want to. –* Why not? (...) Do the rich always want to work? *– Yes. –* If a man wants to become rich what does he have to do? *– Work. –* If he works is he sure to get rich, or not? *– Yes. –* But all those who have lots of money, do they all have the same amount, or not? *– The same.*

It is apparent from these examples that the only progress over the preceding level lies in the solid conviction that money does not fall from the heavens and that it is necessary to work to get it, though there are no discriminations between differing levels of income. Marco, for instance, some of whose responses we have given above, went on to say that his family is rich and that they could buy the whole city if they wanted to; later he argued that by working one did not only become rich but *'rich, very rich even'* and that his father and the other workers could also become very rich. All the same, one should not believe that this lack of any fine discrimination in the diverse levels of wealth depends on an overvaluation of their own family's way of life; it is, rather, an inability on the child's part to represent the way of life of more privileged social strata.

TERESA (6:1) – Do you know what it means to be rich? *– Yes, that you have a lot of money. –* And then? *– That you have lots to eat. –* Do you think your family is rich or poor? *– Rich. –* How come? *– Because they buy lots of things to eat with money. –* Can you buy everything? *– Yes. –* Are you the richest in the world? *– Yes. –* You can buy everything that you want? *– Yes. –* Are there people richer than you or not? *– No. –* Or poorer? *– No. –* How come there aren't any people poorer? *– Because everybody is rich, they all have things to eat. –* But do the rich only buy things to eat, or other things as well? *– Meat, pasta, carrots, eggs. –* But only things to eat, or other things as well? *– Milk, bread.*

The interview went on in this tone for a while with Teresa continuing to confirm the wealth of her own family, even though their only income came from her father's job and they could afford only the most basic necessities.

Level 3: The rich are those who work the most.

At the third level an intermediate condition is added to the rich-poor polarity which the children describe in terms such as 'normal' or 'neither rich nor poor'. They place their own family at this level, thus demonstrating that they have extended the breadth of their experiences to include degrees of well-being slightly superior to those which they enjoy at home. This broadening of the child's vision is, however, still very limited, as can be seen in the examples children give of wealth and of well-paid jobs. They say that factory or agricultural work is well paid, and that, moreover, by working hard and not taking holidays one can earn more, though not every job allows for such extra work.

MARTINO (7:1) – Does everybody have the same amount of money, or not? – *No, because the daddies go to work, but sometimes they only get a little, sometimes lots, it depends on the job they do, heavy or light.* – Do you know what it means to be rich? – *No.* – Who are the rich people? – *Those who have money, houses, villas, cars.* – And do you know what it means to be poor? – *Those who wear rags and other things.* – Do you think your family is rich or poor? – *Not so rich, it's a little poor because we have a very old house; my daddy has asked many times for a house, he's also asked many times for a telephone because we don't have one.* – Could you buy whatever you want? – *No, sometimes my brother wants some toys and my mummy says yes, but then she doesn't buy them because she buys food with the money.* – How come there are rich people and poor people? – *Because the rich, before being rich are poor, then they find a job which is heavy and they give them money and with the money they buy villas like those in films.* – And the poor? – *If they don't look for a heavy job they can't become rich and they'll stay poor all their life.* – How come they can't find a heavy job? – *Because no one wants them.* – Why not? – *Because they look at them and it depends on the muscles they have, if they're strong then they take them on, if not they stay poor all their life.* – Is every job good for getting rich? – *No, there are some where you get a little money and some where they give you lots.* – Which are the best ones for getting rich? – *The heaviest ones.* – If a man has a heavy job is he sure to get rich? – *No, sometimes they start wheezing and they can't go on any longer, because when you work you can't stop for a minute, it's not like school where you can stop and finish things at home.* – Can you also get very rich doing a heavy job? – *Yes, it depends on the boss, how much money he gives you, and you can't squabble about it, you have to take the money they give you.*

In the course of this interview it seems for a moment that Martino manages to understand that the amount of wages paid is not only tied to good will, but also depends on how much the boss has available for pay (something which might lead him to reflect on the possibility of becoming rich or very rich by doing an inferior job). In the end, though, his idea remains that the best paid jobs are those which are heavy or risky. This way of seeing wealth as proportional to work is characteristic of children at this level, and is argued in many of the protocols.

Since working a lot and saving a lot is what counts, becoming rich or very rich is difficult but not impossible. If someone does not become rich it is because they do not want to, or because they are already too old.

RENATA (8:9) – If a man wants to become rich, what does he have to do? – *He must work a lot and not spend very much, he mustn't always buy snacks for the children, or notebooks.* – Is it easy or difficult to become rich? – *Difficult, because you have to work all the time, you must never waste time.* – Can everybody become rich, or not? – *Yes, everybody, they just need to set themselves to work.* – And why doesn't everybody do it? – *Because they want to go and see their friends and spend lots of money instead of keeping it.*

As regards the possibility of a rich person becoming poor there is now the other side of the coin, it is not enough to work a lot, they must also not spend too much.

VITTORIO (10:8) – What do you have to do to be rich? – *You have to save up, only spend a little money and earn lots.* – Could the rich become poor? – *Little by little they have less if they buy things that cost a lot.*

Level 4: The rich do a particular job.

Finally, at the fourth level, children begin to recognise the existence of a more complex economic stratification in which the greater earnings, and hence the greater wealth, are no longer identified with the greater intensity or length of work, since, for a variety of reasons, the children also come to recognise the existence of a wide range of salaries.

RITA (8:10) – Why are there rich people and poor people? – *The rich work, that is the rich find a job which gives them lots of money, while the poor don't find one.* (...) – What are the best jobs for getting rich? – *To be a judge, a lawyer, or a policeman.* – And why are those the best jobs? – *Because you have to take risks in those jobs, policemen risk their lives while the judges are the ones who take people to court and say if they're innocent or guilty.*

GUIDO (8:4) – What are the best jobs for getting rich? – *I don't know, to own something, not to be a worker or a foreman.*

DIEGO (10:9) – Why are there rich people and poor people? – *I don't know how to explain it to you . . . perhaps the rich people have made it happen for themselves, they have studied, they've got an easy job, then from that job they've risen higher, and always earned more.* – And the poor? – *The poor, on the other hand, don't have the chance of going to school, and if they find a job it's as a worker or a labourer.* (...) – Which are the best jobs for getting rich? – *Oh, an engineer, then there are some that I don't know how to explain to you, then there's the head of an office who can always go higher if he's studied.*

These examples seem to identify the 'rich' with the middle classes. In some protocols there was also the idea of a higher state, though this includes a very small number of people and may be achieved, if one does not belong to it by birth, by rising to the highest levels in the management of public affairs, or through illegal activities.

LEONARDO (10:6) – *Some rich people have more money, they are lucky, or perhaps they also steal, or they are rich because of their family, their father was rich, or the grandfather was rich.* – Is there some way of getting rich? – *There are lots of ways, cheating, and these are the dirty illegal ways, or selling cocaine and all those drugs, or doing well in politics, going from being a local councillor to becoming a government minister.*

Together with the idea of a state higher than the middle class there is also the idea, explicitly expressed by MARIA LAURA (10:0), that – *no job makes you rich.* – But how did the rich get to be rich? – *They inherited it from their fathers who were rich, and they too became rich.* – And how did their fathers become rich? – *That I don't know.* – Do you know any rich people? – *No, up till now I've never met any.* – But have you heard of any? – *Ah, I've heard of Leone*[3] *and the ministers.*

The status of the worker comes to be rethought with the knowledge that there exist higher socio-economic levels. At Level 3 the worker was considered as a possible point of departure for becoming rich; now, however, the worker has no hope of being able to improve his own condition.

SIMONE (10:5) – If someone works can they get rich, or not? – *Depends what work they do.* – Which are the best paid jobs? – *Comedians, bankers.* – And which are the worst paid jobs? – *Foundry workman, labourer, all that kind of thing.*

RICCARDO (10:7) – Is it easy or difficult to become rich? – *Very difficult.* – Can everybody become rich, or not? – *No.* – Who can't become rich? – *Workers, teachers and others.*

UGO (10:9) – Can everybody become rich, or not? – *No, because some people work in a factory, they don't have the qualifications to go higher.*

There are many affinities between these results and those obtained from our previous studies. Once again we have found in preschool children the idea that it is easy to obtain money, and that everybody, or nearly everybody, could be rich (Level 1). This is, in fact, a surprising notion, since as soon as the children speak about their own family they describe conditions sufficiently modest as to threaten even the acquisition of notebooks and snacks. From about 6–7 years the connection between money and work is recognised (Level 2), which echoes, from a different perspective, one of the results from the study on the source of money. The idea that earnings should be proportional to the degree of fatigue and amount of time worked is already apparent at this age, becoming more clearly articulated among 8–10 year olds (Level 3). Analogous ideas were expressed, though more sporadically, by the middle-class children interviewed about payment for work (Chapter 2).

These data agree with the picture which emerges from other reported

[3] Translator's note: Leone – President of Italy 1972 to 1978, who had to resign because of his involvement in the Lockheed bribes scandal.

Table 3.2 *What does it mean to be rich?*

Response level	Age groups				Total
	4–5	6–7	8–9	10–11	
0. Don't know	4	1	0	0	5
1. Almost everybody is rich	8	3	0	0	11
2. Everyone who works is rich	7	11	9	4	31
3. The rich are those who work more	1	5	8	6	20
4. The rich do a particular job	0	0	3	10	13
Total	20	20	20	20	80

$r_s = 0.70$, $p < .001$

studies.[4] We have already seen (cf. Chapter 1) that from about 7 years children are able to establish a relationship between wealth and working (Danziger 1958). Goldstein and Oldham (1979) also show that there is an increasing tendency with age for children to consider work as one of the elements determining wealth, and only at around 6–7 years did they some-times find the kinds of fantastic ideas about the origin of wealth (winning a lottery, robbing a bank) reported by Danziger among preschoolers. Connell (1977), finally, shows that it is only at 8–12 years, the second level of the sequence he describes, that children overcome the idea of a bipolar 'dramatic contrast' between wealth and work on the one hand, and poverty and unemployment on the other. In our sample as well it was not until around 8 years that children identified an intermediate condition between wealth and poverty (which they defined as *normal*), and that they understood that working, alone, did not suffice to make one wealthy. At this age children understood wealth to be the result of working hard and, for that reason, being very well paid.

These elements of concordance with responses given by children from other social backgrounds and other countries underlines the way in which

[4] The fact that Duveen and Shields (1984) found a precocious recognition of the existence of differences in the remuneration of different activities is only an apparent disagreement. In actual fact the problem presented to children by these authors was different from, and less difficult than our own. Duveen and Shields presented their subjects with pairs of photographs showing people engaged in different work activities and asked which of them had more money. The children did not, therefore, have to think through for themselves a path from the existence of social stratification to a general explanation. It was this which constituted the problem presented in our own study. The data presented by Duveen and Shields are, however, very interesting since they show that even if young children are not very advanced in economic *reasoning* (as is clear from our own and other studies), they do possess a more adequate *image* of the social world than might have been thought.

the development of the ideas of wealth and poverty mirrors some general characteristics of infantile thinking. For instance, the optimism of 4–5-year-old children regarding the availability of money may be linked with finalism, as we have already suggested. The correspondence established between money and work, especially when it is based on the proportionality of earnings, to the degree of fatigue or the time expended, complements the development of the notion of justice and the emergence of the idea of 'retributive' justice (cf. also Leahy 1983a, 1983b). The passage from an evaluation of wealth and poverty in egocentric terms (Levels 1 and 2) to a recognition of levels of income quite distinct from those of their own families also mirrors a general developmental process. In this case it is the growing capacity for decentration in their evaluation of their own position. These remarks may also be extended to the passage from a bipolar opposition of wealth to poverty, to a series of three terms which takes in the condition of the middle class and, indeed, to an understanding of the difficulties which stand in the way of those who want to become rich.

The determining factor for the conceptions of very young children consists of the typical tendencies of infantile mentality. In effect these children lack adequate cognitive instruments both for understanding the reality which surrounds them, as well as for receiving the interpretations given to them by adults. In short, younger children, in so far as their statements compare with those of older children from similar backgrounds, prove to be less permeable (so to speak) to the specificity of their particular environment. We have, therefore, no reason to expect any important differences between young children from different social classes. Gradually, as their intelligence develops, children become capable of constructing a vision which is always more adequately adapted to reality, and of receiving the interpretations offered to them by different social groups. It would then become highly unlikely that the children of an industrialist, of a clerk, of a farmworker, or of a factory worker would continue to think in the same way about every issue. Connell's (1977) study was undertaken with subjects from different social classes and was extended to higher age levels than those we considered. In his study it is in adolescence that distinctive explanations and judgements about wealth and poverty can be seen to emerge. Conceptions about these themes can be expected to mirror both the mode of thinking peculiar to children's age, as well as the valorisations, the information and the observable elements accessible in their environment (cf. also Emler and Dickinson 1985).

Connell proposes an important distinction between two contrasting environmental influences:

> information which is tied to specific social position, in the sense that one must be in a certain position to get it, and information which is free-floating, available to all regardless of their position in

a structure of social relationships. (...) The assumption of much thinking about class consciousness has been that information about class and class relationships is tied information, that knowledge of class relationships is closely associated with specific position in the class structure. On the contrary, the information about class which these children use in building up their class schemes is almost wholly free-floating information. (Connell 1977, pp. 150–1.)

According to Connell the prevalent influence of free-floating information for Australian children is linked to the social mobility experienced by their families, to the considerable space for free movement available to teenagers, to the public school system, and above all to the diffusion of the television, 'the paradigm source of free-floating information'. If not all, at least some of these conditions are also characteristics of other 'Western' societies in which research has been undertaken on the understanding of social stratification. The prevalence, or at least the presence, of free-floating information available to children independently of their position in the social structure may help to explain the emergence of similar developmental sequences in children from different classes and the difficulty (also noted by Emler and Dickinson, 1985) of distinguishing between social groups in relation to the 'social representations' of stratification.

All that has been said so far about the structural affinities in the reasoning of children of the same age but from different social classes does not establish any basis for supposing that there will not be differences in the contents of children's responses. Such differences have been noted by Leahy (1983) and Furby (1975). In our own study we have also found such variations. When speaking about payment for work, for instance, middle-class children sometimes mentioned criteria other than physical fatigue, such as the greater or lesser utility of the job, or the level of intellectual activity which it demands. What is common to these various responses is the centration on a single characteristic of the activity in question, on which a criterion is then established for the regulation of wages. Following up these differences in content may be only a curiosity in some cases, while in others – and this is so in our view for the ideas of wealth and poverty – they may hold a particular interest for sociology or for social psychology. The evaluation of their own position in the socio-economic scale and the definition of wealth which goes with it are certainly related to children's experiences in using money, and with the social and political ideology of their family. The same may be said of social stratification and the greater or lesser expectations of opportunities for social mobility. Further study of these variables is, however, a task which lies beyond the scope of the present work, and which would need to be addressed through a broad series of inquiries undertaken in diverse environments.

3.3   The bank

In this study we try to clarify what the bank is for the child, which of its functions they recognise and how they connect these functions. We shall see if the bank reappears in the form in which it was spontaneously represented by the younger children in the preceding studies, that of being a benevolent institution. We shall also examine how children understand the way in which the bank realises the function of dispensing money. Apart from contextualising and clarifying the responses found in the preceding studies, examining how children represent the bank holds a particular interest in itself. We shall, in fact, be able to see if children understand the functions of deposits and loans, how they imagine the workings of the bank, if they have any idea of the existence of interest and how they think the bank is able to pay it. Finally, with the older children one can also pose the question of what the bank does with money taken in as deposits, to see if the idea emerges that the bank realises a profit from the management of deposits. As we noted in Chapter 1 some of these issues were also considered by Jahoda (1981) in a study undertaken at the same time as our own, though with subjects of a different age range. Although Jahoda's and our own work were conceived and executed independently of each other, they both used a very similar procedure which has facilitated comparison of the results.

Our interview[5] began with each subject being asked if they had ever been in a bank and if they knew what purpose it served. In this way it was possible to observe the first ideas which came into the children's minds about the functions of the bank. Various replies were possible, from saying that the bank existed to give money to those who asked for it, to saying that it was for putting one's own money in. After asking why this happened, the interview took various paths. If the bank had been presented by the child as a source of money the child was asked why the bank gave out this money and how it came to have the money available. In this way the interviewer sought to establish if it was a question of a donation, or a restitution of deposited money, or a payment for some activity. If the bank was identified as a place for deposits the child was asked if one could also get money from the bank, and on what conditions. If the children spoke of taking out money previously deposited, or of a request for loans, the interviewer sought to ascertain if they were aware of the existence of interest, what reasons they gave for it, and how they explained its origin. For this reason children were asked if the money given

---

[5] There were 100 subjects, 10 boys and 10 girls at each of five age levels: 5–6 years, 7–8 years, 9–10 years, 11–12 years and 13–14 years. These age levels correspond to the following Italian school grades: *scuola materna*, II & IV *elementare*, I & III *media*. The subjects lived in Padova and other towns in Northern Italy; they were the children of factory workers, clerks and salesmen. The data were collected with the collaboration of students attending a seminar directed by one of the authors.

out, or the savings to be withdrawn, were equal to, or more than, or less than, the money received in loans or on deposit, and how the bank obtained the money to pay interest on deposits.

The children's responses were distributed across a sequence of six levels, from a complete absence of knowledge about the bank (Level 0), to a schematic, though complete understanding of the bank's principal functions (Level 5). The idea of the bank as a source of money appears at Level 1, though its function of 'deposits' remains unknown. The second level witnesses a reversal of perspective – the bank now serves as a place to keep money safe from thieves, and one can withdraw money if one has previously put some in, the amount of money one can take out being equal to the amount deposited. At the third level children know that as well as looking after money the bank also lends it, though the ideas of deposits and of loans remain unrelated. Money which is deposited is put in a strongbox; to be able to make loans the bank has to turn to other banks, or the council, or the government, or to the 'banker's money'. Deposits and loans come to be related at Level 4. The bank can loan money because it has received, in its turn, money from savers, the sums coming in counterbalancing those going out. At this level almost all the children know of the existence of interest (on deposits or on loans or on both), but they fail to understand how the bank can pay 'more' on deposits, either because of a lack of coordination, or because they construe the interest paid on loans as a kind of tip, or a payment by the 'banker'. Finally, at the fifth level, interest on deposits and on loans become counterbalanced, while the idea also appears of the bank making money through these transactions.

Level 0: No ideas about the bank.

We can now turn to some examples, beginning with one of the most primitive.

FEDERICA (5:1) – Do you know what the bank is? – *Goes on the sea.* – I asked about the bank not a boat. What use is the bank? – *For the men.* – What do the men do in the bank? – *Go away.* – If I have lots of money and I want to put it somewhere, do you know where I could put it? – *I don't know* – If I need lots of money to buy a house, do you know where I could borrow it? – *I don't know.* – Do you know who makes money? – *To buy things.* – I didn't ask what use is money, I wanted to know who makes it? – *I don't know.*

Federica was not the only one to confuse *banca* (bank) with *barca* (boat). Other children at Level 0 replied to the questions, less picturesquely, with a series of *don't knows*.

Level 1: The bank is a source of money.

Children see the bank as a place where one goes to get money, without any restrictive conditions.

MARCELLO (5:6) – Have you ever been in a bank? – *Yes, with Daddy.* – What use is a bank? – *For giving money.* – To everybody? – *Yes.* – If I want to buy a house and I need lots of money could I go to a bank and get it? – *Yes.* – The bank will give me all the money I want? – *Yes.*

The money which the bank gives out comes, according to these children, from various sources. In some cases it's a question of a '*man*', in others it seems to be a question of a previous deposit, though it is actually a question of multiplication derived from a circular exchange. Other children continue to say '*don't know*'.

ELISABETTA (7:3) – The money the bank gives out, do you have to take it back? – *No.* – They don't want anything in exchange? – *No.* – But how does the bank always come to have money to give out? – *They get it.* – How? – *They go to a man and he gives it to them.* – And who is this man, how does he come to have so much money? – *He gets it.* – But how? – *He goes to some place, asks for money and they give it to him.*

CARLO (5:4) – What use is the bank? – *To give money to those who only have a little.* – So people who only have a little money go to a bank . . . (Interrupting) *They give them a little, then they give them a bit more, and they get to have a lot of money.* – Who gets to have lots of money? – *The man who gave them the money.* – The bank or the man? – *The man gets to have lots of money, then he buys a new house.* – And then he keeps the money forever? – *Yes.* – Forever and ever? – *Yes.* – Do you know if he has to give something back to the bank? – *I don't know.* – The people who go to ask for money, can they ask for a little, or a lot? – *This much* (he gestures with his hand). – What do you mean 'this much'? – *That then he gets to have lots of money and he buys lots of furniture, or a house and then other things, like that.*

Level 2: The bank serves to look after money.

At this level the bank no longer gives out money indiscriminately to everybody. One can go and get some money only if one has previously been to the bank and deposited some to protect it from thieves.

ORNELLA (7:0) says that the bank – *is there to put money in, to leave it there and after to go and get it back.* – Why do people put money in the bank? – *Because . . . to be sure that thieves won't take it.*

It is clear from various indications that it is a question simply of protecting money, to which no other functions are added. Interest is not recognised by subjects at this level, one gets back only the same amount as the money deposited. Furthermore, some children say that one must pay for this service in advance or one will later recover less money than was originally deposited.

ANGIOLA (7:6) says that she has been to the bank to get money – So one can get money in a bank? – *Yes, but only ours.* – What happens? – *You have to go to the bank taking the money, and then you go and get it when you need it.* – If I put 100,000 Lire in the bank and then go to get it out, will the people in the bank give me back 100,000 Lire, or more, or less? – *As much as you say; if you say 100,000 they give you 100,000.* – Could they give me more than 100,000? – *I don't know.* – Can everybody go and get money in a bank? – *Yes, they just have to put some in before.* – And if I haven't put any money in before, can I get money from the bank? – *No.* (...) – Does the bank have a lot of money? – *Yes.* – Who gave it to them? – *Who gave it to them! We gave them the money!* – And then they give it back to you? – *Yes, though we have to, I think, I don't know, though I think that we also have to pay them for looking after the money, I think . . .* – And then that money? – *They keep it.* – The people in the bank? – *Yes, I think so, because I think they also have to look after it at night, because if thieves come, they have to look out that they don't steal it. Because if we kept it at home, then it would be easier . . . so it's better to pay some money than have it all stolen.*

Level 3: The bank gives money on loan.
The children now know that it is possible to get money even if one has no deposits, but they fail to connect deposits and loans, so that they do not understand where the bank obtains the money it lends. To this question they answer '*don't know*', or refer to some external source such as the state, or the council, or to money from taxes, which they believe goes, precisely, to the bank.

DARIO (8:0) – We said that the bank also gives out money . . . (Interrupting) – *But your own! What you had deposited.* – Ah, and if I hadn't deposited any before, can't I ask for any? – *No, because they certainly won't give you anybody else's money. But they will give you a cheque, because the cheque is theirs.* – I don't understand. – *It's the bankers' cheque.* – Ah, it's the bankers who lend you money? – *The money in cash isn't theirs, the cheques are theirs.* – So they can give you cheques and with the cheques you can get some money? – *Yes.* – This money, can you keep it then, or do you have to give it back to the bank? – *If they've lent you some money, 50,000 Lire for example, if after a year . . . however long they say . . . you don't give them this money back . . . not really the same money but 50,000 Lire . . . you can be sent to prison or sometimes hanged.* – The money they lend you, where do they get it from, the people at the bank? – *Oh, I wouldn't know where they get it from, either they get it from other people or they have it themselves.* – Ah, the bankers also have money which they keep in the bank? – *Now I'll explain it to you. They take money from people and put it away in some boxes which are double locked, you have one of the keys, so that thieves can't touch it. But also the money which is there is that there. But they have some money in a till, like in the baker's, like all the shops, they put it there in case somebody asks for money and hasn't deposited anything in the bank.*

We have reported Dario's protocol at some length because it shows clearly the difficulty, typical of this level, of understanding that the money given in loans is the same as that which people deposit. Dario says that it is enough to pay back the 50,000 Lire which had been borrowed, even if it is not the same banknote which they had given out; but as regards deposits he thinks that the money is locked in tills where '*the money which is there is that there*' (i.e. the money deposited, and not any other money). Consequently, even though he recognises the existence of loans, Dario cannot explain where the money for loans has come from; he limits himself simply to saying that it exists. Some children respond to this question with a '*don't know*', and others, the greater number, reply by referring to sources external and superordinate to the bank, such as the state, or the council, or taxes.

PAOLO (9:10) – What use is the bank? – *For depositing money, or also for taking it out, for making loans.* – Can you explain it to me a little? – *To deposit is when someone has some money they put it in a bank, so when they need it they go and take out what's theirs.* – And when you take it out, do they give you back the same amount, or more, or less than you left there? – *Less, I think, because you have to pay for them to look after it.* – And loans? – *When someone has to pay for a house for instance, and they don't have the money, then they go to the bank.* – And they give it to them? – *Yes.* – The money the bank gives them, do they have to pay it back? – *Yes.* – Do they have to give back more, or less, or the same amount as the bank lent them? – *More ... no less ... as much as they borrowed, it depends.* – How does the bank come to have money for loans? – *Oh, I don't know, perhaps from the state.* – Why does the state give it to them? – *I don't know.* – Does the bank then have to give it back to the state? – *I don't know, I've never seen it.*

Level 4: The bank uses deposits to make loans.

The ideas of deposits and of loans, which as we have seen coexist at Level 3 without being integrated, become coordinated by children at the fourth level.

SHEILA (9:10) – *The bank is where people deposit money and they do business.* – Why do they deposit money? – *Because they're afraid that if they leave a lot of money in the house thieves will come and take it all away.* – If I deposit 100,000 Lire in the bank, when I go to take it out will they give me back the same sum, or less, or more? – *It will always be the same.* – Can you only deposit money in the bank, or can you also get money? – *You can also get it, but above a certain limit you have to give it back.* – And when you give it back, do you have to give back as much as you got, or more, or less? – *More.* – Why? – *Because the people who gave you the money want to have, what do you call it, a little to save.* – What do they do with the savings? – *They keep it themselves.* –

It's their salary? – *No, it's a kind of tip.* – And their salary? – *The boss gives it to them.* – Where do you think the money comes from which the bank lends to people? – *From people who have deposited it.* – Only from these deposits? – *Yes.*

PAOLO (10:1) says that people deposit money to avoid theft, and also recognises the possibility of getting loans – Suppose someone deposits 10,000 Lire, and then someone else arrives who wants a loan of 20,000 Lire, how can they give them this money? – *Oh, these 10,000 and 10,000 from other people.* Paolo does not, however, talk about interest, either on deposits or on loans.

Other subjects, however, talk spontaneously about interest which the bank gives to those who deposit money. However, they do not know how the bank obtains the money to pay such interest.

CLAUDIO (9:3) – *A bank is a deposit for money, a house which has a lot of money and where men deposit it; and then there is the interest, which is the money that, when a man who's deposited some money comes to get it back, they also give him the interest which is a little more money which the bank has added.* Then, however, to explain where the bank gets this extra money, he says – *There's also taxes, though they don't have anything to do with the bank . . . I don't think so. I don't know about this.* Indeed, in regard to loans he does not believe that one has to pay interest – Do you give back the same sum? – *The same sum, in instalments, that is to say that you pay a little one day, a little another day.*

MARIA (11:8) – Why do people put money in the bank? – *Because at home they could be robbed and because in the bank after its been there a little the money increases.* – Why does the bank give out this extra money? – *I wouldn't know.* – Where does the bank get the money to pay this extra? – *I don't know.* – But why do the men at the bank keep money for people? – *It's not that they keep it, that is, if you put in 10,000 Lire they keep it there. The amount of money is still there, but this 10,000 Lire doesn't stay in the bank.* – And where does it end up? – *Other people get it.* – How come? – *They ask for a loan.*

Level 5: Understanding of interest.

Finally, at the fifth level, the interests on deposits and on loans are also counterbalanced.

FABRIZIO (14:2) – *The bank is for depositing money and for making loans. If someone finds himself without money the bank can help him. Or, if someone goes to deposit money which he can't keep at home, the bank helps and also gives him interest.* – What would this interest be? – *We leave the money there, and this bank, as far as I understand it, according to how much money we have, gives us interest on top of this money, that is, after a year we have more money and you can go and get the money whenever you want.* – And loans? – *If someone needs money they go to the bank and the bank helps them. (. . .)* – Why does the bank keep money for people? – *It's not that they keep it there, they circulate it, no? If I go back to the bank I don't get back my 10,000 Lire again; that money circulates in the bank. – What do you mean, circulates? – For example, this 10,000 Lire, they give it to someone else, the money doesn't stay there. –* But does the bank earn something by doing this or not? *– I think so, yes. –* How come? *– I've heard tell that when someone gets a loan they have to pay it back to the bank with a certain interest, and the bank keeps all that money. –* But you told me that the bank also pays interest. *– I think they'd be equal, the one and the other.*

As one can see in Table 3.3, the majority of 5–6 year olds either know nothing about the bank, or represent it once again as that source of money which has already been noted in the previous studies (Level 1). Up to this point, then, there is nothing new in the results, except a further confirmation of the extension and diffusion of beliefs whose generality the other studies already left beyond doubt. Greater interest, however, is to be found in the responses at the other levels which reveal for the first time the later successions of these beliefs.

Already by 7 years the majority of children no longer believe that the bank constitutes a source from which anybody may draw. Instead the dominant idea is that of a deposit in which money is lodged to protect it from thieves, and from which one can withdraw it precisely because one has previously put it there (Level 2). The idea that money can also be obtained on loan (Level 3) makes a later appearance. It seems to us that, rather than being related to any intrinsic difficulty in the notion itself, this delay is due to the lesser frequency with which loans occur, and to the consequent rarity of occasions on which children are able to hear them spoken about.[6] Levels 2 and 3, to which the majority of children aged 7–10 belong, in effect comprise the same conception: that there should be an equality between what is borrowed and what has to be given back (in the case of loans), or between what is given and what one can take (in the case of deposits). In this conception we find some features of concrete operational thinking, which is a characteristic of this age level. The actions of giving and taking come to be related in such a way that their respective results cancel one another. By thus connecting the quantity of money taken by a customer with that which they previously gave, the child goes beyond the more primitive conceptions in which the problem of relating deposits and withdrawals was not even posed. This, however, is not sufficient for understanding how the bank functions. Only at 13–14 years do the majority of children understand that the functions of taking in money as deposits and of circulating it as loans are reciprocally related (Level 4). In

---

[6] In a pilot study of the notion of ownership (see Chapter 5) we found that already by the age of three children know how to distinguish and to use correctly the words 'sell', 'lend' and 'give' (the Italian verbs are *vendere, prestare* and *regalare*). The borrowing and the giving back of toys is common among children, as are the limits imposed by adults on the indiscriminate giving and taking of one's own, and other's, things.

Table 3.3 *What use is the bank?*

Response level	Age groups					Total
	5–6	7–8	9–10	11–12	13–14	
0. No ideas about the bank	6	0	0	0	0	6
1. The bank is a source of money	8	4	0	0	0	12
2. The bank looks after money	6	10	5	3	0	24
3. The bank lends money	0	6	9	7	6	28
4. The bank loans the money deposited	0	0	4	4	6	14
5. Understanding of interest	0	0	2	6	8	16
Total	20	20	20	20	20	100

$r_s = 0.77$, $p < .001$

some cases the children also come to understand how the bank obtains the money to pay interest on savings (Level 5). At 11–12 years, however, half the children still operate at Levels 2 and 3. Coordinating deposits and loans appears, therefore, to be anything but a simple task. It becomes effective when children, with the emergence of formal operational thinking, succeed in conceiving exchanges in abstract terms, that is, without reference to the individuals who perform it, nor to the actual activities in question, but by considering only the flow of money coming in and going out.

These results can be integrated with those obtained by Jahoda in which a group of 11–16 year olds were interviewed about shopkeepers' profits and banking, and given various Piagetian-type tests. Jahoda has presented the results of these studies in three different articles (1981, 1984a, 1984b). In this chapter we are concerned only with the first two articles concerning the comprehension of profits in banks and in shops. Other problems raised by Jahoda's work will be considered in the final chapter.

Jahoda assumed that children know of deposits and loans. He asked them what would happen if someone went back after a year to a bank where they'd deposited £100: would they get back more, or less, or the same amount. The subjects were also asked to justify their judgements. Following this they were questioned about money received, such as loans and, finally, to see if they understood the notion of profit, they were asked to explain how the bank gets money to pay for the people who work in it.

The earliest responses which he found were characterised by the absence of any understanding of interest. At a second level, however, children asserted that one would receive more money than one had deposited, though still without any understanding of interest on loans so that they could not explain where the bank found the extra money. This response level is distinguished from the earlier one on the grounds of an increase in factual knowledge rather than any development in economic thinking. Responses at these two levels were generally found among 11–12-year-old subjects. From 13 onwards, however, the majority of children understood about interest on loans. Some believed that interest on loans was less than on deposits (Level 3), some that they were equal (Level 4) and some, finally, that interest on loans was greater than on deposits, though they were unable to offer any justification for this belief (Level 5). Only a few children understood that it was only by charging a higher interest on loans than it paid on deposits could the bank both pay its own workers and realise a profit (Level 6).

The age at which children understand how the bank makes a profit is greater than that at which they understand that shopkeepers must charge more for goods than they pay for them. As we saw in Chapter 1, it is around the age of 11 that children understand how shopkeepers make profits (Strauss, 1952; Furth, 1980; Jahoda, 1979). The majority of children interviewed about the bank already understood this idea. Jahoda (1981, 1984a) studied this idea by explaining to children that a butcher sells chicken for £2.00, and then asking if he had paid more, or less, or the same amount when he had bought it. More than half of the 11–12 year olds, and almost all the older children gave the correct answer. As we have just seen, however, only a minority of children also understood that the bank charges higher rates of interest than it pays, and only a few were able to explain why this should be so. How can one explain this *décalage* between the appearance of the idea of profit in the context of buying and selling and its generalisation to the bank?

In the first place, it seems to us crucial that children only very rarely have the opportunity of being in contact with banks and with what they do, while they have much more frequent and direct experiences of buying and selling; hence they have fewer opportunities to think about banks than about shops. Understanding the former is slower than understanding the latter. As we reported in this chapter, the majority of the 5–6 year olds we interviewed had no idea about banks, or they thought that banks gave money away to people for free. At the same age, however, children knew about shops and that one must pay to buy things (Strauss, 1952, 1954; Danziger, 1958; Furth, 1980; Burris, 1983). Secondly, to generalise to the bank the rules relating to buying and selling it is necessary to construe money itself as goods, as something to be bought and sold. This may be a particular difficulty for children, as we shall see in the following chapter on the development of ideas about commercial exchanges.

Jahoda (1981) also suggests that a particular difficulty in generalising the notion of profit to the bank may be that children assimilate the idea of loans made by the bank to the kind of loans of which they have direct experience, those which take place between friends. They may, therefore, believe that banks are also regulated by the same norms of fairness and strict reciprocity which prevail in interpersonal relations. The assimilation of bank loans to those which take place between friends is most directly expressed in those responses where interest on loans is not yet recognised. However, it is also apparent, if less evident, in conceptions that interest on deposits and on loans are equal. Indeed in this case children justify the interest on loans by saying that otherwise the bank would be in debt when they paid interest on deposits, though without admitting that the bank can make a profit by making loans. Only when the personal and societal spheres become separated do children arrive at a full understanding of the functions of the bank.

We have examined some of the problems arising from characteristics peculiar to the bank; we shall now consider those aspects of its functioning which are similar to other kinds of business. These aspects are reflected in the analogies between children's ideas about banks and their ideas about payment for work presented in the previous chapter. As in the research on payment for work, one can also see here, on various levels, the construction of relationships which are always more numerous and reciprocally related. Another element of similarity is that of the sources (the state, the government, rich men, other banks) to which children at the intermediate levels in both studies made reference. In one case it was to explain the source of the 'boss's' money, in the other, the money which the bank uses to make loans or to pay interest. In short, there are evident analogies between the image of monetary circulation which emerges when children talk about payment for work, and that which emerges from their answers about the bank.

4 Money and goods

The previous two chapters considered economic exchanges related to work, and focused on its organisation and remuneration. In this chapter children's ideas about the economic system are examined from the point of view of the circulation of goods. Other studies of the development of economic understanding have already examined this issue, either as the principle theme of an inquiry (Strauss, 1952, 1954; Jahoda, 1979), or as one theme in a wider-ranging study (Burris, 1983; Furth, 1980; Furth, Baur and Smith, 1976; Goldstein and Oldham, 1979; Leiser, 1983).

In our study, the question of the circulation of goods is first considered in its most general terms by investigating how children believe people obtain some commonly used goods. Secondly we examine how children connect the parallel – though opposite – flow of money and goods. The relation between money and the price of goods is considered in a study of value and the use of money in buying and selling, and in a study of the criteria by which children explain the diversity in the prices of different things.

4.1 The source of goods

Existing research has little to say about the source of goods. This theme has not been the object of any specific investigation, but has figured in wider studies concerned with buying and selling, the idea of profit, and work (Furth, 1980; Furth, Baur and Smith, 1976; Goldstein and Oldham, 1979; Jahoda, 1979; Strauss, 1952, 1954). These studies tried to identify which economic roles and exchanges were understood by children, and if they recognised that shopkeepers have to pay for the goods they sell. Children's conceptions about production, however, have not been studied.

Jahoda (1979), for instance, limited his interviews to asking children if shopkeepers have to pay for goods and found that payment is recognised from the second level on (though he does not give the precise age). Furth (1980) also asked about the source of goods, though the sequence of levels in which he ordered the responses is centred on the idea of payment and, hence, does not consider how ideas about production develop. Strauss (1952, 1954) found that children younger than 6–7 years believe that the shopkeepers replenish their stock from another shopkeeper, who goes to another shopkeeper, and so on. Older children, however, recognise the existence of manufacturers to whom retailers must turn to obtain goods. Finally, Goldstein and Oldham (1979), while confirming that as children get older they come to recognise that behind shopkeepers there are wholesalers, also note that some 6–9-year-old children identify the shopkeeper as the person who made the goods for sale.

Although there is so little research specifically on this theme it is nonetheless possible to advance some hypotheses about the development of these ideas on the basis of Piaget's studies of artificialism (Piaget, 1929). The problem of the source of goods is, for the child, comparable to that of the origin of natural phenomena studied by Piaget. In effect children do not mark any clear distinction between natural phenomena and manufactured objects. Initially children limit themselves to considering the purpose for which things exist, and they respond with finalistic and anthropomorphic conceptions. Every natural phenomenon serves to facilitate some aspect of human life, and that of children in particular. No idea exists of the way in which things come into being, and for this reason this stage is described as 'preartificialism'. Subsequently beliefs develop about the origin of things, which are held to have been made by human beings or by God at some remote time, either independently of natural processes (integral artificialism) or in a manner which combines with the action of natural forces (qualified artificialism). Finally, around 9–10 years artificialism gives way to the idea that various natural phenomena originated independently of human activity.

Piaget wrote little about children's notions concerning the origins of materials such as glass or cloth. The characteristics of artificialism can be more clearly seen by considering such things as the heavenly bodies, mountains or waters which exist independently of human action. Our problem is different, though in some ways complementary to Piaget's. If it is true that children overvalue human manufacturing activity to the point of believing that it can produce mountains, lakes and rivers, will they be able to understand how goods are produced?

On this point one might expect, both on the basis of Piaget's analysis of artificialism and the studies noted above, that very young children would not ask themselves about the origin of goods, but content themselves with establishing their existence. Later, in parallel with the appearance of integral artificialism, a producer might be identified. At first the producer will be confused with the shopkeeper (who is a more well-known figure to children) and only later construed as a distinct figure. Moreover, one can expect that at first children will not be able to specify how production occurs; when they do begin to form some ideas about it they will overvalue human activity (following Piaget's analysis) and consider it as responsible not only for the transformation, but also for the origin of the materials used.

To examine this hypothesis 80 children aged 4–11 years were interviewed.[1] The subjects lived in Padova, and for the most part came from middle-class families. The interviews focused on three types of consumer goods familiar to children, two manufactured (drinking glasses and clothes) and one agricultural (peaches). For each of these objects the opening question was: 'What do you have to do to have ... (a glass, clothes,[2] a peach).' Later questions depended on children's responses. If they said thay had the object at home they were asked how one could obtain some other ones (when the clothes are worn out, or the glass is broken, or the peach is eaten) so as to ascertain whether or not they had the idea that goods have to be procured in some way. If, on the other hand, they said that one could get or buy these things in a shop the later questions were designed to ascertain whether or not they were able to trace back a line to the producer of each article. At that point the questioning sought to establish how the child represented the process of production itself with questions about the appropriate raw materials.

For each object the responses were classified in two separate category systems: one concerned the identification of the economic figures essential for the production and sale of goods, while the other pertained to the origin of raw materials.

4.1.1   The production and distribution of goods

Four types of response were found. At the first level children either did not identify any economic figure, saying simply that they already had each of these goods at home, or could not say where they came from. At the following level children identified the shopkeeper as someone who had an inexhaustible stock of the goods or who could get some from another shopkeeper (a sequence which leads to an infinite regress and the establishment of a kind of *chain of shops*). At a more advanced level there were responses which touched in some way on the necessity for production without, however, separating the producer from the shopkeeper (who might cultivate peach trees, or manufacture goods by repairing old ones or from broken material from the same type of object). Finally at the fourth level the producer is separated from the shopkeeper, and in some cases an intermediary appears between producer and shopkeeper (the wholesaler or commercial traveller).

[1]   The subjects were divided into four age groups with 10 boys and 10 girls in each group: 4–5 years, 6–7 years, 8–9 years and 10–11 years. The data were collected by Sonia Fincato and the authors.

[2]   Translator's note: In Italian this item can be a singular, *un vestito*, while English has only *clothes*. In the interviews it is always a singular garment about which the child is asked.

Level 1: The goods are already at home.

At this earliest level we found some children who did not identify any economic figures and said that they either found or made the things at home, or had no idea of where they came from.

ANTONELLO (4:5) – How do you get clothes? – . . . – What does your mother do when she needs clothes? – *Gets them.* – Where? – *From the wardrobe.* – Who put them there? – *A lady.* – Who is this lady? – *I don't know.* – What did your mother do to get these clothes? – *She made them.* – How did she make them? – *With material.*

Level 2: The goods come from the shop.

For these children goods can be got or bought from a shop, although as to how the shopkeeper got them there are various different ideas.

SILVIA (4:6), for example, believes in the existence of an inexhaustible supply – What do you do to get a glass? – . . . *near my house* – What's near your house? – *They've got lots of glasses there.* – What do they do to have so many? – *They bought them with money.* – Where? – *There.* – What's there? – *A place where they have glasses.* – What did they do to get them? – *They got them from a cupboard.* – How come they were in the cupboard? – *They put them there.* – Who was it who put them there? – *The lady with the glasses.* – What did that lady do to get them? – *They were in the cupboard and she took them out and gave them to my mother.*

ARIANNA (5:10), on the other hand, alludes to a chain of shops – What do you do to get clothes? – *You buy them in a shop.* – And how does the shopkeeper come to have them? – *He went to UPIM,*[3] *and they gave them to him.* – And what did UPIM do to get them? – *I don't know.* – Try and think. – *At the market.* – And what did the people at the market do to get them? – *I don't know.* – Think about it a little. – *In another market.*

The most frequent response to questions about what the shopkeeper did to get the peaches was 'don't know'.

MICHELE (5:1) – What do you do to get a peach? – *You eat it with your hands.* – But how do you get it? – *To get them to my house?* – Yes. – *It's my mother who brings the peaches home, and then I eat one.* – And what does your mother do to get them? – *Down in the square, she goes down a little street, and then she buys the peaches.* – And what does the man who sells them do to get them? – *I don't know.*

Level 3: The shopkeeper-producer.

At this level children comprehend the necessity for a productive phase in the origin of goods. They therefore go beyond the simple affirmation that clothes, peaches and glasses may be found in shops. However, ignoring

---

[3] Translator's note: *UPIM* is the name of a well-known chain of Italian department stores.

how the process of production is organised, they attribute to shopkeepers the task of making what they sell.

CRISTIANO (6:3), for example, thinks that the greengrocer produces the fruit – How do you get a peach? – *You buy the tree, you plant it and wait.* – And what if I want one straight away? – *You can buy one from the greengrocer.* – And what did the greengrocer do to get some peaches? – *He planted some.*

Level 4: The shopkeeper buys from a producer.

At the fourth level children begin to differentiate the figure of the producer from that of the shopkeeper. They affirm that the shopkeepers themselves do not make anything, but obtain their goods from someone else whose job it is to make them. This second figure is frequently assimilated to that of the artisan, someone who works alone in a workshop to produce things either manually or with some mechanical aids.

SIMONE (4:8) – How do you get clothes? – *There are shops that have them.* – What do shops do to get glasses? – *They bring them in a lorry, though packed in boxes so they don't get broken.* – What did the guy with the lorry do to get the glasses? – *He drives around and when he finds a bit of glass he picks it up and makes glasses out of it, then puts them in boxes and takes them to the shop.*

Other children allude to the existence of factories, and some even identify the wholesaler as an intermediary.

CHIARA (6:5) – How do you get a glass? – *You buy one.* – Where? – *From the shops that sell them.* – And what did these shops do to get them? – *They get them from the factory which makes them.*

ANDREA (10:0) – How do the people in shops get clothes? – *From wholesalers.* – How do the wholesalers get them? – *They buy them from the factory.*

Tables 4.1, 4.2 and 4.3 show the age distribution of responses for each object.

As can be seen from the tables, it is only from 8 years that more than half the children recognise the existence of a producer distinct from the shopkeeper. This confirms the result of the study reported in Chapter 2, in which the 6–7-year-old middle-class children interviewed about payment for work showed very little comprehension of the work of labourers or farmworkers. The earlier conceptions revealed by this study confirm and complete the results obtained by other authors. Strauss (1952) also noted the idea, which recurred in our own study, that goods were procured through a chain of shops, behind which no productive activity could be discerned. The notion that shopkeepers themselves made the goods they sold, reported by Goldstein and Oldham (1979), was widespread among our own subjects. Our own study has shown that such notions are preceded by even earlier conceptions. Some of the youngest children did not even mention the shop as a source of goods, limiting themselves to saying that the goods one needed were already available at

Table 4.1 *Where do you get clothes?*

Response level	Age groups				Total
	4–5	6–7	8–9	10–11	
1. Don't know or at home	3	1	0	0	4
2. In a shop	5	4	3	0	12
3. The shopkeeper makes them	9	10	3	2	24
4. The shopkeeper buys them from a producer	3	5	14	18	40
Total	20	20	20	20	80

$r_s = 0.63$, $p < .001$

Table 4.2 *Where do you get a glass?*

Response level	Age groups				Total
	4–5	6–7	8–9	10–11	
1. Don't know or at home	1	0	0	0	1
2. In a shop	5	5	0	0	10
3. The shopkeeper makes it	7	6	10	2	25
4. The shopkeeper buys it from the producer	7	9	10	18	44
Total	20	20	20	20	80

$r_s = 0.43$, $p < .001$

Table 4.3 *Where do you get peaches?*

Response level	Age groups				Total
	4–5	6–7	8–9	10–11	
1. Don't know or at home	2	0	0	0	2
2. In the shop	5	2	0	0	7
3. The shopkeeper grows them	10	16	12	5	43
4. The shopkeeper buys them from the producer	3	2	8	15	28
Total	20	20	20	20	80

$r_s = 0.57$, $p < .001$

home. Although this notion was only articulated by a small number of 4–5 year olds it does raise a question which deserves a response. Are there really some children who have no experience of shops, and who do not know that it is from shops that their parents get things? Such an interpretation seems very doubtful to us, rather such responses should be construed as expressing the fact that the question of the source of goods is scarcely considered. This attitude on the part of these children goes hand in hand with their faith in the constant availability of goods.

Notions that goods come from a chain of shops express the same attitude, and one which is similar to that observed by Piaget (1929) in his studies of children's ideas about the source of some raw materials. That such ideas suggest a deep-seated attitude rather than a limited awareness of economic activities is also attested by the fact that some children express similar ideas in relation to the question of how people get babies. Parents are said to get their offspring from a shop, or that before ending up in their mothers' stomachs they were in that of another woman (Piaget, 1929; Bernstein and Cowan, 1975). Given this state of affairs it is possible to conclude that the transition from Level 2 (goods come from the shop) to Level 3 (the shopkeeper-producer) is determined by the development of artificialistic tendencies in children. As soon as they experience a need to *explain* how things come to be, and assume that their existence must be the consequence of some productive activity, they attribute this activity to the nearest person who they know to be connected with goods, the shopkeeper.

The transition from the third to the fourth level, with the recognition of other economic figures who produce the goods and from whom the shopkeeper gets them, reflects a more detailed representation of social roles and economic exchanges. This interpretation is confirmed by the responses the children gave to questions about the origins of the raw materials used to produce various goods.

4.1.2 The source of raw materials

Children who in some way or another identified a productive phase in the source of goods were also asked to explain how the shopkeeper (or the child's parents, or the farmworker, or the manufacturer) made the object in question. Responses were grouped in four levels: those who were not interviewed about this topic because they had not mentioned any productive activity (Level 0), those who said '*don't know*' (Level 1), those who gave an artificialistic version of the origin of raw materials (Level 2) and, finally, those who identified the natural origins of raw materials (Level 3).

In this case, too, there was a strong positive correlation between response level and age for each of the particular objects.

Level 1: No comprehension.

Children at this level have no idea of what a producer does to make things, or they say that they buy the object or the materials.

ANTONELLO (4:5) – What did your mother do to get the material for the clothes? – *She bought it.* – Where? – *In a shop.* – And the person in the shop, what did he do to get it? – *He went around and they gave it to him.* – But what did he do to get it? – *He bought it.* – Where? – *In another shop.* – And the man in this other shop? – *He bought it somewhere else and then gave it to him.*

Antonello makes the same response about the glass, though he says that one gets peaches from a tree. Even though he says his mother 'makes' things he does not know the origin of the materials used, saying only that they are bought.

Level 2: The producer uses recycled materials.

The characteristic development at this level is the attempt to find the origin of the raw materials used in making clothes or glasses. As Piaget found in his study of the origins of natural phenomena many children at this level resolve the problem by referring to some kind of retrieval or 'recycling' of materials which they know or believe are used in the construction of these objects. Thus clothes are said to be made by retrieving old or worn garments, glasses by putting together fragments or pieces of glass.

This type of response is linked to both Levels 2 and 3 of the preceding categorisation.

MANUELE (6:3) – What do you do to get clothes? – *You buy them in big shops.* – What do the people in the big shops do to get the clothes? – *They make them in a room that you can't go into.* – How do they make them? – *They sew them and they also have a machine.* – How do you sew clothes? – *With a needle and thimble and some thread.* – What do they sew with the needle and thread? – *Cloth.* – How do they get the cloth? – *They take all the worn-out things and make material and then it becomes clothes.* – How do they get these worn-out things? – *Someone with a lorry brings them to them.* – And what does the person with the lorry do to get them? – *They go into people's houses and ask them to give them the old, old, worn-out things, then they put them in the lorry and take them to them.*

Manuele also says that glasses are made in the department stores – *With a machine that they put all the broken glass into, then they wait a moment and out comes a glass.* – How do they get the broken glass? – *They find it.* – Where? – *Round and about in the streets, there's lots of it.*

However curious it may seem, the same ideas about 'construction' also appear occasionally about the peaches.

STEFANO (6:7) – How do you get a peach? – *You buy it in a shop.* – How does the man in the shop get it? – *He puts lots of juice on a stone, and then puts the peel on and it's done.*

GIANLUCA (6:6) says that a lorry brought the glasses to the shopkeeper – And what did the lorry driver do to get the glasses? – *There's a machine in the factory that makes them.* – What did they do to get the glass? – *They found it in the street.* – How come there's glass in the street? – *They throw it away.* – Who? – *People, because it's broken.* Gianluca also goes on to say that cloth is made in a factory with a machine – But what do they do to make it? – *I don't know, you need the machines and the rags.* – What do they do to get the rags? – *From old clothes.* Finally, as regards the peach, Gianluca is convinced that a lorry brings some to the greengrocer after getting them from a factory where – *There are men who make them in a factory and who've got a special machine.* – What do they do to make them? – *They put in something sticky and out comes a peach.*

Only children who did not mention the farmworker gave this type of response about the peach. Once the producer was recognised as the farmworker, all the children easily understood that the farmworker harvested the fruit from the trees.

Level 3: Raw materials have a natural origin.

In the case of the peach it is easy to reach the idea of cultivation. In the case of manufactured things, however, an understanding of their manufacture demands a capacity to represent materials which appear quite different from the finished product. Only at this third level are children able to relate the material of clothes with material such as cotton or lambswool; the glass with sand or (even if incorrectly) 'rocks' or something else. The transform-ation of these materials into finished products can then be described with varying levels of precision; from a cognitive point of view, the most relevant step is the ability to recall simultaneously objects of such differing appear-ances and the realisation that through appropriate procedures the one can be changed into the other.

ELISA (10:8) does not appear to have any idea about how glass is made, but what she says seems close enough to the truth — *That's something I really don't know anything about.* – Have you never thought about it? – *Yes I've thought about it, but I've never asked my mother or my teacher.* – What do you think it could be? – *It could come from a mineral, perhaps there are machines for extracting glass.*

MICHELE (10:6) on the other hand alludes to sand, an allusion which is difficult enough without the help of an adult or teacher – *There's the factory, they have moulds and out comes the glass.* – Where do they get the glass? – *You can make it with sand, you heat it up and leave it, then you take it out and it's become glass.*

The distribution of these responses is shown in the following tables. As can be seen it is only around the age of 10 that a correct identification is

Table 4.4 *The production of clothes*

Response level	Age groups				Total
	4–5	6–7	8–9	10–11	
0. No production	5	5	3	0	13
1. No comprehension	7	8	3	0	18
2. Recycled materials	8	7	3	2	20
3. Natural origin of raw materials	0	0	11	18	29
Total	20	20	20	20	80

$r_s = 0.67$, $p < .001$

Table 4.5 *The production of glasses*

Response level	Age groups				Total
	4–5	6–7	8–9	10–11	
0. No production	5	4	0	0	9
1. No comprehension	2	2	5	3	12
2. Recycled materials	13	12	10	2	37
3. Natural origin of raw materials	0	2	5	15	22
Total	20	20	20	20	80

$r_s = 0.63$, $p < .001$

Table 4.6 *The production of peaches*

Response level	Age groups				Total
	4–5	6–7	8–9	10–11	
0. No production	5	2	0	0	7
1. No comprehension	0	2	0	0	2
2. Recycled materials	2	3	2	0	7
3. Natural origin of raw materials	13	13	18	20	64
Total	20	20	20	20	80

$r_s = 0.42$, $p < .001$

made of raw materials with natural elements. Younger children have no idea of what is used to make glasses or cloth, or they think that the material used is itself the product of some human activity. These ideas are the same as those reported by Piaget (1929) at the same age level in his study of children's ideas about the origins of various natural elements and material such as iron, wood and paper.

4.2   The value and use of money in buying and selling

The majority of children interviewed in the preceding study spoke about the shop as the place where one can get the things one needs. This investigation is concerned with the details of how children represent the transactions between shopkeepers and customers.

Strauss (1952, 1954), the only author to have studied this problem in 3–4 year olds, found some children at this age level who did not even know that to get something in a shop it is necessary to give money. Although 4–7-year-old children know that one must pay, they do not understand why. Typically they explain the necessity for payment by saying that 'that's the way', and that anyone disobeying this rule would 'get put in jail' (Strauss, 1952, p. 277). They do not actually know what shopkeepers do with the money, they believe that it is returned to the customers as change, or kept in the till, or given away as charity. These ideas have also been reported by other authors (Burris, 1983; Danziger, 1958; Furth, Baur and Smith, 1976; Furth, 1980; Jahoda, 1979). It is only from age 7 onwards that children recognise that one must pay shopkeepers because they in turn must pay for the goods, and only around 10–11 years do they recognise that shopkeepers must charge more for the goods than they paid for them in order to earn their living.

Strauss is the only one of the researchers who examined children's ideas about retail buying and selling by means of in-depth interviews. He describes how children come to discriminate various denominations of money and to understand that not any type of money will suffice in a shop, but that there are rules for associating certain types of money with certain types of goods.

These are the themes for the present study. The questions for which we sought a response were: [1] At what age do children recognise that to buy something one needs to pay? [2] And once that has been established how do children distinguish the correspondence between money and goods? [3] What functions are attributed to change at different age levels?

To pursue these issues we returned to some problems already considered by Strauss, though with a younger group of subjects. As we noted in Chapter 1, Strauss interviewed children aged 4:6 to 11:6 years; to complete his developmental description he also spoke to some younger children aged 3 to 4:6 years. There were only 10 of these younger subjects, however, and they were not included in the formal investigation as they were interviewed with a different procedure. The age range of our subjects was from 3 to 8 years.[4]

This study proposes to analyse the relationships which children believe exist between goods and money at that particular developmental level where they understand that one must pay when one buys something, yet are unable to compute monetary values since they lack the necessary arithmetical skills. To establish such relationships on a sound basis children must understand that different goods have different prices, which can be expressed in numbers, and that different monetary denominations also have different values, which can also be expressed in numbers. They also need to understand that to buy something it is necessary to give a sum of money corresponding to the value of the object. This sum may be composed of a collection of notes and coins of different values which together add up to the price of the object, or one can pay with notes or coins of value higher than that of the object, in which case there will be change corresponding to the difference between the sum of money paid and the price of the object. Such understanding demands a comprehension of numbers and the ability to perform the operations of addition and subtraction. According to Piaget (1952) an understanding of these operations is usually acquired around the age of 7–8 years. There is also a particular difficulty for Italian children. The low value of the lira means that the price of even those cheaper goods available to children, such as sweets or comics, runs into hundreds of lire and thus the quantities with which Italian children have to operate in order to understand how money is used are particularly high.

As we noted in Chapter 1 Strauss's research demonstrated the difficulties encountered by children; only around 7–8 years were they able to understand the relations of coins to one another in a systematic way, and the reasons why the shopkeeper must give change. Younger children produced a variety of erroneous ideas. Some children said that one just had to pay, that it made no difference how many coins or how much money, while others said that one could only pay with coins of exactly the same value as the price. Strauss assigned this latter notion, that things which cost a given price must always be paid for with money of a certain denomination, to the second stage of his sequence. He considered it a more primitive idea than that which he classified at the third level, where children maintained that the money given was incorrect only when there was not enough. This notion was assigned to a higher level because, taken literally and in isolation, it appears more correct than the Stage 2 notion. It seems to us, however, that a close consideration of the whole ensemble of the child's beliefs suggests an inversion in the order of

---

[4] There were 100 children divided into 5 age groups (3–4 years, 4–5 years, 5–6 years, 6–7 years and 7–8 years) with 10 boys and 10 girls in each age group. All the children came from the lower-middle and middle classes.

these two levels. The affirmation that a certain denomination of money must always be used to buy a certain thing amounts to the institution of a strict correspondence between each denomination of money and the price of objects. It is precisely because this conception is erroneous that it appears to be the result of an autonomous effort of reasoning by the child. On the other hand, the fact that one cannot pay for goods with money of a lower value than the price may be ascertained quite easily through direct experience. Taken jointly with the wholly erroneous conceptions about the function of change, this fact does not yet provide any evidence for a real comprehension of the relationship between money and price.

In our study these issues are examined through a procedure which Piaget described as the *critical method* (Piaget, 1947). Coins and banknotes were introduced into the interviews as stimulus materials, together with such things as sweets, chocolates and comics so as to simulate the process of buying and selling, thus providing a concrete situation as a starting point for the interview questions. The money used was a 100 Lire coin and three banknotes (500 Lire, 10,000 Lire and 100,000 Lire). There was a simple correspondence between the values of the notes and their size: the more the note was worth the larger it was.

The interview was divided into three phases:

1. The interviewer laid the four types of money on the table in front of the child and asked 'Do you know what these are?', and, when the child had recognised them as money, added 'Can you tell me what they are used for?' and 'Is that all they are used for or are they also used for something else?' If a child failed to identify an appropriate use, we asked 'Haven't you ever been in a shop with your mother?'; 'Did you see what she did?'; 'What did she do to get the shopkeeper to give her the things?', and similar questions intended to ascertain whether the child had any idea of what one does with money in a shop.

2. After this the child was asked about each type of money in turn: 'Do you know what this is called?' and, 'If I went in a shop with this money could I buy a chocolate?', 'Why?' (or 'Why not'?). The same questions were then repeated for a Mickey Mouse comic, a Barbie Doll (or an Action Man for the boys), a 'real' car. In this way the child was asked to distinguish between the various types of money, both in name and in value by having to judge whether each type was sufficient, insufficient or too much to buy each of the named objects. Where the type of money was too much for any particular object it was also possible to see if the child mentioned the possibility of obtaining change.

3. Lastly, the interviewer suggested that the child pretended to be a shopkeeper while she pretended to buy a chocolate or a comic. Holding the

goods she paused for a moment and asked 'What do I have to do now?' to see if the child asked for payment. By repeating the game the interviewer was able to use both the money which the child had previously said was enough to buy the object as well as money of a higher value. It was thus possible to see whether or not the child gave change, and to examine the reasons why. Finally children were asked to take the role of the customer so as to see whether, in this role, they paid or not, what money they used, and also if they claimed any change.

The responses are grouped in 5 levels preceded by a phase in which children show no understanding of money nor used it to pay in the simulation (Level 0). Levels 1–5 were characterised by the acquisition of increasingly accurate rules about the use and value of money. At Level 1 there is a simple recognition of the need for payment, while the idea that there are different types of money to which one must pay attention when buying appears at Levels 2 and 3. Level 4 sees the introduction of a precise criterion for establishing the correspondence between the price of an object and the 'right' type of money sufficient to buy it. Finally, at Level 5, children were able to use money correctly, to give a more or less plausible indication of the price of the various goods and, in the role of shopkeeper, to give the right change when the interviewer paid with a banknote whose value exceeded the price.

Level 0: No understanding of money.
The most primitive responses were those which indicated an almost complete absence of knowledge about money.
CHICCO (3:7), for instance, when he saw the money spread out on the table, said he had never seen anything like it before, nor did he know what it was. When he was asked if he had ever been in a shop with his mother he said no, but that he had played shops. When the interviewer played this game with him he did not use the money when he was either the customer or the shopkeeper.

Other children however, while they did not recognise the money when it was shown to them were able to say something about its use once the word *money* had been spoken by the interviewer. DAVIDE (3:6), for instance, said he had never seen it before when the money was on the table. The interviewer then explained to him – It's money. Do you know what it's used for? – *To pay.* – When? – *When you go out.* – When you go out where? – … – Have you ever seen your mummy or your daddy pay? – *Yes, I go too.* – Where? – *With my daddy, Daddy pays and I give him my hand.*

This child's responses makes it appear that he has very confused and imprecise ideas about what *to pay* means. This impression was decisively confirmed by the simulation of buying and selling. When he took the role of the customer Davide did not pay. When he was the shopkeeper the interviewer asked him – Do I also have to give you something? – *The chocolate.* – But do I have to give you something in exchange for the sweet which you gave me? – *I don't want anything else.* – Don't I have to give you any money? – *Yes.* – Haven't you ever gone shopping for groceries? – *Yes.* – What do you do it with? – *With a bag.*

Some children said that money was used to buy things, though they seemed to lack any effective knowledge corresponding to this affirmation. MICHELA (4:0) and FILIPPO (3:7), for instance, both said that money was used to buy things, but did not use any while playing shops, neither when they were selling nor when they were buying.

Level 1: Money is used to pay when you buy something.
From this level on, children not only say that money is used to buy things, but they also use it effectively when they take on the role of customer in the simulation of buying and selling. They also recognise that payment is obligatory, even if they are unable to give a correct justification for it. Often when they took on the role of the shopkeeper they also gave money to the experimenter who took the part of the customer. Their behaviour is apparently derived from observing shopkeepers giving change, though without any understanding of why they do so. Some children believe it is because shopkeeper and customer are obliged to pay each other, considering *change* to be a custom for which they do not know the reason, or as an expedient to ensure that the customer will never be penniless and always able to buy something else.

FILIPPO (4:7) gives the experimenter 1,000 Lire change after she has paid for a chocolate with 100 Lire – How come you've given me so much money? – ... – Do you give it to everybody who comes to buy something from you? – No. – When do you give it? – *Friday.* – How come? – *Then I give some other money.* – Why do shopkeepers give money to the people who come to buy things? – *Because they have to pay.* – Do they always give it? – *Yes.* – What would happen if shopkeepers gave up giving money? – *They'd put them in prison.* – What would happen if a woman who went shopping gave up giving money? – *They'd put her in prison.*

STEFANIA (5:8) gave 500 Lire after having received, at her own request, 100 Lire from the interviewer for a chocolate – Why did you give me that? – *Because in this bar one gives money.* – Every time that somebody buys something? – *Yes.* – You're very kind! – *They do it in every bar.* – Why? – *I don't know.*

Admitting the necessity of payment and, in many cases, also the ideas about *change*, are also typical of the following level. What is specific to the responses classified at Level 1 is that the children do not discriminate between the different types of coins and banknotes. Any type of money is thought to be sufficient to buy any object, or they describe a single type which will serve for every occasion (generally a 'bunch' of banknotes). In short, when you go into a shop you have to pay, but it doesn't matter what kind of money you use.

ALESSIA (3:6) says that any of the types of money shown to her could buy a doll, or a car or a chocolate. The interviewer then pointed to the 100 Lire coin and the 100,000 Lire note and asked – Can you buy the same things with this money as you can with this one? – *Yes.* – Why did they make one out of metal and one out of paper? – *They made it like that.*

STEFANIA (5:8), whose behaviour during the shop game we have already reported, also said that every type of money could buy these various things – Have you ever wondered why they make one type of money different from another? – *I have, yes, but I still don't know*

Level 2: Not every kind of money will buy everything.

At this level children begin to establish a differentiation between different types of money, even if it is founded on very broad and general criteria. Some, such as MARIA CRISTINA (4:0), simply distinguish between coins and notes – Do you know what this (100 lire) is called? – *A coin.* – Could you buy a chocolate with it? – *I don't know.* – A Barbie doll? – *No, because if someone wants one of those they've got to pay with a note.* – Could you buy a car? – *No.* With the 500 Lire she doesn't think you could buy a Barbie doll or a chocolate – What about a car? – *No-o. Because there aren't any shops, I've never seen one.* – How do the people who have cars get them? – *Jesus gave it to them.* – No, there are shops which sell cars. – *Then, yes.* – Could you buy a car with this (10,000 Lire) money? – *I don't know.* – A Barbie doll? – *I don't know.* – What money would you need for a Barbie doll? – *Paper money.*

Other children, however, gave responses which seemed casual in the sense that one could not understand the criteria of differentiation or their employment in the use of money. ANDREA (4:5) said, for instance, that with 100 Lire it was possible to buy every object on the list. 500 Lire, however, could buy nothing, and 100,000 Lire only the car.

Level 3: Sometimes the money is not enough.

Children recognise that some things cost less than others and some things more, and that therefore certain types of money (differentiated according to size or, less frequently, the number of zeros marked on it, or by name) cannot be used sometimes because they are not enough. It does not matter if the value of the money exceeds that of the object; with 100,000 Lire it is possible to buy either the chocolate or the doll. In their own terms such beliefs are not false. Indeed, if they were allied to correct ideas about the function of change they would be an indication that the child understood the way in which money is used. Children at this level, however, do not understand why the shopkeeper only sometimes gives change, and on this point they give responses similar to those we have already recorded at earlier levels.

What distinguishes the responses at this level from those of Level 2 is the explicit and coherent use of quantitative criteria. Money cannot be used when '*it's too little*' or '*it's not enough*'. Considering the dimensions of the money also allows a finer discrimination between types of money than do criteria based on the form or material (round–square; coin–note). All the same, the conceptions of this level remain rather general and limited. Children recognise that 100 Lire buys very little and that the price of a car is exorbitant compared to the value of the money shown to them.

According to CARLA (5:5), for instance, with 100 Lire one cannot even buy a chocolate, because *it's too little*; 500 Lire, however, is enough for both the chocolate and the Barbie doll, but not for the car *because it's too little*. With 10,000 and 100,000 Lire one can buy everything.

LEO (5:6) says that with 100 Lire one cannot buy even the chocolate *because you need more*. 500 Lire will buy both the chocolate and the Action Man, but not the car *because it costs too much money*; the same goes for the 10,000 Lire. The 100,000 Lire, however, will buy everything, even the car – This (100,000) then is more than this (10,000)? – *Yes*. – How do you know that? – *Because there are more numbers.*

Level 4: Strict correspondence between objects and money.

Level 4 is characterised by the idea that to buy something the 'right money' *is necessary*, which is to say money of exactly the same value as the price of the thing.

ALESSANDRO (6:6) says that the 100 Lire coin will only buy the chocolate or the comic, that it is too little for the other things – With 500 Lire? – *You can buy two chocolates.* – Could you buy the comic? – *You could buy two comics.* – What if you only wanted one? – *Then you need this* (100 Lire). 500 Lire is all right for the Action Man, but is not enough for the car; 10,000 Lire will buy 3 chocolates, 3 comics or 3 Action Men but is not enough for the car. With 100,000 Lire the number of objects which can be bought rises to four.

The idea that one must pay with exactly the right money alternates in some children through the course of the interview with the idea that one could pay with a higher sum and receive change from the shopkeeper. The former idea, however, is more dominant than the second (otherwise the responses would have been classified at Level 5). This mixture of ideas is of particular interest in relation to the hypothesis that 'strict correspondence' is a more advanced response than a simple affirmation that sometimes the money is not enough. Responses in which this strict correspondence accompanies the first signs of the correct understanding of change indicates that this is, in fact, the type of belief which is immediately antecedent to the correct ideas of Level 5.

STELLA (6:3) – Could you buy a chocolate with this (500 Lire) money? – *It costs less.* – If I didn't have a 100 Lire could I pay for the chocolate with this money? – *If you bought two of them.* – And if I only want one? – *Yes, they'll give you the change.* She is less certain about the possibility of buying a chocolate with 10,000 Lire – *It's worth even more than that* (500 Lire). *I don't know if you could buy it ... they'd give you even more change,* and she makes a similar response for the 100,000 Lire. Stella seems, then, to have understood the function of change, but her behaviour while playing shop is not so clear. As a customer she pays for a chocolate with 100 Lire. The interviewer asks – Do I have to do something now? – *Yes, you have to give me the change.* – Will this (1,000 Lire) do? – *Yes.* – How much is it? – *F . . . Fifty?* – Which is more, this or this? – . . . –Which is more, what you gave me or what I gave you? (Stella points to the 1,000 Lire) – Is that all right? – *. . . perhaps less.* – What do they do in the shops, do they give you more or less? – *Less.* When Stella is the shopkeeper the interviewer pays for a chocolate with 100 Lire. Stella laughs and gives 500 Lire as change – Why have you given me 500 Lire? – (Laughs) *Perhaps I was wrong with the notes ... but do they only give notes?* – I'd like you to explain to me when they do give change. – *But there are some things which I never buy by myself.* – But you see your mummy, no? Why do you think they give change? – *I don't know.* – Do they always give it? – *Sometimes they do and sometimes they don't.* – And why don't they sometimes? – *I really don't know that.* – Why does your mummy give money to the man in the shop? – *Because she has to buy something.* – Could she do it without money? – *No.* – What would happen? – *If she didn't the police would come and put her in prison.*

Level 5: Correct ideas.

At this level children have understood how change serves precisely to compensate the imbalance created when the value of money paid is higher than the price of the goods. We have just seen how Stella, at different moments, expresses ideas of Level 4 and Level 5. The continuity between these two levels is also shown in the responses of children who, although classified at the higher level, still exhibit some residues from the earlier level.

VALERIA (7:2), for instance, begins by saying that the change is equal to the price, but during the buying and selling game she is able to calculate it exactly – Can you buy a chocolate with this? – *Yes.* – A comic? – *Some even cost 200 Lire.* – A Barbie doll? – *No, it costs more.* – Can you get a chocolate with 500 Lire? – *Yes, lots, more than one.* – But could you get just one? – *Yes, because then they'd give you the change.* – A comic? – *Yes.* – The Barbie doll? – *Not that.* – With 10,000 Lire? – *Yes.* The car? – *No.* – A comic? – *Yes lots, because they cost 200, 300 Lire.* – But if you only wanted one? – *Yes, because then they'd give you the change.* – What would that be? – *It would be ... if someone gives more money, then there is the change that would be the money he should have given himself.* She says the same thing about the 100,000 Lire. During the shop game the interviewer buys a sweet with 50 Lire – Is that OK? – *There's no change because the sweet costs 50!* – I'll buy another one with 100 Lire. – *50 Lire change!* – I'll buy two with 500 Lire, can you give me the change? – *Wait, I've got to work it out.* – I have to give you 100 Lire and I've given you 500. – *300 Lire change ... no, I've made a mistake, 400.*

These data are both more finely detailed and more wide ranging than Strauss's, allowing us on the one hand to clarify the sense which money, selling and payment have for young children and, on the other, to determine the actual order of appearance of the ideas classified by Strauss in his Levels 2 and 3.

This research has allowed us to observe the first emergence of some of the 'economic' ideas we found in our previous studies. This is so, for instance, with ideas about *change*. It seems that children have contact with money from a very early age, since the majority of children classified at Level 0 knew at least what to call it and that it related to the notion of *buying*. Before 4 years, however, children did not seem to have identified in full the sequence of actions which takes place when something is bought. They speak about payment, but in the shop game all they actually do is exchange objects. By about 4 years, however, children have generally identified a buying and selling 'script' which details some of the actions: the customer asks for something, the shopkeeper gives it to them, the customer gives money, in their turn the shopkeeper gives money, though perhaps not always. These are the manifest and regular acts which children can observe or which they themselves undertake in shops. However, the formation of this 'script' does not imply an understanding of the economic reasons underlying all the events from which it is constructed . For instance, children know that a transaction cannot be concluded after only the first two steps (asking for and receiving something), and they say that it is always necessary to pay the shopkeeper although they are unable to explain why. The explanations of young children tend, in fact, to be either 'because you have to' or to refer to customs and habits. The affirmation that one must pay with the 'right' money constitutes the first attempt at moving from an understanding of buying and selling as ritual purely and simply, to an understanding based on the relation between money and goods.

Table 4.7 *Conceptions about the use of money*

Response level	Age groups					Total
	3–4	4–5	5–6	6–7	7–8	
0. No understanding	11	3	3	0	0	17
1. Money is used to pay	8	8	4	2	0	22
2. Not every type of money will buy everything	1	6	1	0	0	8
3. Sometimes the money is not enough	0	3	6	5	2	16
4. Strict correspondence	0	0	5	10	5	20
5. Correct ideas	0	0	1	3	13	17
Total	20	20	20	20	20	100

$r_s = 0.91$, $p < .001$

Another point of interest in these data is that they provide a more satisfactory resolution to the problem of Strauss's Levels 2 and 3. We have already ascertained that the idea that the money is '*sometimes not enough*' (Level 3 of our sequence) appears in children younger than those who assert a strict correspondence between money and goods. In some cases we also saw that this type of response emerged side by side with the correct ideas of Level 5. A later confirmation that a strict correspondence succeeds the idea that '*sometimes the money is not enough*' comes from a longitudinal extension of the study just described (Berti and Bombi, 1981). We were able to trace the majority of the subjects a year later and re-examine them with the same interview. Almost all the children who had expressed a strict correspondence had, a year later, reached a correct understanding of the function of change. Some of the children who had said that sometimes the money was not enough had changed to asserting a strict correspondence, while others had progressed to a correct understanding of change.

One can conclude that, as opposed to Strauss's argument, the idea of only being able to pay with the right money represents an advance on the notion of being able to pay with money of higher value, since the former rather than the latter is the immediate antecedent of the correct conceptions which children finally form about the function of change.

The mental operations which children need in order to reach the idea that for every object there exists the 'right money' are rather complex. First of all they must understand that different things have different prices, and that different types of money also correspond to different values. They must then associate the different prices with the various types of money. There are logical operations involved here, though not yet arithmetic operations. Even if these children were frequently able to give the name of some banknote, this does not correspond to an understanding of its numerical significance. If that were indeed the case, then they would also have been able to understand the possibility of subtracting the price from the sum paid by the customer. This is just what happens in giving change, but such an understanding is only reached at Level 5 when children finally realise how money functions. At Level 4, however, children recognise the existence of differing amounts, both of prices and of monetary denominations; they are able to put them in order and to establish a correspondence between them. However incorrect they may be, conceptions established on the basis of these operations of seriation and bi-univocal correspondence are nonetheless a great achievement. They allow the child to establish a connection between money and goods bought, while before payment appeared as a kind of ritual included in the whole scenario of buying and selling. Once integrated with an understanding of arithmetic, these conceptions are transformed into the full understanding of the use of money characteristic of children from the age of 7 onwards.

4.3   Differences in price between goods

From about the age of 6, that is at the time when the idea of a strict correspondence between money and goods emerges, children clearly recognise that different goods have different prices. This is also something to which adults frequently draw children's attention: it is not possible to buy something which a child wants because it 'costs too much'; or it is better to go to a shop where such things 'cost less'; some objects are 'valuable' while others are not 'worth anything', and so on. All the same, it is very likely that, notwithstanding the frequency of such remarks, adults do not pause to explain the reasons for the diversity of prices among different goods. It is, then, necessary to determine the reasons children use to explain why such differences occur.

In the first, more limited, of two studies examining this question, we sought to determine if and how children aged 6–11 years explained the reasons for different prices. The second study attempts a more comprehensive view of the issues considered in this chapter, namely, transactions centred on goods and variations in their price between production and consumption.

This section reports the first of these studies in which 60 children aged 6 to 11 were interviewed.[5] The aim of the investigation was to see how the justifications develop for the differences in price between various goods, from an age at which children presumably have already constructed a precise correspondence between price and payment, or at least realise that not every type of money is good for purchase of every kind of object.

---

[5] The children were grouped into three age levels, 6–7 years, 8–9 years and 10–11 years, with 10 girls and 10 boys in each group. All the children were working class and lived in a small village in Trentino, Northern Italy. The data were collected by Marina Lo Scalzo.

The interview was divided into three phases. The first phase began with the question: 'Do you think that the things you see in the shop all cost the same amount of money or not?'. Children who recognised the existence of different prices were asked why things were differently priced; they were then asked to name something which they thought cost a lot and something which they thought was cheap and to explain this difference. Obviously this part of the interview was not presented to those children who said that everything cost the same, though the following phases were presented to all the children and included references to objects of differing prices. In the second phase the child was shown the interviewer's car outside the window and asked if it cost a lot or a little (eventually this led to the question of how much), and why. The same questions were also asked about the gold bracelet on the interviewer's wrist. In the third phase the child was shown a series of objects in pairs and asked if they both cost the same or not, and if not to say which cost more and why (the pairs of objects were: a lettuce and two chicken thighs; a watch and a book; an oil painting and a poster). While the initial questions were designed to assess children's actual ideas, these judgements about pairs of objects were intended to overcome the difficulties involved in giving abstract definitions by recalling to the child's attention the characteristics of some particular goods. These goods were intended to generate the possibility of conflict between various criteria which the child might use to explain differences in price (such as size, scarcity, usefulness, beauty).

The responses are grouped into four levels. The most primitive (Level 0) is characterised by a lack of recognition of price variations, or the absence of any attempt to provide an explanation. At Level 1 (which was the most frequent response) children identify the reason for price differences in some characteristics of the objects. At the second level children indicate reasons of a social nature: prices are decided by someone (generally the shopkeeper) on the basis of utility and of the necessity for everybody to resupply themselves with indispensable things. Finally, at the fourth level, children speak about the cost of labour and materials involved in the production of objects. In every protocol we observed a systematic disjunction of levels between the different parts of the interview (initial questions; judgements about the price of single objects; paired comparisons). The last exercise was in fact the easiest, since children were induced to attend to the different characteristics of the goods and to notice the conflicts in their own responses. The second part, which again used concrete examples, also generally allowed children to give more precise answers than for the first part. Each protocol was classified according to the prevailing level in the child's responses.

Level 0: 'Don't know'.

At this level were grouped the children who did not admit the existence of differences in price, or who repeatedly replied *'don't know'* in the various parts of the interview, or who believed that simply naming or describing the objects we presented constituted a sufficient 'explanation' for their price.

MARCIA (6:8) – Do you think that things you buy in the shops all cost the same, the same amount of money or not? – *Yes.* – A car the same as a roll? – *Yes.* – Can you think of something which it costs a lot of money to buy? – . . . *A car.* – Anything else? – . . . – Can you think of something that costs very little money to buy? – . . . – What can you get with very little money? – *A bracelet.* – Why does a bracelet cost little? – . . . – Look at this gold bracelet, do you think it cost a lot or a little? – *A lot.* – Why? – *Because it's gold.* – But you just told me you could buy a bracelet for not very much? – *Yes.* – So this one too wouldn't cost very much? – *No.* – Why not? – . . . .

KATIA (6:6) says that the things do not all cost the same – Why do some things cost a lot and others a little? – . . . *the bulldozer.* – The bulldozer costs a lot or a little? – *A lot.* – Why? – *Because it costs a lot of money.* – How much, do you think? – *100,000.* – Can you think of something that costs only a little? – *A bicycle.* – Why? – *Because it only costs a little money.* – How much do you think it costs? – *100,000.* – Like the bulldozer? – *Yes.* – But before you said that the bulldozer cost a lot and the bicycle a little, now you say that they both cost 100,000. – *Because they're the same.* – What do you mean they're the same? – *They're just the same, they've both got wheels.* – Does this bracelet cost a lot or a little? – *A lot.* – Why? – *Because it's gold.* – Why does gold cost a lot? – *Because you need a lot of money, they're things for which you have to spend a lot of money.* The remainder of the interview continued in the same vein.

Even if it sometimes appears that these children are using the material qualities of things as justifications for prices, in fact these pseudo-explanations soon reduce to a circular argument: the bracelet costs a lot because it is gold, gold costs a lot because you need a lot of money. Actually the responses of both Katia and Marcia are simply based on the assertions made by adults that they spent 'a lot' or 'a little' for the things which they have bought.

Level 1: Price depends on the characteristics of objects.

At this level children assert that prices vary for different goods and seek justifications for such variations in some salient characteristic of the particular objects being considered. The links established between some quality of an object and its price may be fragile and inconsistent. The same child may justify high prices as much as low prices by recourse to exactly the same quality. The children in the examples given below, however, do maintain a certain coherence in the main criteria which they use.

WALTER (8:11) explains the different prices of goods by saying that *some are big and some are little* and mentions a car as an example of something which costs a lot – Why does it cost a lot? – *Because it's big.* – What do you mean? – *That you can get a lot of people in it.* – Is there something which costs even more than a car? – *Yes, an aeroplane.* – Why? – *Because it's even bigger.* – What do you mean? – *You can get even more people in.* Up to here he is evidently using a criterion of size, but he then begins to add another when he explains that – *A toy car only costs a little.* – Why? – *It's only to play with, it's small.* – Does everything which you play with only cost a little? – *Yes.* – Why? – *. . . Because they're for playing with.* – Do you see this bracelet? – *Yes.* – Do you think it cost a lot or a little? – *A lot.* – Why? – *Because it's beautiful and bright.* – And toy cars aren't beautiful? – *Yes.* – You told me that they only cost a little, why was that? – *. . . I don't know.* – Which cost more this lettuce or the chicken? – *The lettuce, because there's more of it.* – And what if I only bought this much (removing a part of the lettuce), would I have spent more on the lettuce or the chicken? – *The chicken.* – Why? – *because there's more of it . . .* (he checks and sees that this is not so) *no, no, still the lettuce, because there's still more of it than the chicken.*

IVAN (9:1) on the other hand thinks that the price of goods varies as a function of their usefulness. The chicken, he says, costs more than the lettuce because it is more nourishing. Between the watch and the book he chooses the watch – *Because the watch is useful, you can use it to tell the time, if you had an appointment and you didn't have a watch what would you do? And also because a watch is a luxury.* But if you think about it a book is also useful! – *Yes.* – So? – *Yes, with the book you can learn lots of things and with the watch you can learn to tell the time, when you have to go, but for me the watch is worth more, you use it more often during the day.*

Level 2: Price depends on social considerations.

The following extract shows a child who is convinced that the price is decided by the shopkeeper, who has to take account of the needs of the purchasers and of the possible uses for the goods in question.

DENIS (8:11) gives as an example of something which costs a little – *Food.* – Explain that to me. – *Oh, things to eat, and toys.* – Why? – *Because they don't charge very much, because there are poor people who couldn't buy them, so how could they live? So they make them cost only a little.* – And the toys? – *Toys don't cost very much because the grown-ups can't buy them, those who don't have any money, so they buy them just with what they've got, so they only cost a little.* – But who is it who decides how much something costs? – *The shopkeeper when he goes to buy the things.* – He's the one who decides the price? – *Yes.*

Level 3: Price depends on the work done.

Finally children argue that the price of an object depends on the type or amount of work necessary to produce it. Sometimes they also mention other production costs such as the cost of the raw materials and machinery. Work appeared sporadically in the speech of some of the children from the previous level when they considered the painting and the poster (which were the clearest examples of the contrast between something entirely handmade and something produced by a machine). At Level 3, however, this argument is also justified and applied in cases which previously generated only pseudo-explanations, or which could be explained in other ways. Gold, for example, whose price was justified at the earlier level only by reference to its scarcity is now construed in terms of the difficulties in extracting it.

LORENZA (10:8) says that things have different prices – *Because they are different things, some are worth more.* – Why? – *Because they're made better.* – What do you mean? – *... I don't know.* – Can you think of something which costs a lot? – *Lorries, cars.* – Why do they cost a lot? – *Because they're built.* – What do you mean? – *It needs a lot of machines to make them, and then they have to pay the workers who make the machines work.* (Gold too costs a lot) – *because it's worth a lot and costs a lot of money and also because it's worked on.* – Why do things which are worked on cost a lot? – *Because the people who get it out of the blocks have to get a lot of money.*

ADRIANO (8:4) explains the differences by saying that – *... they put more time into things which cost a lot.* – And those things which don't cost very much? – *... they do in less time.* – What do you mean that they put more or less time into it? – *Oh that ... they take a long time, several days to make it.* – Tell me something which costs a lot? – *A motorbike.* – Why? – *Because it takes a long time to make and you need a lot of motors.* – What do you mean? – *Lots of pieces and materials.* – Is there anything which costs more? – *Yes, houses, land.* – How come? – *Because ... houses take a long time to build and lots of material, land, on the other hand fields are big.* He says that gold costs a lot because – *You need to make it.* – What do you mean? – *You have to find some and then make it into something.* – Why does it cost a lot then? – *Because there's a lot of work to do.* – If this bracelet was made of iron would it cost the same? – *No, less.* – Why? – *Because you can find iron everywhere, but gold is more difficult to find.*

Sometimes these ideas about work are more openly tinged with subjective reasons; work is then considered in terms of tiredness.

FABRIZIO (10:7) – *Things which people work on more cost more and things cost less which people get less tired making.* – Can you think of something which costs a lot? – *An aeroplane, a ship.* – Why? – *Because they get very tired making them, and they need years of work.*

The results demonstrate that the criteria most frequently used by children aged from 6 to 8–9 years in explaining the existence of different prices are those referring to various characteristics of goods (Level 1). Only around 10–11 years, with the emergence of Level 2 and Level 3 responses, do children begin to acknowledge social and economic processes. A study undertaken by Burris (1983) after our own had been completed produced very similar results. She too used a paired comparison procedure, asking children which of

Table 4.8 *Differences in price between goods*

Response level	Age groups			Total
	6–7	8–9	10–11	
0. Don't know	5	0	0	5
1. Price depends on the characteristics of objects	13	12	1	26
2. Price depends on social considerations	1	4	9	14
3. Price depends on the work done	1	4	10	15
Total	20	20	20	60

$r_s = 0.68$, $p < .001$

two objects cost more and why. In her research the 4–5 year olds argued that price depended on the physical size of the object. The 7–8 year olds thought that price depended on the utility or the functions of an object; these ranged from providing pleasurable reassurance to whether or not it might be harmful to one's health. Such responses are very similar to those of Level 1 in our own study. Finally only about half of Burris's 11-year-old sample spoke about production costs.

Taking our own results together with those reported by Burris it seems reasonable to conclude that before 10 or 11 years, and even later for many children, price appears to be an intrinsic property of goods, something directly derived from its characteristics. Younger children consider only perceptible characteristics, such as size, while from about 6–7 years children speak of other less perceptually evident characteristics, though ones which have an importance for the consumer.

Burris (1983) also considered the development of the concept of commodity, producing responses similar to those she obtained in respect of price. Children were asked to name some things which could be bought and sold, as well as some which could *not* be bought and sold. Children were also asked to classify a number of objects into one of these two categories. Here too younger children most frequently used an object's physical characteristics as the criterion for deciding whether or not it was something which could be bought or sold. In particular things which were large or immovable or difficult to transport were not recognised as commodities. A cow, for instance, could not be bought and sold 'because it's too big to fit in the car' (Burris, 1983, p. 797). Even half of the 7–8 year olds gave this kind of response; it was only among the 10–11 year olds that such thinking had practically disappeared.

We can conclude, therefore, that for a long time children do not distinguish between the physical properties of an object and its economic properties, and that they represent buying and selling as a purely physical act, even if it is a social relation regulated by a particular type of norm. In the following section we shall see how such conceptions are reflected in the way in which children construe retail selling within a wider network of exchanges, including production.

4.4   The formation of prices

This section is concerned with the issue of commerce, and we shall examine how children come to coordinate the movement of goods with the movement of money, from production to retail sale. As we noted in Chapter 1 this is a theme which has been considered to a greater or lesser extent by many other authors, with converging results. Both Danziger (1958) and Burris (1983) report that only around 7–8 years do children become aware that the shopkeeper uses money received from customers in sales to replenish stocks of goods for sale. Strauss (1952, 1954), Jahoda (1979) and Furth (1980) also lead to similar conclusions; moreover these authors examine the difficulties which children face in understanding how the shopkeeper realises a profit.

Our own study of this theme dealt with more specific issues than other researchers. Children were asked about some goods with which they were familiar, apples and comics. In particular they were asked to describe what happened to both the goods and the prices between production and consumption. The interview[6] began with the children being asked if they had ever been to the greengrocer's (or newsagent's) and if they could remember roughly how much apples cost (or a comic which they knew). They were then asked if these things cost the same in every shop, and who it is who decides the price. This question produced various responses such as the shopkeeper, the producer, a commercial middleman, or sometimes even the state, the council or the bank. The children were then asked how these people or institutions determined the price. This was followed by some questions about the origins of goods, and if the child spoke about a producer distinct from the shopkeeper they were asked if the latter also had to pay, and if so how much. The interview concluded with some questions about the variations in price from year to year and, for the apples, from season to season. Thus it was possible to see whether or not children were aware of the various factors which contribute to the determination of prices: the costs of raw materials, machinery and labour, as well as the profit for every participant in the economic chain through which the goods pass before reaching their destination.

The same five types of response were observed for both the price of apples

---

[6] The subjects were 80 middle-class children from state schools in Padova. They were grouped into four age levels: 5–6 years, 7–8 years, 9–10 years and 11–12 years. Half the children were asked first about apples and then about comics, while for the other half the order of questions was reversed.

and the comic. The question of price variations is not applicable in the first two levels. Children either still do not understand that there is a precise relation between the money paid in shops and the goods bought (Level 0) or (Level 1) having understood this connection, they still retain some very primitive ideas about the origin of goods or believe that the shopkeeper gets them for nothing. Subsequently, children understand that the producer sells the goods to the shopkeeper; some of these subjects also introduce intermediate commercial figures such as the wholesaler or transporter. They can thus compare the prices set by all these participants. At Level 2 children are convinced that the price of goods remains invariant, or is even reduced, across the various commercial transactions. Only in the final two levels (3 and 4) do children understand that the price increases with every transaction, representing in ever more complete forms the significant factors influencing the formation of prices.

Level 0: Lack of understanding of buying and selling.

Children at Level 0 have not yet reached an understanding of how money is used in retail trade. Payment by the customer and change from the shopkeeper are considered to be the same thing, that is, the way in which the two partners to the deal replenish each other with money. The quantities which they exchange depend on their willingness to give and their wish to have, rather than on any characteristic of the goods which pass from one hand to the other in the course of the transaction. Some children believe that it is actually the customer who decides how much money to give, while others believe that the amount is determined by the shopkeeper. In either case, however, it is a question of an arbitrary decision, in which no consideration is given to any characteristics of the goods.

SERERNA (5:3) describes her mother buying apples – *She ... she ... she said 'give me some apples' and then gave him the money and he also gave her money* – Who gave the money? – *The greengrocer.* – And your mother also gave him money, or not? – *Yes.* – Who decides how much your mother has to give? – *Mummy.* – And how does she decide how much money to give? – *Thinks.*

MARCO (6:0) explains how the greengrocer decides how much money to ask for the apples – *Because they want to spend ... because they want to give people the money that I gave them.* – I don't really understand what you mean. – *Because they have to give money to the others, because I gave money to the greengrocer and when someone else comes to buy something they give that money to them.* – How does the greengrocer decide how much money someone has to give them? – *Because they want to have a lot of money.* – And can they ask for as much as they like? – *Yes.* – You told me that when you go and buy apples you give money to the greengrocer and that then he gives it to – (Interrupting) *To someone else.* – Why? – *Because otherwise they wouldn't have any money to give him.* – How does the greengrocer get the apples? – *He finds them on the trees.* – Does someone own the trees, or not? – *Yes, there is an owner.* – Who is the owner? – *The man, the greengrocer.*

Level 1: The shopkeeper does not buy.

The responses of Level 1 differ from those of Level 0 because of their more correct view of retail trade, although they remain very primitive. Change and the reciprocal exchange of money between customer and shopkeeper are no longer mentioned, while children now believe that it is the shopkeeper who decides how much money people have to give. Thus the idea begins to emerge that money is given in exchange for the goods bought, but the connection between goods and price remains very vague. The shopkeeper's decision rests on arbitrary criteria, and only in the oldest children is there any attempt to locate the reason for differences in prices in characteristics of the goods themselves.

CLEIDE (6:0) – What did you do to buy Topolino (a comic)? – *There's a man there who gives us Topolino and we give him money.* – Who? – *Us.* – You and who? – *My brother and Mummy.* – Who gave the money? – *I did.* – Do you remember how much you had to give? – *Two coins and a note.* – Who decided how much money you had to give him? – *He was the one who told us.* – Who? – *The man in the newsstand.* – And how did he know? – *Because before he went to the newsstand he went to school and they taught him.*

As regards the source of goods these children believe that either shopkeepers make them, or that they are made by a friend or an associate, who gives them away for free, or delegates the function of selling them while sharing the income. Some of the older children say that the shopkeeper obtains the goods from a transporter who brings them from the factory where they are produced. Even in this case, however, the idea does not occur that the shopkeeper pays for the goods, rather they say that the transporter is paid by the boss of the factory.

MONICA (8:0) says that the greengrocer gets the fruit from wholesale warehouses – And how do the people in the warehouses get the apples? – *Pick them from the trees.* – Why do the people in the warehouses give apples to the greengrocer? – *Because it's his job as a shopkeeper to sell the apples.* – And do the people in the warehouse also work? – *Yes, picking apples.* – Do they get paid? – *Yes.* – Who pays them? – *There's a boss who gives them money if they've worked well, if not he gives them less.*

Level 2: Prices remain the same or increase between the factory and shop.

It is only from Level 2 that as well as understanding the transactions which take place in retail trade, children also have a conception of the movement of goods from production to consumption, even if in a simplified way. They distinguish the figure of the shopkeeper from that of the producer and frequently, especially for the apples, present intermediaries (wholesalers or transporters) between shopkeeper and producer. Moreover, every time goods change hands money also changes hands. Thus it is at this level that children begin to make sense of the problem of the relationships between the various prices of goods at each transaction.

This passage of money is interpreted by children at Level 2 in two completely different ways. If we have nevertheless grouped these responses into a single level it is because each of these ways seems to be the product of a particular centration, while the responses at the later levels are characterised by coordination between these centrations.

The first type of response, shown by the majority of children, considers the passage of money which accompanies the movement of goods as payment for the goods themselves, as is the case for retail trade. The price is fixed by the shopkeeper (or occasionally by some public institution) either on the basis of an arbitrary decision or, in just the same way as recorded in the preceding study, according to some characteristics of the goods in question. The second centration, less frequent than the first, is based on the assertion that the money is given as payment for the work done by those who give up the goods.

We shall begin with the examination of the first type of response, in which children maintained that price remains invariant through the course of these various transactions. As a justification for this fact children allude to reasons of a moral order, saying that it is not fair for the shopkeepers to sell goods for a price higher than they paid; these answers provide evidence that children believe in the existence of a *fair price* related to the intrinsic properties of the goods in question.

LUCA (7:8) – The apples which the shopkeeper sells at 1,000 lire per kilo, how much did he have to pay when he got them from the lorry driver? – *The same.* – And how much did the lorry driver have to give the farmer? – *Still the same.* – So the money which the farmer gets, and which the lorry driver gets and which the greengrocer gets are all the same? – *Yes.* – In that case how does the shopkeeper make any money? – *... the greengrocer?* – Yes. – *From us.* – How come the greengrocer sells apples at the same price he paid for them? – *Because if he paid more for them then the farmer too ... would have to pay more ... on the other hand if the farmer paid less then the greengrocer would have to pay less.* – If the shopkeeper wanted to take more money could he sell the apples he bought for 1,000 Lire a kilo at 1,500 Lire? – *No!* – What would happen if he did? – *There wouldn't be enough money.* – Which money wouldn't be enough? – *The money which the greengrocer gives wouldn't be enough.* – He has to sell them at the same price he paid for them? – *Yes.* – But if he sold them for more what would happen? – *He couldn't do it, it's the lorry driver who says what the right price is, otherwise I don't know.* – The lorry driver says 'You have to give me 1,000 Lire for every kilo of apples'. Could he then sell them to the mothers at 1,500? – *No, it must always be the same price otherwise the farmer too would want to buy for 1,500 rather than 1,000.*

Luca has no doubt that the shopkeeper makes money (*'from us'*) by selling apples at the same price he himself had paid. How this happens is illustrated by PAOLA (7:8) who says that the shopkeeper – *give his money to the farmer, and wants his money back, so he gave him 500 Lire and he wants 500 Lire.* – Does he sell the apples for the same price he paid for them? – *Yes.* – The shopkeeper has to spend money to buy the apples? *Yes.* Then he sells them again and gets back exactly the same money? – *Yes.* – So how does he come to have the money to buy things for his children? – *The shopkeeper sells and people have to give him money, he puts it in the till, then other people come, take something and give him money, so the money is always increasing. When there's enough he buys clothes, shoes.* – Is the money in the till enough to buy clothes, food to eat and apples to sell? – *Yes.*

Paola, then, loses sight of the equivalence between the sum paid by the shopkeeper and the total received from customers because she is beguiled by the reiteration of the very act of buying and selling in relation to the total quantity. The shopkeeper's numerous daily sales seem to amount to much more than the payments he has to make every now and then, when he buys the goods from the warehouse. There is here an error of quantification analogous to the classical Piagetian conservation task in which children assert that the quantity of liquid increases when it is poured into several smaller containers (Piaget, 1958). As a consequence of this error, children at this level are able to believe that the shopkeeper makes money while buying and selling at the same price without being aware of any contradiction.

On the other hand the centration by some children on the work under-taken by the producer, wholesaler, retailer or other commercial actors, leads them to believe that the price of goods gradually decreases as they pass from the place of production to the shop, since the quantity or quality of work which is necessary at each stage also appears to them to diminish gradually. According to CLAUDIO (7:10), for instance, apples cost more when bought from the farmer *'because the farmer grows them'.* However for these city children the work of industrial production is seen as more tiring and consuming. Fruit appears to be more of a work of nature than the product of human activity. Responses of this type are therefore more frequently observed in relation to comics than apples.

GIORGIO (7:8) – If the paper seller pays 400 Lire for the comics, how much could he sell them for? – ... *200.* – For less? – *Yes.* – How come for less? – *Because he gives 400 Lire to him who made it, and it costs more to make something; he makes it for him, then he gives it to him and then he sells it for less.*

– I didn't understand very well, could you explain it to me a little more clearly? – *He sells it for less because* . . . – You were telling me about the man in the factory . . . (Interrupting) – *Yes, because he makes it, writes it, makes the paper, writes on it, and draws the pictures, he does everything you have to do to make a comic.* – And you told me that he gets more money than the paper seller? – *Yes.* – Why? – *Because he* . . . *it's something, it's difficult to make; the paper seller, if he gives it to him, it's not difficult to sell it.*

ELISA (9:6) on the other hand believes that the paper seller buys and sells comics at the same price, 400 Lire, but that the lorry driver pays 10,000 Lire for each comic when he in his turn buys them from the factory – The lorry driver who brings the comics to the man at the newsstand, is the price he charges more, or less, or the same as the price he paid at the factory? – . . . *more.* – Why? – *Because otherwise the man who goes to get the comics from the factory* . . . *no, that is less, because it's very tiring to make the comics and so they give them more money, on the other hand when they go to give the comics to the shopkeeper they pay less.* – How come? – *Because comics don't cost much, only a little, for instance the one who goes to get the comics pays 10,000 Lire to the man in the factory; though he can't decide to go to the shopkeeper and say 'this comic costs 10,000'. A comic couldn't cost 10,000 Lire, only 350 or 500.* – But he gives 10,000 Lire to the man in the factory? – *Yes, or perhaps 8,000, because it's tiring, it's not easy to make comics.* – So the man at the factory is paid, 8,000 Lire for a copy of Topolino, so how much will the shopkeeper pay? – 400. – And the children who go to buy it? – 400. – Doesn't that mean that the lorry driver will lose out? – . . . – He pays 8,000 Lire for the comics and then sells them for 400. – . . . *well, he loses, yes.* – He loses? – *Eh!.*

Elisa therefore comes to understand that selling goods for a lower price than was paid for them leads to losses. This is a case of a subject whose beliefs are in transition towards those of Level 3. Pressed by the interviewer's objections she comes, towards the end of the interview, to admit that prices increase with each new transaction. Other children at this level, however, are not sensitive to the objections made to them and maintain that one can make money even by selling goods below cost price. Their explanations for this are the same as those we have already reported as to how the shopkeeper makes money while buying and selling at the same price.

CLAUDIO (7:10) – You pay 500 Lire for Topolino, how much did the paper seller pay? – *More.* – Why did he pay more? – *Because the person who makes it charges more.* – Doesn't the paper seller risk not having any money if he pays more for the comic? – *No.* – How does he come to have money? – *Because everybody who buys newspapers gives him some.* – But if every child who buys Topolino gives him 500 Lire, and he pays 800 Lire for it, for instance, in the end won't he be left without any money? – *No.*

As we saw above, GIORGIO (7:8) says comics cost more at the factory. His convictions seem a bit shaken by the experimenter's first objections. – If he pays 400 Lire for each comic and sells them for 300 won't he be left without any money? – ... *Left without money ... (ruminating) ... he buys them for 400 Lire, and they give him 300, then ... he'll be left without any money.* – What should he do then so as not to be left without any money? – *He gives 400 Lire, he buys them for 400 Lire, he gets 300, then he's left without money ... he's only got the 300, not the 400.* – So what does he do? – *... costs, it costs more where they make it than where they sell it, where they make it costs 400, and where they sell it it costs 300 but according to those who buy it. You need to see how many get bought!* – You mean that if the people buy comics ... (Interrupting) – *So he gets the money to buy them from the person who makes them.*

Level 3: Prices diminish between the shop and the factory.

The last two levels are both characterised by a recognition that shopkeepers sell goods at higher prices than they pay for them, and that in general prices increase through the course of the various transactions. However, children at Level 3 reconstruct the changes in price between the factory and the shop step by step and in reverse order, beginning with the retail price and reaching the factory price by progressively subtracting the sum added by each intermediary. At Level 4, on the other hand, there seems to be a comprehensive vision of the sequence of transactions already constructed by the child prior to the interview. From their first response such children speak about production, and assert that the final price depends on a series of successive additions.

Children at the third level begin by saying that prices are determined by the shopkeeper, either on the basis of criteria they do not know how to define, or according to the quality and size of the goods for sale. Only when they are asked how the shopkeeper obtains the goods do these children talk about producers and wholesalers and admit that the price paid by the shopkeeper is less than that paid by the consumer. In some cases they also come to understand that each increase in the price is necessary to allow the different economic actors to realise a profit; more frequently however the increase remains just a given fact for these children, which they do not know how to explain.

MARIANNA (9:5) – Who is it who decides the price of the apples? – *The person who sells them.* – And how do they reach that decision? – *Perhaps they look at the apples, see if they're good quality or not, perhaps they taste them to see if they're good or bad.* – How do the shopkeepers come to have the apples and vegetables that they sell? – *They go to the warehouses.* – And they give them to them, or do they have to give something in exchange? – *They buy them.* –

Who is it who decides the price they have to pay? – *The people in the warehouses.* – And how do they decide the price? – *Well, the wholesalers always sell it for less . . .* – Why do they sell it for less? – *Because they're bigger, there's lots of things . . . and lots of people go there.*

When asked how the producers decide on prices, children at this level tend to respond with notions similar to those already given about shopkeepers. According to PAOLO (9:2), for instance, shopkeepers set the price of apples according to quality, and farmers because they *know by the trees they have whether they're good.*

This is not always the case, however. MARIANNA, for instance, who as we have just noted said that the shopkeeper tasted the apples to decide the price, spoke instead about work when asked about the farmer – How do the farmers decide the price? – *They decide.* – Whatever comes into their mind? – *No! For instance, I think, that since they grew the trees from which the apples came, and had to look after them, the time they spent looking after these trees perhaps, also the apples, the way they are, good apples according to them, I think they would sell them for a higher price rather than a lower price.* And later – Do apples cost the same in every season? – *I don't think so.* – It changes? – *I think so, yes, because, for instance, in winter they have to be more careful.* – So in winter do they cost more or less? – *More I would say.*

If children take into account the length and quality of work as operative factors in the formation of prices, this is so only in those moments during the interview when they speak about production. When they speak of the retailer they revert to implicating arbitrary criteria or the quality of the goods.

Finally here, as in Level 2, there are children who speak about various public institutions as having responsibility for setting prices. This does not substantially differentiate such protocols from the other children of Level 3. The public institutions are seen to use the same criteria as those which the children ascribe to the shopkeeper; their authority is limited since it seems that the prices they set can be changed by the traders; or sometimes their functions are only to orient and to control, being limited to establishing the range within which prices can vary for any particular merchandise.

ANDREA (10:0) says that the price of apples varies from shop to shop – Why? – *Because in one shop they want to make a little more and so they add a little to the price of apples.* – Who is it who decides how much apples cost? – *A man.* – Who, the greengrocer or someone else? – *Someone else.* – And this person decides that one shopkeeper should set one price and another one a different price? – *No, perhaps this man sets a price of 100 Lire a kilo, for instance, and if the shopkeeper wants to make more he can increase the price to 1,200.* – But this man, what does he do? – *Decides the prices they have to charge in the shops.* – And the greengrocer has got to listen to him at least? –

Yes. – But how does this man decide? – *Because he's the boss of it all. I don't know, the country, the city.* – There's someone whose job it is to ... (Interrupting) – *Whose job it is to say how much to charge for apples, oranges.* – But the others don't listen to him, you told me ... (Interrupting) – *Well, the others don't listen to him, so they charge a little more or a little less.* – And how does this man decide what price to charge? – *He has to think how much the apples should cost.*

Level 4: Prices increase between the factory and the shop.

We shall now consider some examples of Level 4 responses. For the first time the idea appears that the retail price does not depend so much on the evident quality of the goods as on the costs of production, including all the various commercial intermediaries and the profit which each economic actor wishes to realise. When they say that it is the shopkeeper who sets the price (as the majority of children do for the apples), the children explain that he does so by calculating what he's spent and adding to it the sum he wishes to realise as profit.

NICOLA (11:6) – Who is it who decides the price of apples? – *The shopkeeper.* – What does he do? – *Sees how much he's spent to buy the things ... apples, fruit, adds what he wants to make and sets the price.* – And who does he buy the apples from? – *From the farmers* – And who is it there who decides the price? – *The farmer.* – How? – *He charges for his labour and adds what he needs to earn.* – What do you mean? – *He goes to cultivate, as they say, cultivate the land, plant the trees, water them, the money he needs for fertilisers, all these things.*

ANNA (12:2) – Do apples cost the same in every shop, or not? – *No, it changes, but not much.* – Who is it who decides the price? – *Perhaps the shopkeepers ... it depends how much they paid the farmer and they distribute the money they want to make and add 100 Lire to every 100 grammes.* – How does the farmer decide the price? – *I think he's free to sell at whatever price he wants to, but it depends on how much he had to spend to produce them, for fertiliser, and ... I don't know, the time it took to grow the plants, and besides he had to work a lot.*

In the case of the comic the producer is immediately introduced as the person who decides the price by adding the costs of production and a profit.

PIERO (11:2) – How much does Topolino cost? – *500 Lire.* – Does it cost 500 Lire in every newspaper stand, or not? – *I think it's 500 in every one.* – Who is it who decides the price? – *The publisher.* – How? – *He sees how much the paper costs, the other materials, and he adds something more.* – To set the price then he takes account of what he spent on the paper ... (Interrupting) – *And think of how much they want to make, and then they set the price.* – How much does the comic cost the man at the newspaper stand? – *Less, otherwise they wouldn't make anything; 100 or 200 Lire I think.*

This was the kind of response which, as we have noted above, was given by the majority of children for the comic, though some children also produced it for the apples.

STEFANIA (12:0) – Who is it who decides on the price of apples? – *I don't know ... the person who sells them ... no, the farmer.* – How does the farmer decide on the price? – *Depends how many apples he grew.* – And so if he had a lot? – *They cost less.* – Why? – *Because they would soon go bad.* – But wouldn't he think that if he sold them for more he would make more? – *No, because people wouldn't want to buy so many.*

It is at this level that some ideas about the market begin to appear. When she says that if prices are high that consumers will buy fewer apples Stefania is alluding to a market dynamic. At the preceding levels children think that completely arbitrary variations in price are possible, without considering the effects this would have on sales, or else they believe for reasons of a moral order that variations are impossible. At Level 4, however, some children spoke about various factors influencing the demand for goods, both when trying to explain how sellers fix their prices as well as at other moments during the interview.

ARTURO (12:2) – How does the wholesaler decide what price to set for the apples? – *He works on the basis of the prices which others charge, because if one of them sells the apples for 1,000 Lire a kilo, he can't then sell them at 2,000 otherwise no one would buy them from him because they would cost too much, so he has to base himself on what the others do.*

MIRIAM (11:9) – Do apples cost the same in every season? – *No, the early apples cost more.* – Why? – *Because they're the first, whoever buys them will buy them even if they are a higher price. It happened to me with strawberries, it was a long time since I'd had any, and I wanted some even though they cost a lot.*

In the preceding levels children, thinking only of the price or the characteristics of the goods, said that apples cost less out of season because they are not yet ripe, or they are shrivelled.

NICOLA (11:6) – If the man in the newsstand wanted to, could he sell Topolino for a 1,000 Lire instead of 500? – *I don't think it would be worth it.* – But wouldn't he make more money? – *No, because the other shopkeepers would sell it at a lower price and so it would be worth buying it from them. If he sold it for 1,000 very few people would buy it.*

Notice how Nicola in this last extract refers to a notion of convenience or economy rather than fairness.

Finally, there are also children at this level who refer to public institutions. In some cases the superficiality of such notions becomes evident in the course of the interview as later responses contradict these ideas, or they simply do not recur.

GUIDO (12:3) – Who decides the price of comics? – *I think it's the minister, I don't know ... it could be the publishers ... I don't know, I think it's the publishers but I'm not sure.* No other reference to the minister occurred in the remainder of this interview.

MARCO (12:4) – Who decides on the price of apples? – *Perhaps it's the shopkeepers, perhaps there's the same price for everybody which is fixed by law, I'm not sure.* – What do you think would be fair? – *That there's the same price for everybody.* – Could you explain what you think happens? – *Oh, the shopkeepers decide, but it would be better if there were the same price for everybody.*

It is apparent from the two tables, 4.9 and 4.10, that the response distributions show little difference between the apples and the comics, and therefore the following discussion will consider goods as a whole. The description of the levels given above has already indicated where differences between the two types of goods exist.

The youngest children were nearly all grouped at the more primitive response levels. These children consider the shop as the place where, apart from getting goods, people obtain money (Level 0) or, when they are able to form more precise conceptions of retail trade, they believe that the shopkeeper either makes the goods or receives them free of charge (Level 1). By the age of 7 or 8 years the majority of children have differentiated the figure of the shopkeeper from those of the producer and intermediaries, and they are able to represent the passage of money which flows parallel to the passage of goods. It is only around 9 or 10 years, however, that children begin to understand that the movement of goods is associated with an increase in price, and only at around 11 to 12 years do they finally understand that at every transaction in the passage of goods there is an increase in price and that this is how every economic actor is able to realise a profit.

As regards the type of response and the order of successive response levels this sequence largely corresponds with those proposed by Furth (1980) and Jahoda (1979). There are however qualitative differences between Jahoda's answers and ours. When reporting conceptions that shopkeepers sell goods at the same price they have paid for them, Jahoda notes that children at this level also believe that shopkeepers do not, thereby make a surplus. In order to explain how shopkeepers are able to pay their assistants or to buy new goods for the shop children suggest that they have recourse to some source of money external to buying and selling, such as social security or the bank. As we have just seen, however, our subjects did not mention such sources; they were convinced that shopkeepers could make a lot of money even without increasing prices, since the number of times they received money far exceeded the number of occasions on which they had to spend it. Furth (1980; Furth, Baur and Smith, 1979) reported the responses about buying, selling and profit together with those relating to other themes examined in the interviews and there is not sufficient detail on these precise notions to understand if the ideas

Table 4.9 *The formation of the price of apples*

Response level	Age groups				Total
	5–6	7–8	9–10	11–12	
0. Buying and selling is not understood	8	1	0	0	9
1. The shopkeeper does not buy	10	7	2	0	19
2. The price remains the same or increases from shop to producer	2	12	6	1	21
3. The price decreases from shop to producer	0	0	11	8	19
4. The price increases from producer to shop	0	0	1	11	12
Total	20	20	20	20	80

$r_s = 0.86$, $p < .001$

Table 4.10 *The formation of the price of comics*

Response level	Age groups				Total
	5–6	7–8	9–10	11–12	
0. Buying and selling is not understood	8	1	0	0	9
1. The shopkeeper does not buy	10	6	2	0	18
2. The price remains the same or increases from shop to producer	2	13	6	1	22
3. The price decreases from shop to producer	0	0	11	9	20
4. The price increases from producer to shop	0	0	1	10	11
Total	20	20	20	20	80

$r_s = 0.86$, $p < .001$

children expressed in these interviews were similar to those reported by Jahoda or by ourselves.

A second point of disagreement between our sequence and those described by Furth and Jahoda is the age at which the various response levels emerge. The idea that the shopkeeper increases prices appears in our subjects at a lower age (9–10 years) than the 11 years reported by these authors. Furth's interviews covered a wide variety of topics (not all of which were pursued with each child), while the developmental sequence he proposed was based on responses to all of those themes. It seems likely, then, that there would be some uncertainty in his age-level associations. The difference between Jahoda's (1979) results and our own may be explained by taking into account the characteristics of his sample. He interviewed children from several semi- and unskilled working-class areas of Glasgow, a substantial number of whose fathers were unemployed and obtaining financial support from social security. The idea that shopkeepers might also obtain money from sources other than their own trade might be a generalisation from these children's own family experiences. The delay among these children when compared with our own middle-class sample might well reflect a more general delay in the development of thinking as a consequence of socio-cultural disadvantage.

It is now possible to see how these results compare with those presented earlier. What do they have to say which is new, and on what points do they give us greater certainty?

Once again, the ideas about 'change' have emerged in young children. The conceptions about the source of goods and the formation of prices are similar to those we found in the other studies described in this chapter. The more specific topic of this research (variations between prices) now allows us to consider afresh the problem of the circulation of money. In Chapter 2 and Chapter 3 this problem was considered from the point of view of payment for work. In commenting on these results we shall be able to draw on those reported earlier, and thus to reach a first, partial, conclusion on the investigation as a whole.

Only at around 7–8 years does the question of variations in price take on any meaning for children, since it is only at this age that they first become able to form a conception of both the passage of goods and the parallel passage of money. Most children consider the connection between prices and goods to be very stable, witness both their conviction that price cannot change across the various transactions, and the fact that in some cases children explicitly affirm that a 'fair' price exists which depends on the quality of goods, and that while the shopkeeper, or some intermediary, might change it, to do so would be unjust. The reader will recall that 7–8 years was also the age at which children were able to establish stable and endurable connections between money and work. The research on the source of money and the ideas of 'wealth' and 'poverty' also showed that, again, it is at around this same age that children justify payment in terms of the work done and no longer in terms of the finalistic conceptions of the needs of the worker. They also try to relate various characteristics of the work done (such as the time spent or the effort made) to increases in payment. This type of response was also observed in this research among those children who said that goods cost more when bought from the producers because they had to make a greater effort than the shopkeeper. We can, therefore, conclude that around 7–8 years children distinguish two types of economic relation: in the first money is given in exchange for objects, in the second money is exchanged for work. At this age, then, the finalistic beliefs of the earlier levels has given way to a recognition of various acts of exchange which can properly be described as economic.

This recognition, however, occurs within two clearly separated fields. The relations which the child distinguishes take place in two distinct universes, that of buying and selling and that of work, which are not yet integrated. As Jahoda (1979) says, children at this age construct both a 'profit-system'[7] and a 'job-system' without yet being able to integrate them into a single system. This lack of integration is evident in the responses of Level 2 (exactly those of 7–8 year olds): when they say that the price always remains the same, they focus on buying and selling; when they say that the price decreases, they focus on work, without ever coordinating these two centrations. Such coordination begins to be established around 9–10 years and is fully developed by the age of 11–12 years. At that age children assert that retail prices are determined by the various expenses incurred in the production and distribution of goods. Payment for goods and for work are no longer actions of a different nature since to buy something one pays for the labour which is incorporated in it; the industrialist in deciding on the price to ask the wholesaler takes account of the costs of production, among which is included the cost of labour.

A question arises when these results are compared with those of the previous chapter on payment for work. We noted there that before 10 or 11 years children did not mention the sale of goods or services when they were asked to explain where the money came from to pay the workers. Instead they said that the boss found the money from other sources. We interpreted this result as an indication of the difficulty children experienced in integrating different economic relations within a single network of exchanges. In the present study (as well as in that on the source of goods in Section 4.1) we have seen that already by 7–8 years the majority of children say that the newspaper seller buys the comics from an artisan or a factory. Thus they connect the shop with the factory. There seems to be an incongruity between these two results, though it is only apparent; the two problems which are resolved at different ages present, in fact, different levels of difficulty to the child. In the two studies of the present chapter children have to trace their way back through a chain of mediations from what passes between shopkeeper and customer to what connects the shopkeeper more or less directly to the producer. In the earlier study it was a case of closing a circle which included customers, workers and industrialists, a much more complex problem.

The results which we have just described enable us to understand something of the difficulty which children younger than 10 years old experience in trying to close the circle. When asked where goods come from, children are led

---

[7] Though we would rather call it a *system of buying and selling.*

to focus on the system of buying and selling, representing links in the chain through which goods pass from factory to shop. At the head of this system there is also the figure of the industrialist (according to the varying representations which children hold), but who appears here only as the person initiating the chain leading to the goods being available to the customer. The two faces of the entrepreneur (the payer of workers and the producer of goods) remain therefore separate and uncoordinated.

In the research on payment for work we noted that the image of a single system in which money flowed circularly only began to emerge around the age of 10, when children said that the boss obtained money from sales. In this way the boss comes to be represented in the dual aspects of head of the system of work and also at the origin of the system of buying and selling, thereby also taking on the function of being the hinge between the two systems which were previously unconnected. Here too, from another point of view (that of buying and selling), we can trace a similar sequence. At first the publisher or the farmer are only seen as the person who initiates the movement of the goods they produce; they give them a price and sell them to wholesalers or directly to retailers. Around 9–10 years children begin to understand the double role of the shopkeeper as provider of both goods and work (i.e. the service of selling). Some children at this age even reach the point of saying that the price at which producers sell their products is calculated to take account of the costs incurred, including the cost of labour, though this response only becomes general among 11–12 year olds.

Difficulties of an arithmetic order also obstruct the development of children's understanding of the way in which the different economic actors make money and, especially, the way in which costs of production and profit come to be apportioned within a single product. The examples which we reported when describing Level 2 may stand as the proof of this. Relying on primitive forms of quantification, children believe that the shopkeepers can make a living even if they sell at cost. They fail to take into account the contradictions that emerge from the lack of integration between the system of work and the system of buying and selling. But why should it be so difficult to integrate these two systems? A primary consideration on this point is that children's understanding of buying and selling and of work are distinct not only in their origins (direct experience in the first case and verbal information in the second) but also in terms of the spontaneous questions which they are able to answer. We have already seen in the research on the source of money (Chapter 2 and Chapter 3) that children are very quick to understand that money is necessary to buy something, and to form various beliefs to explain how people obtain money. From the first the shop is construed as the place where one obtains goods, while work is the means through which one has access to money. Intellectual development and increased opportunity for experience ensure that knowledge about buying and selling and about work become more and more correct. Initially, progress occurs in each field independently of the other. For children's understanding to become integrated into a single system, it is necessary for them to put their own personal experience to one side, and to group together in the same field information derived from different contexts and related to different issues. According to Piaget (Inhelder and Piaget, 1958) such an achievement is a product of the period of formal operational thinking when knowledge is expressed in abstract propositions which can be connected through logical relations. Children's own subjective experience induces a separation between the systems of buying and selling and of work. It is only by abstracting from their own experience that children become able to realise an integration in which producing and selling, working and buying are all individual moments coordinated in a single process.

5 Means of production and their ownership

Existing research has thrown very little light on the problem of children's understanding of industry or productive activity. We have already noted the few points which can be extracted from the work of Danziger and Strauss on the ideas of the 'boss' of a factory and the origin of goods. While there is some data relating to the secondary sector, we have been unable to trace anything relating to children's understanding of the primary sector. As regards the tertiary sector, the only services considered by previous research have been commerce and banking; children's ideas about services such as transportation which are vital to the organisation of work were insufficiently studied. In his study of children's understanding of occupational roles Furth (1980; Furth, Baur and Smith, 1976) did ask some questions about the work of, among others, the bus driver: 'Who owns the bus? . . . Who paid for it? . . . Can the driver go wherever he wants? . . . Where does the money for the tickets go? . . . Where does the driver get the money he needs to live?.' However, the developmental sequence which Furth described was not intended to capture the details of children's understanding of each particular theme of the interview. Rather he traced a more comprehensive sequence in which it is not possible to identify the development of specific notions pertaining to the bus.

Our own research, however, has produced many interesting indications about children's understanding of the means of production. In Chapter 2 we reported the scarcity of knowledge about agricultural and industrial production in children up the age of 8 from differing social backgrounds; the difficulty which children of this age have in grasping the existence of hierarchically ordered roles in the world of work, as well as the gaps in their representation of the relations between industrialists, workers, and merchants which persist up to the age of 10 or 11. In Chapter 4 we encountered some children who confused the shopkeeper and the producer, others who identified the producer as an artisan, even some children to whom it did not occur that a producer exists. Among those children who recognised the existence of productive phases prior to retail trade there were many, even among the older children, who did not understand how it was possible to make a profit. Artificialistic conceptions about the way in which goods are produced and the origin of the means by which work is accomplished were observed in quite a number of the studies.

Data on children's ideas about transportation can be found in the studies on payment for work and the source of money (cf. Chapters 2 and 3). According to the youngest children the bus driver gets money in the same way as everybody else, from the bank or through change. Around 6–7 years the idea emerges that perhaps the driver is paid by the passengers. This notion persists even among 8–9 year olds, an age at which most children recognise that other types of work are paid by a variety of 'bosses'. Finally around 10–11 years the bus driver comes to be described as a public servant paid by the council or the state.[1] Children's ideas about these institutions also undergo a gradual development. At first they are seen as rich men who generously provide for the needs of people. Later they appear as associations which supply the different services, and which it is possible to enter either through a career or some relevant scholastic training. Only around 13–14 years did children begin to construe these institutions in terms of popular control exercised through electoral choice. The theme of transportation, then, broadens into the related area of political institutions and thus also provides an opportunity for pursuing this latter theme.

All these data concur in suggesting that knowledge of the world of production is almost entirely lacking up to the age of about 7–8 years, and remains sporadic and imprecise until 10 or 11 years. This conclusion, however, is constructed from a mosaic of data drawn from different studies none of which were directly focused on the means of production. The present chapter is devoted to the explicit study of the ideas which children form in relation to some of the means through which goods are produced and services are supplied. First of all we examine the way in which children represent the ownership of both the means of production and what may possibly be produced, then we consider what children construe to be the aims of such ownership.

5.1 Previous research about ownership

As well as corroborating from a different perspective some of the results already obtained, the present study also addresses an entirely new theme, that of ownership. In spite of its clear importance there is very little other data about ownership (cf. Burris, 1983), and what there is has, in part, been derived from research not primarily oriented toward economic socialisation (cf. Furby, 1978a, 1978b, 1979).

Burris (1983) adopted an indirect approach, asking children questions

[1] Translator's note: In Italy local bus services are run by companies owned by the local council.

about stealing (What does stealing mean? Why is it wrong?) and trying to infer their concept of property. She found different conceptions which developed according to a stagelike pattern. For the youngest children one must not steal simply because '*it's forbidden*', and because otherwise one will incur the disapproval of adults or some kind of punishment. Later (from about 7 years) children justify ownership on the basis of personal needs; stealing is wrong because of the injury it causes the victim. Finally the majority of older children (10 years) are able to conceive of property within the rationality of the total system of economic production: ownership now consists of a coherent system of reciprocal obligations. In this context stealing contradicts principles of equality, since one person obtains for free what others only obtain through sacrifice.

Lita Furby, on the other hand, was interested in the development of motives for possession, both through reviewing the various theories, and what little empirical evidence exists, about possession in animals and in some human societies (Furby, 1978b), and by conducting her own research on the significance of, and motivation for, possession at different ages and in diverse cultural contexts (Furby, 1978a, 1979). This latter problem we shall leave to one side as our interest here is only concerned with some aspects of definitions of possession. In one of her studies Furby (1978a) asked subjects aged 6–16 years as well as a group of adults (average age 48) to explain what it meant to say that something belongs to someone, and also to give concrete examples. A content analysis of the responses (conducted entirely *a posteriori* without any reference to pre-existing categories) revealed a large number (290) of types of answers, though very few recurred frequently. Some of these types concerned the acquisition of property through buying, gifts or making something; others referred to established ownership and mentioned the use of a personal possession or the right to such use. These results correspond to the analysis of the conceptual core of the word 'possession' presented by Miller & Johnson-Laird (1976). These authors maintain that the right to use is one of the fundamental elements of ownership, together with the right to allow or to refuse others to use what one possesses, and the right to transfer to others these rights, by selling, for instance, or through a gift or other means.

These 'ingredients' of the concept of ownership were not all present with the same frequency and in the same way at every age. Furby does not report any test of statistical significance on her data, simply describing the various kinds of response which she observed. Use and/or the right to control use are the most salient feature of possession at each age level, though younger subjects mentioned use more often than the right to control use (which they often phrased as 'allowing someone else to use the object'). The acquisition process also appeared at every age, but shifted from being a passive process among younger children (others buy or give) to an active one among the older ones (the owner buys or works for something). Moreover, although the interview included questions about the reasons or motives for ownership only adults mentioned the pride and satisfaction attached to it.

In our own research presented in the previous chapters we have often noted the emergence of the idea that the owner of some means for working must be the person who uses it. One can recall, for instance, the response of Davide about the way in which a train driver makes money: '*If someone doesn't get money they can't drive a train . . . haven't you ever seen those long, long trains? To buy those trains you need to have lots and lots of money.*'[2] Here the idea that the train driver must be the owner of the train is clearly visible. Silvia seems to think much the same about the road sweepers: '*They bought the lorry, they gave them change and they too get money.*'[3] It seems, therefore, that for young children the use of an object and its ownership coincide.

The term 'use' is intended in a fairly wide sense which at most extends to simple spatial proximity. Miller and Johnson-Laird (1976, pp. 562–3) observe that the language in which ownership relations are spoken about is very similar to that in which other relationships are expressed, including location as well as kinship and the parts of the body. A short analysis of the concept of possession by Piaget also shows that young children confuse three different types of genitive relationships, the partitive, the possessive and the attributive. Piaget concludes that the child's undifferentiated conception corresponds to the idea of *property* (Piaget 1928, pp. 94–5).

The close relationship between use, proximity and possession which distinguishes early ideas about ownership also emerged in the results of a pilot study undertaken with children aged 3–11.[4] A preliminary phase of this study established that by the age of 3 children were able to use the terms 'mine', 'yours' and 'owner of'[5] when talking about familiar objects. They were also able to distinguish correctly between loans, gifts and thefts. In the interview children were asked if the sun, the sky, the mountains on the horizon, the lawn in front of the school, the tree on the lawn or the river running nearby 'belonged to somebody' or 'had an owner' and, if so, who it was and why. The interview also sought to establish what rights the children

---

[2] Cf. Chapter 3, Section 1. (Level 2) p. 63.   [3] Cf. Chapter 3, Section 1. (Level 3) p. 64.

[4] The subjects were 48 children from kindergarten (16 at each of the following age levels: 3–4 years, 4–5 years and 5–6 years), and 60 children from primary school (20 at each of the following age levels: 6–7 years, 8–9 years, 10–11 years). All the subjects were middle-class children attending Catholic schools in two different cities. The data were collected by Elvira Bordet and Flora De Bernardi in the Kindergarten, and by Alessandro Frezzato in the primary school.

[5] Translator's note: The Italian words are *mio* which can mean both *my* and *mine*, *tuo*, which similarly can mean both *your*, and *yours*, and *padrone di* which might be literally translated as *owner of*, but which would correspond pragmatically to the question *who does this belong to?*

attributed to any possible 'owner'. The results showed that the most primitive answers were those based on use or proximity or some syncretic combination of both these notions. Thus the 3–5 year olds attributed an ownership to everything which, rightly or wrongly, they considered reachable or useable. The sun might thus belong *'to the aeroplanes'* which own it because they *'fly close to it'*, the river to the fisherman because they go out on it in boats and fish in it, even to the fish themselves because they swim in it. Responses based on use tend gradually to become less generic and inappropriate with age. Around 5–6 years artificialistic responses begin to appear in addition to these other explanations. Such responses, which we have had occasion to describe previously, construe ownership as justified by the actions of making or transforming an object. At the same age level the response of *'by buying'* also begins to appear as a definition of the way in which the real or presumed owner of an object acquired it. In the primary-school years responses were divided according to whether the objects were considered to be private things (which was frequently the case for the tree and the lawn, whose owner was someone who had bought them or planted them), or collective things (in which case children denied that there was an owner). Some children said that these things belonged *'to everybody'* while some also attributed ownership to God as the *'maker'*.

5.2   Previous research about political conceptions

For the present study it is also important to take account of the development of political conceptions, both because there is an objective intertwining of the political and the economic, and because children do sometimes refer to political figures and institutions in explaining economic relationships. Furth, Baur and Smith (1976), for instance, report that the youngest children they interviewed attributed to the 'queen' the 'government' or the 'law' the functions of dispensing money and assigning jobs. In this case children's confusion of work roles with political roles seems to mirror their inability to differentiate between various fields of social life. In older children, however, one may expect to find a distinction, at least in general terms, between private and public economic subjects, as well as some outline of the relations between them.

It must be admitted that research on political socialisation has not been well developed (Stacey, 1978; Renshon, 1977) and for the most part it has been undertaken by political scientists interested in examining childhood antecedents of adult political choices, or in outlining from whom, and in what circumstances children obtain political information (cf. Greenstein, 1969). The question of how children use their cognitive abilities to construct an integrated vision of political life has generally been ignored; where it has been considered (Adelson and O'Neil, 1966) investigators have only been interested in preadolescents and not younger children.

One exception to this approach is the work of Robert Connell (1971), who studied Australian children aged 6–16 years using a method very similar to a Piagetian clinical interview.[6] The interviews began with questions about television programmes on the presupposition that these were the principal sources of political news for children. Then came some questions about public figures frequently in the limelight (the queen, the president, the prime minister) or who played an important role in the local community. The conversation then turned to parties and elections, flexibly following the responses given by the children.

Connell grouped the responses into four levels, which he related to Piagetian stages. At the lowest level (6 years) there did not yet exist any consciousness of a sector of social life which could be characterised as political. The 'social world' of children at this age is divided into two sectors. One sector comprises the environment closest to the child including the family, the school, and the neighbourhood; and the other includes everything which is more distant from the child and which merges into a single indistinct universe. Fragments from conversations with adults or television programmes are the only sources from which children of this age derive information about presidents and queens, and such persons are thus confused with the heroes of other television programmes and with the protagonists of fairy tales and stories. When they speak about political activities or personalities, these children juxtapose pertinent particulars and details of varying importance and mix them with others which are quite irrelevant. In this way these children reveal in their 'political' conversations some typical features of intuitive thinking. Connell emphasised that it is the absence of higher cognitive abilities rather than a lack of information which prevents children younger than 7 from constructing conceptions about political reality.

Around 7 years, with the beginnings of the stage of concrete operations, the child achieves a less confused and fantastic vision of those sectors of the adult world with which they are not in direct contact, and they begin to distinguish the world of politics and government from other spheres of reality. The first political notion which is formed at this stage is that of *political role*. This arises from the intersection (logical multiplication) of two other notions; that of *important persons* and that of *command*. The child represents queens, ministers or mayors as important persons whose principal function is to command. The power attributed to them is, however, limited and concrete. It is manifested in relation to the restricted entourage with whom such figures are in direct contact (servants, guards and various types of 'helpers') and whom they can

[6] More than 100 children from various social backgrounds were interviewed.

'tell what to do'. There is no differentiation between political figures; the queen, the mayor, the president of the republic all do more or less the same things in different places. There is even less distinction between various levels of government; legislative power is not differentiated from executive power, nor ceremonial positions from positions of effective power. At this stage the child constructs a very summary idea of *political role*, putting together the fragmentary and disparate information which they have happened to collect about various figures such as the head of government, the mayor, a member of parliament.

The advent of the next level (which most subjects reached around 10 or 11 years) marks a great leap forward for the child. For the first time children are able to construct an integrated vision of the political world, that is they construct what Connell calls a 'political order'. Different figures are now differentiated from one another through the attribution of varying degrees of power and through being ordered in a hierarchy. The queen, for example, commands the prime minister, who in turn has the premier as an assistant of lower rank. This vertical ordering of different roles is associated with the inclusion of territories within which each figure exercises their power. These series are composed of only two, or at the most three terms. Connell suggests that the reason these hierarchies extend to only two or three terms is that children hear about the highest political offices on television, while at home or at school it is the local authority which they hear being discussed. They have, however, little or no knowledge of intermediate levels of power. The notion of a hierarchical ordering is also shown in the conceptions which children at this level develop regarding access to political roles. They imagine a sort of career in which one begins by being a mayor and ends up a prime minister through successively occupying a series of ever more prestigious roles. This hierarchy is associated with a more abstract and correct idea of power. The various authorities are no longer seen as exercising their power only over a few persons close to them, but rather over the whole population through the enactment of laws and the control of an apparatus of power. At this age children also know that political parties exist and that their activities have to do with elections. However, they do not understand that such parties represent different social classes and express different ways of ordering society. These are later acquisitions, belonging to the following level which coincides with the emergence of the stage of formal thinking.

The capacity for abstract and deductive thinking not only allows adolescents to articulate in a more precise and direct way their conceptions of political institutions, it also allows them to conceive of conflicts of opinion and interests, and to express their own opinions about the conduct of political leaders. This is not to say that adolescents have an ideology, if by ideology one means an explicit theory about society from which they derive their own opinions and choices about specific issues. Among the 15–16 year olds interviewed by Connell only a few who came from particularly politicised families showed any ideological thinking. Even among adults, however, only a minority ever formulate conceptions which could be described as 'ideologies' in Connell's terms.

For Connell, then, children are not limited to receiving political information passively, but, rather, elaborate an understanding of politics according to whatever cognitive structures are available to them for organising their thinking. The parallelism with the stages of the development of the intelligence described by Piaget is explicit and tightly defined at every level except the third. Connell's third level does not coincide chronologically with any of Piaget's stages, although it is at this level that the child realises the greatest progress as they are able for the first time to construct an integrated vision of political reality. The notion underlying this vision, and which also allows for the organisation of many diverse elements, is that of *hierarchy*, and the operations which this notion requires are the groupings of asymmetrical relations which are acquired with concrete operational thinking. There is, then, a delay between the moment in which the child begins to elaborate a coherent vision, even if incomplete, of physical reality and that in which they become able to organise their understanding of political reality. According to Connell it is not difficult to specify the reasons for this *décalage*:

> We must distinguish thought about immediate social relationships, intimate and personal contacts, from thought about society on the large scale. Politics is part of the latter; and here is the first main difference we must allow for. The children's political thought differs from their thought about such well-studied features of the physical world as number, weight and volume, spatial relationships, etc., in that the objects of thought are at a distance from the child rather than immediately accessible to him. (Connell, 1971, p. 228)

Connell refers to two types of distance; the first is subjective and psychological, it coincides with the disinterest which children, especially when very young, show towards political themes. The second distance is objective and social, deriving from the fact that children do not participate personally in political events, but only hear about them through talking with adults. Children do not, therefore, have the possibility of verifying their own understanding through action. On the contrary, the understanding of the physical world is acquired through actions on objects and that of the intimate social world through interactions with other persons. In both these cases the effects achieved by actions allows the child to verify the validity of their own understanding and to effect corrections to it; such opportunities are, however, absent in the case of political understanding. Connell's arguments on this point thus re-echo those of Furth concerning the development of an understanding of social institutions.

5.3   Research outline

We interviewed 120 children about the ownership of factories, agricultural land and buses.[7] The children all lived in Marghera, a heavily industrialised area facing Venice surrounded by cultivated farmland, and would thus not only have had the opportunity of seeing fields and buses – much as any child sooner or later would have – but also the great factories which are studded across the Venetian mainland. To this direct, though external knowledge of the factory our subjects, as children of workers and housewives, would also have had the possibility of additional information derived from adult conversations about their father's work. Each of the three means of production selected for the interview thus represent themes important from both an economic and a psychological point of view. We can try to examine how children's responses are influenced by the diverse characteristics of each of these means of production.

The interviews for the factory, the countryside and the bus, included the following themes: who owns the means in question and any eventual produce, and what did they do to become the owner; what purpose does ownership of these means serve for the owners, and – for the factory and the farmland – what use is their produce to the owners. The interview began with questions designed to reveal what children already knew about each of these means; for instance, in the part of the interview devoted to the factory they were asked, 'Do you know what a factory is?' and 'Have you ever seen a factory?'. If such questions evoked negative responses, their attention was drawn to their father's work. 'What does your father do?', 'Where does he work?' and 'What does he do at work?'. The themes of the farmland and the bus began in a similar fashion. 'Have you ever seen fields full of maize?', 'Have you sometimes seen the buses that go through Marghera', etc. Once it had been ascertained that the child at least knew something about the means in question the interview continued with questions about ownership: 'Does someone own the factory (farmland or bus) or not?'; 'Whose is it?', 'Are they really the owner?', 'What did they do to become the owner?', 'What use is the factory (farmland or bus) to the owner?', If the child spoke about industrial or agricultural products we also asked about the ownership of these: 'Whose is the corn (or the T-shirts or whatever)?', 'How come they own them?', 'What do they do with them?'. Needless to say, the interviews did not proceed in a

---

[7] The subjects were divided in five age groups (4–5 years, 6–7 years, 8–9 years, 10–11 years and 12–13 years) with 12 boys and 12 girls in each group.

rigid or too schematic a fashion. A more precise idea of how they were undertaken will be apparent from the numerous extracts presented below.

Given the complexity of the theme every protocol was divided into three parts corresponding to the three different means. For each part two developmental sequences were identified, one relating to ownership of the means and its products, the other to the economic aims of the owner and the advantages conferred by ownership of these means and products. These data are described in the following sections, and they both confirm and make more precise some of the results presented in the previous chapters. The concluding section of this chapter presents an overview of the development of the idea of ownership.

5.4 The factory and its products: who owns them, and how one becomes an owner

Responses to this section of the interview were divided into 5 levels. At Level 0 are the children who know absolutely nothing about the factory. At the first level some very general conceptions of the factory appear, though there is still no precise idea of the owner. In Level 2 the descriptions of the activities which take place in the factory become more precise and the owner is now identified as one of the workers or someone who shares the same tasks. At the third level the factory belongs to the 'owner-boss'. Finally at the fourth level the proprietor is distinguished from both the workers and the boss, and is identified as someone who is not in direct contact with the workers, but who is an administrator in contact with the world of commerce.

Levels 0 and 1: First ideas about the factory.
There is very little to say about Level 0; the children's responses demonstrate that they have no idea of what a factory is, nor that what goes on inside is something which is called 'work'.

MARA (4:8) – Have you ever seen a factory? – *No.* – Do you know what the word 'factory' means? – *No.* – What work does your father do? – *He goes to Venice.* – And when he gets there what does he do? – *Works with his friends.* – What does he do when he works? – *My mother gives him money.* – Does he need money to work? – *Yes.* – What does he do with it? – *Because then there is water and he goes fishing.*

MASSIMO (5:0) – Have you ever seen a factory? – *Yes.* – How's it made? – *With all the animals.* – What do they do in it? – *They work.* – Do you know what work your father does? – *No.*

The first vague conceptions about the factory, which begin to appear at Level 1, are composed of two types of elements. Firstly there are images in which children fix some salient items of knowledge which they are able to ascertain directly, such as the large dimensions of the buildings or the smoke which comes from the chimneys. Secondly there is the knowledge that the factory is where their father does something which is called 'work', whose tangible result is that it enables him to bring home money.

MIRIAM (5:4) – Have you ever seen any factories? – *Yes.* – What are they like? – *I don't remember.* – Big or small? – *Big.* – Are there people inside? – *Yes.* – What do they do? – *They make the smoke come out.* – Why do people go to the factory? – *To work.* – Why do they work? – *To get money.* – How do people get money in a factory? – *They put a ticket in and out comes the money.*

CINZIA (6:4) – Have you ever seen any factories? – *Yes, when I go to my uncle's I see my father's.* – What's it look like? – *All metal, with smoke coming out.* – In that factory is there only your father or are there also other people? – *Other people, my uncle Mino and his friends.* – What do they do in the factory? – *They work.* – What work do they do? – . . . –Does someone own the factory? – *I don't know.*

Children at this level know very little or nothing about the owner of the factory. When asked about the owner most of them, like Cinzia, respond with a '*don't know*', or say only that there is an owner without adding any other information which might indicate who they identified as the owner.

Level 2: The factory belongs to the workers, or the owner is someone who does the same work.

For the most part the understanding of the factory at this level remains more or less what it was at the preceding level; it continues to be the place where parents go '*to work*', an activity which is itself synonymous with '*getting money*'. Only a few children show the beginnings of a more specific idea of what happens in a factory, when they speak of things being '*made*' or '*mended*'. What differentiates this level from the earlier one are ideas about the owner; children now say that the factory belongs to the workers, or to an 'owner' who is indistinguishable from the workers in terms of activities performed.

For GIANNI (8:1) factories – *Belong to those who work there.* – What use is the factory to them? – *Do you know why? . . . it's where they make things, glasses.* – Do the glasses they make in the factory belong to someone? – *Yes, to the men.* – How come? – *Because they did the work.*

ROBERTO (10:0) – Whose is the factory? – *Whoever built it.* – Who did build it? – *The workers.* – What use is having a factory to them? – *For making money.* – How? – *By working.* – What work do they do when they're in the factory? – *I'm not very sure.* – Are there only the workers in the factory? – *The workers.*

GIORGIA (6:6) – What do people do in the factory? – *They work.* – Who works in the factory? – *Everybody . . . no not everybody, the daddies.* – And what do they do? – *Watch out that it doesn't explode* (her father works for Montedison, a major industrial conglomerate). – What might explode? – *I don't know.* – Is there machinery? – *Yes.* – Why do the daddies work? – *Because they have to make money.* – Is there someone who gives it to them? – *Yes.* – Who? – *The owner.* – Does the factory belong to the daddies or to the owner? – *The owner.* – What does he do in the factory? – *He works as well.* – Does he do the same work as the daddies or a different job? – *The same.*

Various different beliefs exist about the way in which somebody becomes the owner of a factory; they range from 'don't know' to the assertion that they just need to be grown up, or to live near the factory or use it. There are also artificialistic myths in which the workers and the 'owner' and a group of friends built the factory with their own hands. Such responses will already be familiar from Chapter 2, and no further examples will be given here. These ideas re-emerge, however, in relation to the ownership of the factory's products in those few cases where children admitted the existence of such products. When they spoke about the factory as a place where things are built or mended, these children were convinced that the objects thus created belonged to the workers because it was they who had made them, and also because being in such close contact with these things it would be easy for them to take them and bring them home.

CRISTINA (6:9) – What do the men make in the factory? – *Little birds, boxes . . .* (her father works in a glass-works in Murano). – And in the factories in Marghera? – *Other things as well.* – Who do the little birds and boxes that they make in the factory belong to? – *The people who make them.* – Do the little glass birds belong to your father? – *Yes, he brings them home.* – What use is the factory to the owner? – *I don't know.* – What does he do? – *He's someone who also works in the factory.* – Like the other daddies? – *Yes.*

MONICA (8:6) – *The factory is where they make . . . there's one near my house but I don't know how to tell you.* – What kind of things do they make in the factory? – *Iron things.* – Does someone own the factory, or not? – *The council.* – The council is the owner? – *Yes.* – What use is the factory to them? – *It's somewhere for the men to work.* – How did they get to own the factory? – *They bought it.* – In a factory there are lots of things; sheds, machines, tools. Does the council own all of these things or only some of them? – *The sheds.* – And who owns the machines? – *The men who work.* – What use are they to them? – *To make things.* – Who owns the things which they make in the factory? – *The people there who made them.* – How come they're theirs? – *They're theirs because they made them, though the factory isn't theirs.* – And what use are they to them? – *Because later someone will buy them and so they'll have some money for food.* – Are there only the workers in the factory? – *No.* – Who else is there? – *Oh, I don't know.* – What's the council? – *It's a man.* – What does he do? – *I think . . . he calls the men to work, so then he gives them money.* – What did he do to become the council? – *He bought it, the factory.*

Monica's responses are an example of a somewhat unusual belief expressed by a small number of children. The factory belongs to the council (a kind of boss) but the workers are also owners to some extent in so far as they own the tools. Perhaps such responses should be considered as a kind of compromise formation between Level 2 and Level 3 where the figure of the 'owner-boss' becomes differentiated from the workers.

Level 3: The factory belongs to the 'owner-boss'.

Children at this level now have some idea about what goes on in a factory. The conceptions of the younger subjects classified at this level still remain permeated to a greater or lesser extent with artificialism. The older ones, however, speak in a simplified though substantially correct way of things being made or built.

All the children now distinguish the owner from the workers. The majority believe that the owner is a 'boss'. Only three subjects identified the owner as the council or the state, describing them as rich and powerful men. The idea of the 'owner-boss' has already been noted in the studies of Chapter 2; here we shall only record some examples of the way in which children represent the activities which take place inside a factory.

LEILA (8:8, whose father is a worker at Montedison, the major industrial conglomerate) – What do the men do when they're in the factory? – *They work at lots of things: machines, pipes, curtains, lots of things.* – What do they do with the pipes, the curtains? – *They repair them.* – They take in the broken ones and repair them? – *Yes.* – Who do the things repaired in the factory belong to? – *The owner.* – What use are the curtains? – *To give shelter to the men who work so they don't get cold.* – And the pipes? – *They put them inside the factory.*

TIZIANO (7:11) – *The factory belongs to the commissioner.* – What did he do to become the owner? – *He did it by himself, he built it.* – By himself? – *With someone.* – What do the workers do when they're in the factory? – *Get things ready.* – Do they make them or do they repair them? – *They repair them.* – Why? – *To sell them.*

Both Leila and Tiziano explicitly defined the work which goes on in factories as the repairing of broken things. Other children, however, began with the affirmation that in the factory they '*make*' objects and materials, and only during the course of the interview did it become apparent that for them the construction of things occurred through the recycling or repair of objects out of use. There is an echo here of the conceptions described in the research on the source of goods (cf. Chapter 4.1).

Even in responses concerning the ownership of a factory's products traces of artificialism remain. Some children still say that these belong to the workers, in so far as they made them, or to the workers and the owner at one and the same time.

MAURO (8:6) – Whose are the toys which they make in the factory? – *They take them to the shops and sell them.* – Who takes them? – *The workers.* – But do the dolls belong to the workers or to the boss? – *The boss, I think.* – You don't seem very convinced? – *I'm not really.* – Why not? – *Because it's the workers who make them.* – Why don't the workers keep them? – *Because they have to sell them.*

MICHELE (8:0) – Does somebody own the cement they make in the factory, or not? – *Yes, because they made it, so it belongs to the boss.* – But who made the cement, the boss? – *No the machines made it.* – Is the boss the only person in the factory, or are there also others? – *Yes, the workers.* – What do the workers do? – *Make the cement, the houses.* – How come the cement belongs to the boss and not to the workers? – *To the workers as well.*

More often, however, the ownership of a factory's products is attributed to its owner, sometimes just as a given fact, sometimes justified with the observation that while the workers may have worked on them they have received a payment in exchange.

MONICA (7:1) says that the T-shirts which the factory produces – *Belong to the owner.* – Why don't they belong to the women who made them? – *Because they work to get paid, not to have the T-shirts.*

CRISTINA (12:2) says that a factory's products belong to its owner – *because the worker didn't buy the materials, he works like a labourer with things which belong to the owner; the worker doesn't have the capital to buy the material.*

At this level artificialism has almost completely disappeared from explanations about the way in which the owner came into possession of the factory. The majority of children say that he had some workmen build it, or that he bought it. For the others becoming a 'boss' (and hence also an owner at the same time) is part of a career, as we have already seen in research on the boss in Chapter 2.

Level 4: Differentiation between 'boss' and 'owner'.
Finally, children at this level recognise that the 'boss' and the 'owner' are distinct figures. This type of response has also been noted in previous chapters and so we shall only report here data which either clarify earlier statements or add something to them. Of particular interest in this respect are answers in which the owner is not construed as an individual but a group of people. Such answers were more typical in response to questions about large factories. The idea that where there is more than one individual owner each one possesses a piece of the factory shows the persistence even at this level of an extremely concrete conception of ownership.

ALESSANDRO (12:11) – Does the factory belong to someone? – *Of course, small factories though; Montedison for instance doesn't belong to a single person. I think it belongs to a lot of people.* – Why do you think that? – *Because it's impossible that one man could have such a big industry. There would have to be lots of people. On the other hand a small factory which makes furniture or shoes has a single owner.* – Why couldn't there be just a single owner for the big factory? – *Because he would have to have an enormous amount of money to keep all those workers.* – What do the owners do? – *They have to maintain contacts with the middlemen, so that if someone wanted a certain type of shoe they would send their representatives around to show them theirs . . . I think they would sit in an office with lots of telephones.* – They wouldn't supervise the workers? – *No.* – Whose are the things which they make in the factory? – *They must belong to the owner, who sells them to someone, who then sells them to someone else who has a shop.* – How come these things belong to the owner? – *Because he pays the workers who do this particular job.* – Does the owner own everything in the factory, the sheds, the machines? – *If they're partners one owns a half, if there's only one he is the owner of it all.* – And if they're partners? – *They have to divide it, one has a piece of the shed, another one another piece, another one another piece and so on.*

FRANCESCA (12:8) – Do the factories belong to someone? – *Not exactly to someone, the factory belongs to lots of people, there's not just one owner but a lot.* – Are these owners the owners of all of it, or just some of it? – *Some of them are owners of it all, others just own a bit.* – What do these people own? – *Well, a factory is divided into lots of departments, so one owner could have some departments, that is some of the things which they make in those departments.* – What did these people do to become owners? – *They had to study a lot.* – And then? – *You have to see if you find something straight away . . . or anyway you need to have friends who help you . . . someone who knows you and does it for you . . . if you're rich you have opportunities, first you can study, then you can build a factory or something.* – What do these owners do? – *They look for . . . they try to find projects.* – The shift supervisor or the head of a department, do they belong to this group of owners? – *No.*

We have included in this level also those children who identified the council or the state as the owners of factories (or some of them). These institutions are seen to have the function of directing public interests, and to derive their power from the consensus expressed by the citizens through elections. Children's conceptions of political institutions will be discussed in relation to the ownership of buses, since that was the theme which most frequently drew responses of public ownership by the council, state or government (see Section 5.4 below).

These conceptions about the ownership of the factory are the same as those observed in the studies of the 'owner' and the 'boss' described in Chapter 2. The first ideas about ownership appear around the age of 6–7 years when children assert that the factory has an owner, even if this figure is not distinguished from the workers. In some cases even the workers are explicitly identified as the owners, which is of some interest when one thinks that

Table 5.1 *Who owns the factory?*

Response level	Age groups					Total
	4–5	6–7	8–9	10–11	12–13	
0. No knowledge of the factory	12	3	1	0	0	16
1. Doesn't know who the owner is	6	4	3	0	0	13
2. The factory belongs to the workers, or to one of them	3	10	4	5	0	22
3. The factory belongs to the 'owner-boss'	3	7	16	15	14	55
4. The factory belongs to an owner distinct from the boss	0	0	0	4	10	14
Total	24	24	24	24	24	120

$r_s = 0.80$, $p < .001$

without a doubt these children would have had the opportunity to learn that their father and his workmates are all employees. It seems in fact that spontaneous ideas about ownership, in which proximity and use play a predominate role, may prevail over correct information available to children, even when it is presented in the context of their own family. The syncretic idea of the 'owner-boss' was again found around the age of 8–9 years, and this reinforces all that was previously said about this notion. Even among the 12–13 year olds only a minority distinguished the owner from the 'boss'.

This further questioning about the factory has enabled us to see how the development of representations of the factory and the work undertaken there parallels the various conceptions of ownership. However, before commenting on these data it would be useful to consider also the responses obtained to questions about the aims of this means of production.

5.5   What use is the factory to the owner?

The question 'What use is the factory to the owner?' produced responses whose various levels reflected the development of ideas about the factory and its ownership described in the preceding section. The youngest children, who expressed the most generic ideas about both the factory and its owner, produced equally generic responses to this question; the factory is merely a source of money for the workers. Somewhat different responses begin to appear around 8–9 years when the child can clearly distinguish the owner from the workers and understand that a factory is where various kinds of things are made. From this age onwards some children say that the factory enables the owner to distribute to consumers cars, clothes, or whatever, while others define the principle aim as that of making money, and yet a third group continue to believe that the owner's intention is to give work to people so that they can take money home. It is worth noting that a third of the children aged 8–9 years and older gave this latter type of response, which represents a more elaborate version of ideas which we have found many times in even younger children.

The way in which the workers, or the owner, or both, make money is described differently at different ages. Three levels could be identified. At the first level children have no idea about productive activities and the factory is represented solely as a source of money. At the second level children recognise that production exists, and very often buying and selling as well, but believe that the money with which the owner pays the workers comes from the bank or from 'subscriptions' paid by the workers themselves. Finally, at the third level, children recognise that it is through the sale of goods produced that the owner obtains money. Those children who knew nothing about the factory (Level 1 of the preceding sequence), or about the owner (some of the children from Level 2) were excluded from this part of the study, and were thus not classified.

Level 1: The factory is for making money.

The characteristic conceptions of this first level will already be familiar from the preceding sequence and the study of the source of money (Chapter 3). Consequently only two examples of these ideas are given here.

MASSIMILIANO (6:11) – What use is the factory to the bosses? – *To give work to the others.* – What do the daddies do when they're in the factory? – *They work and ... work.* – What does the boss do? – *Watches how they work, if someone messes around and plays instead of working they put him in prison.* – What use is the factory to the boss? – *Well, because they say to those who don't have work, who are poor, they say to go there and get some money.* – Who is it who gives money to the people who work? – *The council.*

MARINA (8:9) – What use is owning Montedison to the owner? – *To give men work.* – What do the men do when they're at Montedison? – *They work.* – Why do they work? – *Because ... because they make a little money.* – Who pays the workers? – *The owner.* – What does he do to get the money he pays them? – *He goes to the bank, or if he has any he gives it to them.*

Level 2: The factory produces different things and makes money.

At the second level children have some idea about the kind of productive activities which take place in a factory. Various different things are made, and this is also one of the objectives attributed to the owner. The aims more frequently mentioned, however, are for the workers, and eventually also the owner, to make money. The sale of products and the earnings remain unrelated. Some children are not even aware that the products are sold, even though the interviewer tries to prompt them.

For MICHELA (6:3) it is the workers who are the owners of the factory – What use is the factory to the workers? – *To make cars, otherwise there wouldn't be any.* – Why do the workers make cars? – *Because they've learnt . . . from a book perhaps.* – But why do they go to work in the factory? – *Because otherwise there wouldn't be a single car, and then how would I get to Venice?*

Primitive responses such as this were produced by a very small number of children. Generally there was at least some mention of the sale of products, even if this was only construed as a means for enabling the products to reach the consumer.

MICHELE (10:3, whose father is a worker at Montedison) – *The factory belongs to the council perhaps, or to the bosses . . . no, because they go to work, I think it belongs to the council.* – What use is it being the owner of a factory? – *For one thing to make work for the others and also to make money.* – How do you make money with a factory? – *When the men have to pay to go to work . . . not always.* – When? – *For instance when they begin, and . . . the workers too need to get paid every month.* – Who is it who pays the workers? – *The council or the boss.* – What does the council do to get the money to pay them? – *I think that when the workers . . . they pay the council, or the boss.* – I didn't understand that too well. – *I think that when the workers start to go to work they give money to the boss.* – And then the boss pays the workers with this money? – *I think so, because . . . because I don't know.* – What do they do in the factory? – *Repair machines.* – Just repair them? – *Oh . . . my daddy for instance repairs lorries and cars.* – Do you think that all factories repair things? – *They repair ships, there's also factories which make iron.* – They make it? – *They make it, they produce it.* – Does this iron in the factory belong to someone? – *To the people who buy it.*

GABRIELLA (10:1) – *The factory belongs to the owners who direct the workers.* – What use is the factory to them? – *Nothing really, to . . . to make money, but also to spend it, because they pay the workers.* – So how did this owner buy the factory? – *I don't know, you'd have to see what idea he had.* – What do they do in the factory? – *Work, make metal, though my dad works in a factory where they unload oil, they make petrol.* – Does the iron they make in the factory belong to someone or not? – *No, because after they send it to the shops, they make it into little statues or something, and then people buy them.*

Even though they know that industrial products are sold, these children do not recognise that this is how the owners make money for themselves and to pay their employees. Payment for work and payment for goods remain two completely different things. This was so in Michele's responses, for instance, where, from the moment they went to work, both the boss and the workers had to receive money from someone. Such payments, however, had nothing to do with the money paid when buying things. Exchanges which take place in the world of work remain confined within this

world, providing yet another example of the 'reciprocal exchanges' between owners and workers.

The responses of Wilma and Marisa throw a clearer light on the difficulties which children have in relating payment for work and payment for
goods. These two protocols deserve to be quoted at length especially
because these two girls explicitly admit to having asked themselves the
same questions as those posed by the interviewer, and explain the difficulties they found in discovering answers.

WILMA (12:8). The owner of the factory – *Calls people to work, then gives them
their pay, but he too earns something in return.* – What does he do to earn? –
That's something I've never understood. – Have you thought about it before? –
*Yes ... I even asked my mummy and daddy ... but it was too difficult to
understand, and they weren't able to explain it too well, and then sometimes they
said to me 'I'll explain it to you later'.* – What do you think happens? – *Maybe
the owner gets the money from the state or the council.* – And how does he get
the money to pay the workers? – *I don't know.* – But do you know what a
factory is for? – *Yes, to give ... build ... like Montedison for instance makes
plastic bags, and ... there are others which make iron, and others which make
other things like metal.* – Who owns the things which are made? – *Well, the
workers make them and then the owner sends them to the shop.* – What use are
these things to the owner? – *Not for him, for the shopkeeper.* – It's to do a
favour for the shopkeeper? – *No, it could be that he also does it to get some
money.* – What does he do to get some? – *If he sells them to the shopkeeper it
could be that the shopkeeper gives him some money.* – You think that could
explain how he gets money? – *No.* – Why not? – *Because he also works in the
factory, that is, he gives orders, what to do, and it could be that there's someone
else who gives him some money.* – For the work of giving orders? – *Yes.* – Is the
money he gets from selling the things enough to pay the workers? – *No ...
because the bags for instance don't cost much and ... he also has to ... with the
money he gets ... he gets very little, not much for so many workers, the plastic
bags which Montedison make don't cost very much at all.* – Does Montedison
only make plastic bags? – *No, it makes ....*

Wilma's attempts to understand how owners make money seem to
flounder on two rocks. The first is that of considering payment for goods
and payment for work as two distinct things independent of each other. The
second is that she only has very limited ideas about what Montedison
produces. The first of these points has already been discussed in Chapter 4,
and Wilma gives a particularly clear example (as, for instance, in her
response to the question as to whether the owner might not make money
through sales: *No. Because he also works in the factory, that is he gives orders,
what to do, and it could be that there's someone else who gives him some money.*
As regards the second problem it certainly is difficult to imagine how a

company the size of Montedison could balance expenditure and receipts if they only produced plastic bags. Nevertheless, anyone who understood that the price of goods must necessarily include the costs of production could find a solution. They might for instance say that Montedison could not *only* produce plastic bags, or they might think that the bags were made in such a quantity so as to allow the costs to be recouped from the large number sold. It is possible that this problem arises from Wilma's inability to connect the system of buying and selling with that of work.

Marisa expresses a similar set of perplexities as Wilma. However, she finally comes to recognise that, if sales go well, the owner could pay the workers with the receipts.

MARISA (12:9) is convinced that only small factories have a single owner, while large factories have many owners – *Because for a small factory you need less money to buy it, and there are less people to pay.* – What use is owning the factory to the owner? – *Because he too makes money, and then he hires men who have to work to keep their families.* – How does he make money? – *That's just what I've wondered, lots of times!* – Did you manage to find an answer? – *I thought about it but I don't know.* – Didn't you ever try asking someone? – *No, at school we don't talk much, and after school we play and think about playing.* – What do they do in the factory? – *I don't know, there's the person who dries the metal, someone to carry the sacks onto the ships, someone who makes parts of ships.* – Who owns the things they make in the factory? – *The person who made them.* – The worker? – *... Perhaps the one who is in charge, because afterwards he puts them up for sale, I think it's the boss.* – What does the boss do with these things? – *He puts them up for sale, sends them to lots of other shops, the shopkeeper pays the owner.* – And what does the owner do with that money? – *Maybe he gives it to the council, no, it could be that he puts it away to pay the workers.* – You said that you didn't understand how the owner makes money, don't you think that by selling ... (Interrupting) – *He could take so much money to be able to give to the workers ... no, that is not enough, I think ... if there is not also something from the council ... though they often sell lots of things.* – Try and think how much a car costs. In a factory, the more workers there are the more cars they make. – *Oh yes ... yes, I've often wondered, in a glass factory there are things that get sold, I went to see a factory at Murano, they sold them for 1,000 Lire, they were just little things ... but afterwards I asked myself if they only get this money how do they manage to pay the workers.* – So? – *If they sell lots of things then they will be able to pay the workers.*

Level 3: Money is made by selling the produce.

Finally at Level 3 children recognise that the owner pays the workers with the money received from sales. In some cases they also argue that the owner retains some of this money, either as payment for the work which he himself has done, or simply because he is the owner. In other cases, however, the owner is paid by the council or the state.

FRANCESCA (12:8) – The factory is useful to the owner because it allows him – *To get back more than he spent. – How? – By making aluminium and selling it. –* Why do the workers go to the factory? – *In order to get paid. –* Who is it who pays them? – *The owner. –* Where does he get the money from to pay them? – *From the aluminium. –* And the money for himself? – *Maybe the council gives it to him.*

MICHELE (12:6) – *Factories make money for the owner, for the people, on the other hand they produce useful things . . . they make the things we need. –* How does a factory produce money? – *Through the workers who work there. –* But where does the money come from? – *Selling the things they make.*

DORINA (11:0) – What use is the factory to the owner? – *For making every kind of material. –* For instance? – *They could make plastic, for instance, or a wood factory makes furniture, or another makes metal. –* Who owns the things they make in the furniture factory? – *The owner, then they sell them and the cashier who sells the furniture is not the owner but he gives him half the money. –* If I bought a small table in a furniture shop, let's say it cost 100,000 Lire, then 50,000 . . . (Interrupting) – *. . . Goes to the owner of the shop and the cashier keeps the rest. –* So he makes money from the things they make in his factory? – *Yes, but then he has to pay the others, his workers, though he always gives them less than he makes himself. –* He keeps a part of it? – *Yes? –* How come? – *Because, I don't know, because he's the owner of that factory and it's him who directs the factory.*

According to PIERLUIGI (12:0) the owner of the factory is sometimes the state and sometimes a private person – What use is the factory to the owner? – *Oh, I don't know, helping people and the state. –* To do what? – *To produce things. –* And what use are these things? – *They can be exchanged with goods from other states, sell them to whichever state needs them. –* For instance? – *One that doesn't have the raw materials to make them. –* How does the state come to have the money to pay the workers? – *From the money it gets from the other states for the things. –* If the factory is in private hands, where does the money come from to pay the workers? – *From the money for the things they sell.*

The children interviewed about the factory, its ownership and the economic activities which take place within and around it, have produced an image of industrial work in which various elements which appeared separately in the preceding studies now find their place in relation to one another. The 4 and 5 year olds knew little or nothing about this topic; for most of them the factory remains completely unknown. Those who do have some idea see it only as the

Table 5.2 *What use is the factory?*

Response level	Age groups					Total
	4–5	6–7	8–9	10–11	12–13	
Not classified	17	5	2	0	0	24
1. The factory is for making money	6	11	5	1	0	23
2. The factory produces different things and makes money	1	7	13	10	6	37
3. The factory makes money by selling its products	0	1	4	13	18	36
Total	24	24	24	24	24	120

$r_s = 0.83$, $p < .001$

source from which their father gets money. This idea (already familiar to the reader) re-emerges in 6 to 7 year olds. At this age there are also the first signs of an understanding of productive activities, even though such notions are sporadic and impregnated with artificialism. Furthermore, the figure of the 'boss' also begins to be distinguished at this age, and slowly to become more clearly differentiated from that of the worker. The activities which go on inside the factory are always aimed at making money for the workers. We already know from the study on the source of goods (cf. Chapter 4.1) that children of this age think of shopkeepers and artisans as the producers of goods, without saying anything about the existence of the factory. It is only from 8 or 9 that the factory also comes to be seen as a centre of production. This new function is at first only juxtaposed to that of making money for the workers and the owner; it is not until the age of 10 or 11 that the child is able to integrate the 'system of work' with the 'system of buying and selling'. This conclusion confirms much of what has already been noted in the preceding chapter, and which will be yet further enhanced by the analyses of the data on farmland and the bus.

5.6   The ownership and use of farmland

Children's responses to questions about agricultural land are notably different from those concerning the factory, both in terms of the criteria used to identify the owner of the fields and their produce, as well as the way in which the objectives of ownership are described.

The first thing to note about the identification of the owner is that, unlike the developmental sequence associated with the factory, there are no subjects at Level 0. Even the youngest children have some ideas about farmland, however vague or partial these may be. At the first level these primitive representations are associated with an absence of knowledge about the owner or erroneous and generic replies. Some children only indicate that it is '*a man*' without being able to specify or justify this answer, other children speak about particular cases (farmland belonging to friends, for instance), while some others identify the owners of agricultural land as persons such as gypsies who can occasionally be seen there. At Level 2 children use spatial proximity as a criterion for identifying the owner, who is someone living in the countryside, though they make no particular reference to agricultural activities. Such references are the distinguishing characteristic of Level 3 in which the owner is defined as a farmer who became the owner by buying the land or, sometimes, merely by cultivating it. Finally, at Level 4, children assert that the owner is a 'boss' who also generally works the land himself with the help of companions or employees. We did not isolate a further level in which the owner was no longer perceived as cultivating his own fields, since very few subjects mentioned this.

Understanding of the reasons for owning farmland can be classified in three levels. The first level includes such diverse replies as the ideas that the fields are for playing in, walking in, or camping in, as well as the idea that they produce fruit and vegetables which anybody can gather. At the second level children assert that the produce is consumed by the farmworkers, or those who live on the farm. Only at the third level do children arrive at the idea that the surplus can be sold or recognise clearly that the sale of produce is in fact the principal aim of agricultural activity.

These two sequences about the ownership and use of agricultural land are intimately connected: the more primitive responses in the one are associated with the more primitive responses in the other, and thus they are presented together in the following discussion.

Level 1 of both sequences groups together diverse responses which are all based on extremely primitive representations of the countryside. Some children make no distinction between meadows or uncultivated land and cultivated plots, they have no idea that there exist such people as farmworkers and can indicate only incorrect and egocentric objectives.

ENRICO (4:2) – *The fields belong to the owners.* – And who are the owners? – *Children.* – What use is it to the children to own the fields? – *To play in.* – Are you also an owner of a field? – *No.* – What about the other children? – *Yes.* – All of them? – *Yes.*

Enrico does not recognise the existence of produce, though other children do have in mind some ideas about cultivation, albeit confused. They deny that there is an owner, or identify him as someone they know or a relative, perhaps on the basis of trips or visits. Responses of this type are

Table 5.3 *Who owns agricultural land?*

Response level	Age groups					Total
	4–5	6–7	8–9	10–11	12–13	
1. Don't know, or anyone passing by	8	2	1	0	0	11
2. The people who live there	13	12	5	3	0	33
3. The people who cultivate the land	3	10	16	17	11	57
4. A boss	0	0	2	4	13	19
Total	24	24	24	24	24	120

$r_s = 0.75$, $p < .001$

Table 5.4 *What use is farmland?*

Response level	Age groups					Total
	4–5	6–7	8–9	10–11	12–13	
1. For playing or walking, etc.	10	1	1	0	0	12
2. The farmworkers eat or give away the produce	14	20	12	4	0	50
3. The produce is sold	0	3	11	20	24	58
Total	24	24	24	24	24	120

$r_s = 0.79$, $p < .001$

generally accompanied by a complete incomprehension of the ownership of the produce and the uses to which it is put.

MARA (4:8) – Have you ever been to the countryside? – *Yes.* – Did you see any fields? – *Yes.* – What was there? – *Cows . . . horses . . . and also sheep.* – Did you also see any fields with corn? – *. . .* – Any with grapes? – *Yes . . . I also saw some dogs.* – Do the fields with the grapes belong to anyone? – *No.* – To nobody? – *Yes.* – And do the grapes have an owner? – *No, there's no one.* – If the children want some can they just take them? – *Yes.*

CHIARA (5:1) says that the fields – *Belong to my uncle.* – What does your uncle do with fields full of maize? – *When children touch it, they shouldn't touch it.* – You mean your uncle shouts at the children? – *Oh yes!* – And what does he do with the corn? – *The birds eat it.*

At the following levels farmland is always described as a place where corn, lettuce, vines or other plants grow, or where cows and chickens are bred or just live. For the most part these remain partial and inexact images, although they include the idea that the countryside affords the production of various types of foodstuffs. From the moment at which agricultural land begins to be represented in this way, children also begin to identify the owner (either of the land or the produce) using less generic criteria. A few subjects, whose responses can be considered as transitional between Levels 1 and 2, say that the owner is simply someone who wanted to be an owner, an idea which we have already seen in younger children's responses to questions about access to work roles (cf. Chapter 2.2).

FABRIZIO (4:10) describes farmland as a place where – *There are butterflies . . . flowers.* – Have you ever seen a field of corn? – *No.* – Or grapes? – *No.* – Or lettuce? – *Yes.* – Do those fields of lettuce belong to anyone or not? – *Yes.* – To whom? – *The owners.* – What do these owners do? – *Dig up the earth to see if there's a worm, otherwise it would eat all the lettuce above.* – What did they do to become the owners of the field? – *Because they wanted to.* – Who owns the lettuce? – *The owners.* – Why is it theirs? – *Because afterwards they take it to where the others sell fruit.* – They give it them? – *They make a present of it.*

Fabrizio, then, can only really say that owners exist, without understanding clearly what they do or why they do it. In his responses there is also the same confident belief in the availability of the produce as was seen in the children of Level 1.

The most frequent responses at Level 2 are those which identify the owner as someone living in the country.

NICOLA (6:9) arrives at this idea in the course of the interview after having expressed some doubts about the existence of an owner – What are those fields near your house like? – *There's maize, grass and wheat somewhere else.* – Do they belong to someone or not? – *I don't know, I've never seen anybody there.* – In the other fields near your house . . . (Interrupting) – *There's only one.* – But those which you see when you drive along the motorway? – *They belong . . . to a man who has two or three houses there.* – So he's the owner? – *Yes.*

Nicola does not know how this man might have become the owner. FRANCESCA (5:5), on the other hand, does give an explanation, even if a very primitive one – *The fields belong to the men.* – Which men? – *The ones who live there.* – What did they do to become the owners? – *They were born and found that house for themselves.*

Other children say that the house had to be built or bought, though the emphasis is always on the spatial proximity to the fields rather than the performance of any specific activity.

MASSIMO (5:0) – *The fields belong to the men.* – Which ones? – *The ones who live there, yes!*

The farmworker, construed as someone who works the land and not merely as an inhabitant, appears in responses of the third and fourth levels.

MARCO (6:7) – *Farmland belongs to the owners.* – What do they do these owners? – *They bought the seed, then they planted it, and then all the tulips, corn and flowers for camomile grew.*

According to the children classified at Level 3 there are two ways of becoming the owner of a field, by buying it or just by beginning to cultivate it. The latter idea is by far the more common, and emerges particularly when children are asked how someone becomes the owner of an uncultivated plot of land. It seems that such plots do not belong to anyone, and fencing it in and beginning to cultivate it is all anyone has to do to become the owner. This is how the conversation with Marco continued, for instance – What did these owners do to become the owners of the fields? – *Cultivated them.* – What about uncultivated land, where there's no corn growing but only weeds and thistles, do they belong to anyone? – *No.* – If someone wanted to become the owner of a plot like that what would they have to do? – *But are they near by or a long way away?* – From who? – *I asked if they are near by or a long way away.* – Near to who . . . I think there's land like that everywhere. – *Well then, this is what they have to do. They have to go there, cut all the weeds and plant some good grass . . . .*

Sometimes the idea that cultivation of a field is the means for becoming its owner is also associated with the idea that the permission of the council or state is necessary before beginning.

LARA (7:11) says that all the farmworkers became owners because – *They planted it all themselves.* – What about the land that isn't cultivated, where nothing grows, does that belong to anybody or not? – *No.* – If someone wanted to become the owner of it what would they have to do? – *Tell the council and then go there.* – What's the council? – *The people who control the fields.* – Just the fields or other things as well? – *The flowers, the trees . . .* – And then? – . . . – What orders does the council give to control the fields? – *To look after it well.* – What is the council? – . . . – Is it a man? – *Yes.* – What do you have to do to become this man? – *Pay.* – Who? – *I don't know.*

Finally at Level 4 the farmer-boss always has to pay to get the land; but, as we said earlier, only very few subjects reached the stage of understanding that the ownership of farmland is not bound up with the exercise of any agricultural activity. The more common replies were those such as Alberto's.

ALBERTO (12:7) – *The farmer works to get the produce, but he's not alone, there's also his companions.* – Others who work with him? – *Yes.* – His companions, do they also own some land or not? – *They could be owners of land, or they might just be workers who work there just for the money . . . in order to live.* – Could the owner of the fields be someone who didn't do any work there? – *. . . They could be only . . . the workers.* – What did they do to become owners? – *They bought the fields and the house as well.*

Only very few children among those who recognised the existence of produce denied that it might belong to someone or said that anybody could help themselves to it.

CRISTINA (5:2) – What use are the fields to the farmers? – *For putting down grass . . . and the earth.* They put down the earth themselves? – *Yes . . . also the trees and the ditches.* – And what about the grapes that grow on the trees, what do they do with them? – *They . . . we eat them.* – They do or other people do? – *We do.*

In the majority of cases it is farmers and farmworkers who are identified as the owners of the produce, and the reasons given for this vary according to the child's view of these people as either inhabitants of the farm (Level 2) or as cultivators (Levels 3 and 4). In the former case it is their proximity to the plants which is emphasised, in the latter case it is the effort or time expended in cultivating the fields.

ELISABETTA (5:9) speaks about cornfields – Who do they belong to? – *The people who live in the house.* – The one close by? – *Yes.* – Why are they theirs? – *Because they bought the house and the corn was already there.*

SALVATORE (8:0) – What use is farmland to the farmers? – *For growing fruit.* – Who does the fruit belong to? – *The owner who planted it.* – Is that the farmer or someone else? – *The farmer.* – How come it's his? – *Because he put a lot of effort into it.*

Other children, however, from the second, third and fourth levels, related ownership of the produce to ownership of the land, tools or other materials.

NIVES (6:6) – Who owns the corn growing in the field? – *The farmer, always the farmer.* – Why is it his? – *Because he paid for the field.*

LUCA (9:9) – *The fruit belongs to the farmer because the land is his and he paid for the seeds.*

Once the produce is no longer considered to be available to everybody, it is construed as being food for the farmers (Level 2). When the interviewer tried to cast doubt on this idea by pointing out the large quantity of foodstuffs produced and suggesting that there might be a surplus, Level 2 children never came to recognise the possibility of selling the produce. Generally they said that the farmers could give away what they did not need. This idea is perhaps the last vestige of the finalistic conceptions typical of Level 1, according to which anyone can take what they need from the fields.

MARCO (6:7), as noted earlier, described a farmer who grew corn, tulips and camomile – What use is the corn to him? – *He can eat it.* – Does he eat all that he grows? – *Yes.* – And what if it's a lot? – *He eats it another day.* – But what if there's really a lot, an enormous amount? – *Some he gives to whoever asks for it, some he keeps and eats.*

Some children say that the produce is stored.

NIVES (6:6) – What use is the field to the farmer? – *To grow grain.* – And then? – *He gives it to his chickens.* – All of it? – *No, some to them and some he uses to make polenta.* – But if he had a huge amount of grain would he eat it all? – *No.* – What would he do with the rest? – *Put it away for when he needs it.*

GIOVANNI (6:6) – Who owns the grapes that grow in the field? – *The farmers.* – What use are they to them? – *For making wine.* – And then what do they do with the wine? – *Drink it.* – What if they really have a vast amount, do they drink it all? – *No, they put it in kegs.* – And what do they do with the wine in kegs? – *When one keg is finished, there's a thingummy, there's a straw, and they put it there and then it fill up.* – You mean that when they finish one keg they fill another one? – *Yes.*

In some cases the destination of the surplus can be a little surprising.

SABRINA (5:0) says that the grapes belong to the farmer – *Because he grew them on his land.* – What does he do with them? – *He eats them.* – Does he eat all of them? – *No, he makes wine as well.* – But if he makes a lot of it, what does he do with the rest? – *Gives it to the calves.*

Finally we shall finish with some examples from Level 3 in which the idea of buying and selling first emerges only in response to prompting from the interviewer, and is seen as a secondary objective for the farmer, a way of getting rid of his excess, before becoming recognised as the principal aim of agricultural work.

ALDO (12:8) – What use is the corn to the farmer? – *They harvest it ... or something.* – And then? – *They make polenta.* – Do they eat all the corn they grow in their field? – *Perhaps, but they may also sell some.*

ANNA (12:5) – What use are the fields to the farmer? – *For growing grapes.* – What does he do with the grapes? – *They use them to make wine, they eat them, and sell them to the wholesalers.* – Only what's left over? – *No, most of them.*

MICHELE (12:6) – What use are the vegetables he grows to the owner of the farmland? – *He sells them, like in a factory. Selling these things brings him money.*

Perhaps the most unexpected and interesting result from this part of the study is the idea, expressed by a large number of children, that farmers themselves consume all the produce from the fields and the animals. This is not only a very common notion but also one that is firmly entrenched; from the examples given above it is clear how the children resist our suggestions when we draw their attention to the fact that the quantity of corn or wine produced by farmers is far more than they themselves could consume.

However unexpected they may be, these replies tally perfectly with what we know from the study of the source of peaches (Chapter 4). Until the age of 8–9 years children continue to say that greengrocers themselves grew what they sold. When speaking about farmland, then, children forget the figure of the greengrocer whom they often see at the market or in a shop. The opposite happens when they talk about the shopkeeper; the farmer is left in the shadows. As we have observed in so many of these studies, it is only around 10–11 years that children develop a more or less clear view of the chain that includes commercial transactions and production for consumption.

5.7   Who owns the bus?

We mentioned earlier that children's ideas about public transportation have not been considered by any of the existing research. Yet means of communication constitute an essential aspect of economic and social organisation, both for the distribution of goods and the mobility of people. Furthermore in many countries, including Italy, there are elaborate systems of public transport, so that investigating children's ideas about this kind of service also throws some light on their ability to distinguish between public and private, and even touches on their understanding of the functions of public institutions such as the council and the state.

Responses about the ownership of the bus were divided into five levels. The first level groups together the most primitive answers, even though they may not all have been the same. This level includes children who have nothing to say as well as those who identify the owner as the people on the bus. The second level consists of children who say that the owner of the bus is the person who drives it. It is from the third level on that the owner and the driver of the bus are differentiated. At first the owner is identified as a 'boss' (Level 3a) or as the council or the state (Level 3b), even though these institutions are construed as a 'man' and are thus only distinguished from the 'boss' by a difference of name. At Levels 4 and 5 the owner is also the council or the state, but the characteristics of these institutions are now defined in more correct and precise ways. Firstly they are distinguished from private owners by the greater extension of their property and the control which they exercise over different activities; later children recognise that people enter into and take part in these institutions through elections.

Level 1: The bus belongs to the passengers.

  Many children at this level simply respond with a '*don't know*' to questions about the ownership of the bus, others deny that there is an owner or say that it belongs to everyone who gets on it.

ROBERTO (4:7) – Have you seen the buses that go through Marghera? – *Yes.* – What use are they? – *To go and make a trip.* – Do these buses belong to someone? – *No.* – Nobody owns them? – *No.*

FRANCESCA (5:5) – *The buses belong to Mummy and Grandma.* – Are they the owners of the bus? – *Yes.* – Do they own just one bus or all of the buses that go through Marghera? – *All of them.* – Are the other mummys and grandmas also owners of the buses or not? – *Them as well.* – What about the children? – *Them too.* – What did the mummys and the grandmas do to become the owners of the buses? – *They were born.* – And the children? – *When they go out then they get on them.* – If your mummy and grandma wanted to, could they take one of the buses home? – *No.* – Why not? – *Because it's too big and would make them tired.* – Can the mummies and grandmas tell the driver what he has to do? – *Yes.* – But the man who drives the bus, how does he come to be driving it? – *Because the mummies have to go out.*

CHIARA (5:1) – *The buses belong to my daddy.* – Your daddy's the owner of the bus? – *Yes.* – Of just the one or of all the buses in Marghera? – *All the buses in Marghera.* – What did he do to become the owner? – *He worked.* – What use are they to him? – *For going to work.* – Are the other daddies also owners of the buses, or just your daddy? – *The others too.*

Level 2: The bus belongs to the driver.

The explanations given by children at Level 1 of how their mothers and fathers became the owners of the buses are extremely primitive. With the idea that the owner is the driver, more differentiated conceptions also appear about the way in which this person became the owner. These conceptions range from explaining ownership purely and simply in terms of wishes to notions of possessing the necessary abilities for using the bus to the assertion of the need to acquire the means of transport.

MICHELA (6:3) – *The bus belongs to the driver.* – So he's the owner? – *Yes.* – And what did he do to become the owner? – *He learnt to drive.* – And as soon as he'd learned he became the owner of a bus? – *Yes.*

CATERINE (8:7) – *The buses belong to the men who've already learnt to drive a car, and then they've changed and gone to drive the buses.* – What did they do to become the owners of buses? – *They bought them.*

Level 3: The bus belongs to a 'boss' or to the council.

The differentiation of the owner from the driver follows one of two lines. Either (3a) the owner is identified as a 'boss', an idea which is soon abandoned; or (3b) the owner is identified as the council or the state, a notion which persists into the following levels as the child's knowledge of public institutions continues to become more precise.

CLAUDIO (8:7) – *The bus belongs to the factory.* – The one that made it? – *No, the one that makes it go, that says 'you will be this number and go to this street' etc.* – And how did they become the owner? – *By studying.* – And then? – *He bought it.*

MARIANGELA (7:1) – *The buses belong to the council, because they made it, first they built the houses and then they also thought of making the bus.* – What use is the bus to them? – *Because the people who haven't got a car go on the bus.* – Who drives the bus? – *The men who work for this boss.* – Why doesn't he drive? – *Because he just sits down like in a factory.* – What else does he do? – *He writes on a typewriter or talks to his friends.* – What is the council? – *A big house with a boss inside.*

As can be seen in Mariangela's protocol, artificialistic conceptions appear among some of the younger children. These were not observed in the earlier levels where children were convinced that the bus belonged to the driver. Both the 'boss' and the 'council' are sometimes represented as the people who built the bus. In other cases, just as we saw in relation to the factory, one becomes the boss (or the Council) either through one's career or by buying the means necessary to undertake that activity.

Levels 4 and 5: Later development or conceptions about the council and the state. Like Mariangela, children at Level 3b represent the council as a man who is only distinguishable from any other boss by means of the particular name. The responses which are classified at Levels 4 and 5, however, include representations of the council, state or government as associations composed of more than one individual which exercise (in territories of various dimensions) the functions both of control and of various economic activities. As well as providing an urban transport system they also build schools, gardens and hospitals. They are often the owners of the factories and sometimes also of houses for which they receive rent from the tenants. The resources which permit the undertaking of such activities are manifold, including the payment of taxes and tariffs by the citizens and the proceeds of industrial activity. The state, the council and the government are distinguished from private owners by the various public interest functions attributed to them.

Children at Level 4 think that it is necessary to choose the appropriate career to enter these institutions, or else to be co-opted by someone already working for them. If the word 'elections' is used, it is to indicate either the selection of the mayor by 'the men in power' and the ministers, or the choice of a new minister by the existing ministers.

EROS (10:9) – *The bus belongs to the council.* – The council owns the bus? – *There's the company but the council controls everything.* – What company? – *There's the council which gives orders to a company.* – And what does the company do? – *Follows the orders. The council gives the orders to the company, and the boss of the company gives them to everybody who . . . the people who carry them out.* – What is the council? – *The boss of all the city. For instance, Mestre, Venice, Marghera. In the square in Marghera there's a notice saying 'Council of Venice'.* – And what does this boss do? – *Makes the roads, the houses, the hospitals, the cinemas.* – What do you have to do to become this boss? – *You*

have to be elected. – By whom? – The ministers. – Who elects the ministers? –
The ministers who were there before.

DAVIDE (13:3) – *The state is a kind of regime which governs Italy. –* Are there
people who control it? *– Yes. –* How do you become one of these people in
control? *– You take a degree in political science, you become a lawyer, and then a*
minister, always going higher, trying to win the support of large sections till you
become a minister like Andreotti[8] *. . . I think there are elections every seven years*
and the one who gets the the most votes becomes the head of State.[9] *–* Who votes?
– The ministers. – What do you have to do to become a minister? *– It's only*
those who are specialists. – Who chooses the ministers? *– The professors of the*
schools where they study.

ALESSANDRO (12:11) when asked who is in charge of the bus drivers says *– I*
think it's the mayor, the deputy mayor and all the other people who meet there. –
What is the mayor? *– The leading person in the place, who's elected by the*
citizens. – What do the citizens do to elect him? *– The citizens elect the people*
who are the council, like the deputy mayor and the other people there, I don't
know what they call them. They elect them because they're the most intelligent
people, the most humane as well. – When there are elections, who votes? *– The*
people who are always on the council, or are close to them, who know them well. I
don't think that all the citizens of a town go to vote. – Only a group of people? *–*
Yes, because, a big city like Milan, I don't think that everybody goes to vote, there
would be such confusion wouldn't there? – But the people who go to vote, are
they special in some way? *– They're more intelligent. I don't mean that one*
person is more stupid than another, just that some have studied more. – Would
they be the people who work for the council? *– Yes. –* And how do you
become one of these people? *– I think by studying, and by behaving properly,*
not like the Red Brigades, going round blowing everything up, becoming a good
person.

MARCO (13:6) – What is the state? *– A group of people who make the laws and*
then . . . who ask . . . every group of people who are not part of the state send a trade
union to see if the laws . . . if it's all right, if they pass those laws, and if not to make
them rethink. – What do you have to do to become one of the people who
make the laws? *– You have to study, do interviews, understand what to do. –*
And them? *– You have to join a party, become one of their workers, from there*
you go from one job to another till you get to the state.

The term 'elections' is used correctly by those children we have classified

[8] Translator's note: Giulio Andreotti, leader of one of the factions in the Italian Christian
Democratic Party and many times a minister and Prime Minister in post-war Italian
governments.
[9] Translator's note: The Italian Head of State is the President of the Republic, who is elected for a
term of seven years by the members of both Houses of Parliament, the Chamber of Deputies
and the Senate.

at Level 5. They assert that all the inhabitants of a city or the nation choose who is elected to the council or the government. None of them, however, distinguishes between legislative and executive power. This is clear both from their descriptions of the state and the council as well as their statements, frequently made spontaneously, that the citizens directly elect the head of the government and the ministers, as well as the mayor or the president of the republic, which is not in fact the case in Italy.[10]

CRISTINA (12:2) – *Does the bus belong to someone? – . . . It's a public thing, it must belong to the council, a group of people, because the mayor couldn't look after everything himself, telephones, lights etc. So it's the council which is an association, that is a group of people, who use the taxes which people pay to provide the things which people need. A public thing belongs to everybody, and they pay through taxes.* – How did the council become the owner of the bus? – *In the beginning Marghera was just a few factories which belonged to private owners; then by investing money the council provided what the people needed. In the beginning they ran up debts, but then with the money from taxes the debts were paid off.* – How do you get to be a member of the council? – *By election.* – Who votes when there are elections? – *Everybody who lives in Marghera.*

These conceptions about the ownership of the bus can be placed mid-way between those which we described in relation to agricultural land on the one hand and to the factory on the other. As we found for farmland, the youngest children (4–5 years) identified the owner of the bus as those who are physically close to it, either occasionally (the passengers) or constantly (the driver). By 6–7 years nearly all the children said that the owner of the bus was the man who drove it. By the same age nearly all of these children had also said that the owner of the fields was the farmer, either because he lived there or because he cultivated the land. The parallelism between conceptions about farmland and the bus continues until around 8–9 years. While many of the older children continued to identify the owner of the country as the farmer, from 10–11 years the idea emerges in relation to the bus that the owner is someone distinct from the driver, either a private 'boss' or the council, or, less frequently, the state.

The responses about the council (or the government or the state) are the most interesting aspect to have emerged from this part of the study. Although children have spoken about these institutions in various other studies, this theme has remained marginal. Here children's responses have enabled us to distinguish in some detail between levels of awareness about political institutions.

Children's conceptions of political institutions constitute an area of inquiry

[10] Translator's note: Only local (councillors) or national (deputies and senators) representatives are directly elected in Italy. The local mayor and the president are then elected by these representatives.

Table 5.5 *Who owns the bus?*

Response level	Age groups					Total
	4–5	6–7	8–9	10–11	12–13	
1. The passengers	7	2	3	0	1	13
2. The bus driver	17	20	14	2	1	54
3a. The boss	0	1	2	8	5	16
3b. The council as boss	0	1	3	6	2	12
4. The council as an association	0	0	2	7	9	18
5. The council as an elected body	0	0	0	1	6	7
Total	24	24	24	24	24	120

$r_s = 0.74$, $p < .001$

at least as vast as their economic conceptions. Our focus has been on the latter, and we have collected only limited data about the former. However, these data are, by and large, convergent. In the course of our studies the children who spontaneously referred to the council or the state described them in one of the ways mentioned above. It is possible, therefore, to extract from our data some general considerations.

We have seen that the council or state are represented first as individuals, then as associations, and finally as institutions which the local or national community entrusts with looking after its affairs, and whose membership is chosen by election. This latter conception is still not firmly established even by 12–13 years. As Table 5.5 shows, only 7 children in all gave this type of response. The sequence we found generally resembles that described by Connell (1971). One difference, however, does need to be underlined; the majority of the Australian children already knew about elections by the age of 7; notwithstanding the frequency with which non-elective offices were mentioned (ministers, and even the Queen), elections were correctly described. Indeed Connell notes that while they may lack some of the details of the procedures, from the beginning children understand that elections are a way in which a group of people reach a decision, and that a majority is decisive. According to Connell this precocious understanding is related to that fact that even in primary school Australian children have the opportunity themselves to participate in elections. In some cases this even induces children to assimilate political elections to these school elections which take place among small groups of pupils, leading them to assert that only some people go to vote. This, however, was a rare occurrence; the great majority of children interviewed by Connell said that the whole adult population participated in elections.

Many of the children we interviewed, however, misunderstood the organisation and significance of elections. We found children who said that only some inhabitants who possessed the appropriate qualifications could vote, but also some who said that new ministers were elected by the out-going ministers. More frequently however, elections were not even mentioned. This difference between Connell's and our data probably arises for a variety of reasons. Firstly, our subjects did not have any experience of elections in school. Secondly, certain of the conceptions we found (e.g. *'civilise yourself more and more'* or *'trying to win the support of large sections'*) may be considered caricatures of common-sense ideas found particularly in social groups with conservative political tendencies. Thirdly, the Italian electoral system operates through party lists rather than individual candidates; this gives the electoral system an abstract and complex character which may make it difficult for children to understand. These data suggest some questions and indicate some possible directions for future research. The overall cultural differences between our subjects and those interviewed by Connell, as well as the different interpretations to which they lend themselves, suggest the possibility of comparisons between children of different nationalities, and between children of different socio-economic areas of the same countries. The primitive and erroneous conceptions which we found among preadolescents also indicate a need to extend these inquiries to adolescent and adult subjects.

5.8   What use is the bus?

We have already seen that, for our subjects, the factory is useful above all to the workers for whom it provides work, and hence a wage; the countryside is useful for the farmer who is able to eat and to sell the products of the earth. Up to now children have emphasised the worker's and the owner's points of view of the functions of the means of production. The perspective of the consumer (in this case the passenger) emerges with respect to the bus. Indeed the majority of the children said that the bus was for taking people around, at the younger ages in egocentric terms (*'otherwise how would I get to Venice?'*), later taking account of other people as well (*'the bus is for carrying people'*).

As for the factory and agricultural land, we have found a sequence of levels based on economic exchanges which, according to the children, relate the bus to the various people who have something to do with it. Four levels were identified. At the first level the figure of the driver is barely present, the bus belongs to the mothers and fathers and is for taking them on their various trips. At the second level it is the driver who becomes the owner of the bus, and it is useful to him in making his own disinterested contribution to the good running of the world. Some children do not even know that it is necessary to buy a ticket to get on, others do, but do not know where the money ends up. At the third level children believe that the driver keeps the money from ticket sales, or, if he is construed as an employee, they think that he is paid by a 'boss' who, in his turn, obtains money from the same sources we have already seen many times (the bank, change, etc). Finally, at the fourth level, the 'boss's' money (whether this is a private person or the council or the state) comes from the sale of tickets. However, this provides an insufficient income, and it needs to be increased through various other means.

Level 1: The bus is for going around.

Level 1 includes both children who believe that the bus belongs to the passengers as well as those who, while identifying the driver as the owner, also believe that he uses it for personal ends, as though it were just a large car. The first type of response has already been illustrated in the sequence about the ownership of the bus. Monica provides an example of the second type.

MONICA (8:6) – *The bus belongs to the man who bought it.* – And what does he use it for? – *To go around, but a long way from here, if it was close by he could go on foot.* – But a car would do just as well for him! – *Eh!* – What use is the bus with all those seats? – . . . *because he likes it better.*

Level 2: No understanding of payment for tickets.

For children at this level the bus is of use to the driver, who is its owner, for carrying people about. He is not moved by any economic motive; in some cases children explicitly state that he does it out of kindness.

MARCO (6:7) said that buses belonged to the drivers – What use is the bus to the driver? – *You know, to give people a ride.* – Why take people for a ride? – *Because he's kind.* – What do you have to do to go on a bus? – *You just have to get a ticket, get on, if you haven't got a ticket you need some coins and you put them in the machine and a ticket comes out.* – The money just stays there, or does someone take it? – *The police, and then they go and put it in the bank, and then they give it to the children again.* – Do the police also give you money? – *No, but my dad goes to get it from them on Mondays.*

Like Marco, children at this level do not understand the reasons why tickets are paid for; for the most part they simply note that payment is obligatory.

According to MARIA (6:5), for example, the money which goes in the 'the box' does not stay there because – *The driver takes the key, opens it and then takes the money.* – Why? – *Because if he just left it there, it would get full and then wouldn't work any more.* – Why do you have to have a ticket when you get on a bus? – *Because otherwise if the inspector comes and you can't show a ticket he gives you a fine.*

Other children are not even aware that when one gets on a bus it is necessary to have a ticket.

MARISA (5:6) – *Buses are for taking people about.* – Why does the driver take people around? – *To take them to Venice.* – And why does he take people to Venice? To do them a favour, or as a present? – *Eh!* – To get on a bus what do you have to do? – *You have to ask.* – Who? – *The man.* – And then? – *You get on and he takes you to Venice.*

Level 3: The driver is paid.

Even at Level 3 the majority of children still say that the driver (who is also the owner) uses the bus to carry people around. At this level however, children recognise that he is paid because he keeps the money for the tickets.

ANGELA (10:6) develops this idea through the course of the interview – What did the drivers have to do to become the owners? – *They found a job and then they became owners of the buses.* – What job? – *Taking people around in a bus.* – Why do they take people around? – . . . – Why do they work? – . . . – Why do people in general go to work? – . . . –What do you have to do to go on a bus? – *You get on . . . I sit down.* – Don't you get a ticket? – . . . *Yes, I get a ticket . . . oh, but then . . . then . . . the money goes to the drivers because we've paid for the ticket!*

NICOLA (6:9) says that the owner of the bus is the driver, who uses it to transport people – Why does the driver take people around? – *To take them to where they ring the bell to get off.* – What do you have to do to get on a bus? – *Get on, put money in and out comes a ticket.* – Where does the money for the tickets end up? – *In the machine, and it stays there till he sees that it's full, there's a little hole, he opened it once when I was on the bus and I saw a bag with all the money.* – And then who keeps the money? – *The owner, who buys himself something.* – Which owner? – *The owner of the trolley-bus.*

NIVES (6:6) – What use is the bus to the driver? – *For taking the people who don't have a car.* – What do you have to do to go on a bus? – (She imitates the gesture used to stop the bus at a request stop.) – And then? – *Get on.* – Is that all? – *Then you pay.* – Where does the money end up? – *Then the driver takes it to buy something for himself, then it just goes from one hand to another, from one hand to another.*

At this level we have also included the responses of children who said that the driver is paid by an 'owner-boss' (or by the council) who uses the proceeds though these have nothing at all to do with the sale of tickets.

ANDREA (8:9) – Why does the director give money to the drivers? – *Because they do his work for him, then he pays them for their work.* – Otherwise he would have to do it? – *It's not exactly that they do his work for him, as if I asked you to go to school for me; it's that he is the director, that's all.* – How does the director come to have the money to pay the drivers? – *He works in another place, or he's rich, if he gives away money.*

GABRIELE (12:8) – What use are the buses to the council? – *To bring in coins which are now very rare.* – Only that? – *Also for taking people from the suburbs of Marghera into the centre.* – What money do they use to pay the driver? – *Money from taxes.*

Only seven children in all gave these kind of responses (2 8–9 year olds, 1 10–11 year old and 4 12–13 year olds). It was not, therefore, appropriate to group them in a distinct level as we did for similar conceptions about the factory. Indeed, it is interesting to ask why such conceptions are so rare in relation to the bus; this is a point to which we shall return at the end of this section.

Level 4: The driver is paid by the owner with money from the tickets.
At this level the children say that the driver is paid by the owner, nearly always identified as the council, which uses the money received from tickets and sometimes from other sources if necessary.

CATERINA (12:1) sometimes says that the buses are owned by the council and sometimes by the ACNIL:[11] Where does the money from the tickets end up? – *Goes for petrol or repairs.* – Are the drivers paid? – *Yes.* – Who pays them? – *The owner.* – And who's that? – *Someone from ACNIL.* – Where does he get the money? – *Some from the tickets, some ... I don't know ... he keeps a little of what he gets for himself and gives some to the driver.* – Just from the ticket money? – *No, also from other things.* – For instance? – *From the vaporetto, and the other buses where you pay more, 1,000 lire.*

MARISA (12:9) – How does ACNIL come to pay the drivers? – *I think that the money people pay for tickets ... but that's not very much ... I think the council pays as well.* – How does the council come to have the money to give ACNIL? – *From the money we pay for rent ... taxes, lots of other things that we pay.*

GABRIELLA (10:1) says that the owner of the bus is – *the boss of all the men who drive buses.* – What use are the buses to him? – *For making money, because now there are machines for putting money in. Some he gives to the workers and some he keeps for himself.*

Table 5.6 shows that the majority of children aged 4 to 6–7 years do not know that one must buy a ticket to ride on a bus or, when they do know that a ticket is necessary, they do not consider this payment as being for the benefit of the transport service. Drivers drive the buses so that people don't have to walk (as we have already noted in the research on the source of money in Chapter 3); you have to have a ticket otherwise you'll be fined; the money stays in the machines and when someone takes it out it is only to avoid the machines overfilling and breaking down. Even though children do go on buses and buy tickets, or see other people buying tickets, this personal experience is not sufficient for them to form more developed ideas than they display at the equivalent age levels in respect of the factory or agricultural land.

The example of Angela, who constructed the idea that the driver is paid by the passengers in the course of the interview, showed clearly that, however

[11] Translator's note: ACNIL is the acronym for the local public transport company run by the council.

Table 5.6 *What use is the bus?*

Response level	Age groups					Total
	4–5	6–7	8–9	10–11	12–13	
1. The bus is for taking people around	13	4	2	0	2	21
2. Payment for tickets is not understood	8	11	8	0	0	27
3. The driver is paid	3	9	9	4	4	29
4. The owner pays the driver with money from sales of tickets	0	0	5	20	18	43
Total	24	24	24	24	24	120

$r_s = 0.73$, $p < .001$

wrong or primitive it may have been, this idea arose on the basis of reasoning which integrated the recognition that the driver must get paid with the knowledge that one must buy a ticket to ride on the bus. This type of reasoning was generally accessible to children around the age of 8–9 years; at this age we found children saying that a factory's products are for sale, and an understanding (even if limited to only half the sample) that the farmer sells wine and vegetables. By 8 or 9 years, then, children are able to reconstruct the hidden side of some conceptions derived from direct experience. In shops one buys industrial and agricultural products, one pays to go on the bus; from these data children are able to infer the reciprocal, that products come to be sold from agriculture and the factory and that the money for the ticket goes to the bus driver. If our economic system consisted only of individual producers of goods and services, children would already be in a position to understand at least the essentials of its mode of functioning by the age of 8 or 9. Things, however, are not like this, and only when children begin to understand that in different situations workers are dependent on an owner who pays them does a more complicated picture begin to emerge. The idea of a 'boss' is applied first of all in the factory. By 8 or 9 years nearly all the children say that the factory belongs to an 'owner-boss' and, while recognising that he makes and sells various types of goods, they believe that the owner pays the workers by working himself, or by receiving money from the bank or the government. Farmers and bus drivers, however, remain autonomous workers who sell their products or are paid by their users.

We have frequently had occasion to note the difficulties which children experience in representing the passage of money from consumers to workers through the mediation of various bosses and owners. Chapter 2 emphasised that children only gradually come to differentiate between economic roles and to coordinate relations among them in a widening and more integrated network. The research on the formation of prices in Chapter 4 showed that for a long period children consider payment for work and payment for goods as two distinct things, and are thus unable to recognise that money to pay for work comes from the sale of produce. With the factory children encounter both of these problems, while in relation to the bus they have to deal only with the former, and it is this which appears to facilitate the formation of the idea that the 'boss' pays the drivers with money received from the sale of tickets. It is difficult to compare conceptions which emerged about the factory in this respect with those which emerged about the bus, because only 7 of the 8–9 year olds differentiated the owner of the bus from the driver. It is possible, however, to make a comparison among the 10–11-year-old age group, in which nearly all the subjects recognised the existence of a 'boss' for both the factory and the bus. At this age level, the more developed ideas about payment were more often observed in relation to the bus. Indeed 20 children said that the money to pay the driver came from tickets, while only 13 connected the sale of industrial products to the workers' salaries. At this age, then, children do not meet any particular difficulty in relating various payments in a comprehensive system when these all involve similar kinds of exchanges; the task is more complex, however, when the exchanges to be coordinated come from different areas, such as commercial transactions and work relationships. According to the results of the study on the formation of prices (Chapter 4) this difficulty is overcome around the age of 12. The data from the present study point to a similar conclusion. At this age, in fact, an equal number of subjects gave higher level responses for both the factory and the bus.

5.9   The development of the idea of ownership

It is clear that the sequences of responses for the various themes of this chapter concur with the data reported in the preceding chapters. Together these data indicate some of the crucial stages in the development of an increasingly more precise image of economic reality. In this section we shall try to sketch a comprehensive line of development of children's ideas about the ownership of means of production.

At the beginning of this chapter we emphasised that an essential component of ownership is the capacity for owners to use that which belongs to them; use, in so far as it is direct and continuous, implies a close tie between ownership and the thing possessed. Naturally ownership can exist without being expressed at all in any direct use of the goods possessed, and even without there being any close spatial relationship between the possessed and the possessor. Nevertheless, it seems that the historical (and, we should also like to add, the psychological) origins of ownership are to be found in just those situations of constant and privileged relationships with objects, relationships whose echo is present in language (cf. Miller and Johnson-Laird,

1976, p. 563). Our data suggest that the development of ideas about the ownership of the means of production consists of passing from an extremely concrete conception of possession, in which the syncretic nexus of proximity and use is the determining factor, to an abstract one, in which ownership can be exercised indirectly. The developmental succession of different ways of conceiving ownership, which go from the primitive to the more detailed and complex, emerges to varying degrees in the responses given in relation to the factory, agricultural land and the bus. In fact there are marked differences between these three means in terms of their economic purpose, their ownership and the experience children have of them.

The question 'Who owns the bus?', and to a certain extent the analogous question about agricultural land, are the ones which have produced the best evidence about the more primitive ideas, as when some of the younger children said that the bus belongs to the passengers, or that the fields belonged to the people who go through them. In these conceptions ownership is related to a momentary situation of proximity, or, put another way, the transitory use of an object. In any case, ownership is not construed as a strict relationship determined by an appropriate and specific use (i.e. the worker and his tools). These conceptions are very similar to those found in our pilot study with very young children (3–6 years). The factory, on the other hand, is a place inaccessible to children's direct experience, and gave rise, once its existence was acknowledged, to assertions that while there must be an owner children did not know who it could be.

A step forward in the elaboration of the concept of ownership can be seen in those responses, most frequent around 6–7 years, which assert that the countryside belongs to those who live there. Indeed in this conception the use-proximity relationship which children consider most relevant is both constant and appropriate. There is a gradual transition between responses in which habitation purely and simply is the important point, and those where being in the countryside is specified in terms of the typical actions of the farmer. Although this latter idea might be thought to be a later development, a clearer sense of this developmental stage can be grasped from the answers given for the factory and the bus, where ownership is identified with the workers or the bus drivers. Farmers, workers and bus drivers are all people who concretely use their means of production and who, precisely because of this, remain in stable proximity to these means. One could describe the relationship between these figures and their means of production as one of *contiguity*.

The idea that the means of production could also belong to someone other than the person directly using them appears at different ages according to whether one considers the factory, the bus or agricultural land. The factory is the first means for which the child constructs an idea of this type – already by 8–9 years it is seen as belonging to the 'boss'. It is only at around 10–11 years that the majority of children understand that the owner of the bus is not the driver but someone else, a 'boss' or the council. For agricultural land it is even later – only around 12–13 years do children recognise that there could be a 'boss-farmworker' or that there might be an owner who has nothing to do directly with fields and tools. There are here different opportunities for knowledge and different difficulties in understanding who owns these various means.

Clearly, our subjects hear most about the factory, their fathers' workplace, at least as regards the particular question of the existence of an owner distinct from the workers. The direct observations which children are able to make in the course of their journeys on buses or through the countryside do not reveal to them the existence of 'bosses' or owners. Children are, however, able to see farmers working with their tools in a fashion which could seem completely free and without constraints. Thus the best opportunity of direct experience may directly consolidate erroneous ideas which children might have developed for themselves. Children may hear about the council at home or at school, or at least hear it named, and indeed they gradually understand that it is the council rather than the driver which owns the bus. The situation regarding the possibility of bosses in agricultural production with day-labourers working for them is different; indeed, such things are rare in the area around Marghera. The emergence of ideas such as those expressed by 12–13 year olds seems rather to be the result of their efforts to represent purely hypothetical situations, something which is already possible at their level of cognitive development. They generalise to the agricultural sphere forms of ownership which they have mainly heard spoken about in other contexts.

In addition to the type of experience and the greater or lesser amount of information likely to be available to children, it is also necessary to emphasise another element which may have a certain weight in determining the development of ideas about the ownership of various means. While the driver works alone, and the farmers, at least in the area around Marghera, spread their work across the fields, the workers join together in great numbers in a single place. The children we interviewed had had the opportunity to observe the entrance and exit of great crowds of workers from the big factories; this situation of collective work, which children perhaps assimilate to school in some way, very easily attracts the idea that there must be someone who controls and coordinates the mass. And indeed, as we have often noted, the idea of the 'boss' first appears syncretically fused with the idea of the 'owner'. This consideration mitigates against considering as advanced those responses in which the owner of the factory is described as the 'boss'. Here the children perceive a figure that is present inside the factory and directly involved, if not with the manipulation of tools, at least in relations with the workers.

The proximity-use criterion for identifying ownership is finally overcome when some of the 12–13 year olds argue that the owner need only manage the business and direct, not the workers themselves, but the department or section heads. Similarly some children of this age also argued that the owner of the fields need not always cultivate them.

In children's ideas about products we also find an analogous development from a realistic conception, in which ownership is linked to the direct exercise of an activity, to a more abstract conception, in which ownership could also be the consequence of another ownership relation. Young children around 6–7 years who can identify industrial products say that these belong to the workers. Very quickly however this idea clashes with the notion that the factory belongs to the 'boss'. At first this conflict produces various compromise solutions in which products somehow are seen as belonging a little to the workers and a little to the 'boss'. Finally the idea emerges that they belong unambiguously to the owner. This is initially recognised simply as an unmotivated fact. A justification of why the products belong to the owner comes later when children say that it is because the factory, the machines and the raw materials belong to the owner, while the workers '*work to get paid, not to have the T-shirts*' (MONICA, 7:11). Generally it is not until around 12–13 years that children are able to state this explicitly, which implies the idea that ownership is mediated by other relationships.

This account of the development of ideas about ownership is based on the *type* of ownership described by children, rather than their explanations for the *way* in which ownership comes about. On this second question we found a variety of responses, ranging from those which made some explicit reference to proximity or use, to those artificialistic concepts which we have frequently noted, as well as those which speak of buying things. This latter notion appears fairly frequently, and even among young children who identified the workers as the owner of the factory and the driver as the owner of the bus. Children can borrow the idea that the buyer becomes the owner from experiences which are common enough for them but whose sense, as we have frequently noted, can vary from age to age (cf. Chapter 4.2). Proximity-use or artificialistic criteria appear to be two foci which can co-exist, alternating in their importance for the child. Some of the protocols are particularly revealing with respect to this phenomenon. ANDREA (8:9), for example, shifts between three distinct explanations. He describes ownership first as being related to proximity, then in an artificialistic way, and finally brings in the notion of the 'owner-boss':

– Do you think the bus belongs to someone or not? – *I don't think so, because everybody gets on, lots of people, children.* – Does the bus have an owner? – *I wouldn't know.* – Think about it. – *I think so, because . . . the man who made it.* – And who is this man? – *I wouldn't know.* – Some children said to me that the bus belongs to the man who drives it. What do you think? – *Yes, I agree with* them. – Did the man who drives it also build it? – *No.* – What did the man who drives it do to become the owner? – *I don't know.* – What use is the bus to him? – *First so that he can do what the boss told him to, then to take money and do a job.* – Does the bus driver have a boss? – *Yes.* – Why does he take people around? – *Because people who haven't got a licence can't go in cars.* – But why does the driver do it? – *Because he's kind, but also to make money.* – How do you make money with a bus? – *Take the people around, and when your shift is finished go to the garage and they give you money at the end of the month.* – Who does? – *The director.* – At the beginning you told me that the bus doesn't belong to anyone because everybody gets on ... (Interrupting) ... *But the person who made it, it's his; he sends it out and then everyone can get on; then it goes where it's stored, oh ... where there's the garage, he gives him money. But when it's just going around it belongs to everyone.* – And when it's in the garage who does it belong to? – *To them, because they leave it there.* – Who? – *The drivers.* – When the buses are in the garage they belong to the drivers? – *Yes, and when they drive them they belong to them, but everyone can get on.* – (...) – Listen, the director you told me about before, how does he come to have the money to pay the drivers? – *He goes to work somewhere else, or else he's rich, he saves money.* – Is the director also a driver? – *No, because he just stays there to tell them how to drive buses around.* – How did he become the director? – *Because he made it, and he said, 'If you want to come and work you have to pass a test'.* – So he's the owner? – *Yes, but when they're on the streets they belong to the drivers. If it wasn't for the director just anybody could drive the bus.*

6 Children's conceptions of economics: a developmental synthesis

Having examined each of these different economic notions independently, it would seem useful to attempt a synthesis of our results which can also take into account the data of those other authors we have cited in the course of the preceding chapters. In this chapter we will attempt to integrate within a unified framework the economic ideas which we have found at each age level. A synthesis of this kind has first of all a practical aim. It should help prepare those individuals, such as teachers, who find themselves in front of groups of children, to deal efficiently with the economic conceptions which might emerge in the course of a discussion. It should also make clear the point which children of different age groups can be expected to have reached in their understanding of economics. However, the sequence we shall present does not claim to predict what any particular child of a given age will think, nor to infer from an examination of conceptions about a certain theme (such as the value of money, for example) the presence of conceptions about another theme (such as the source of goods). A longitudinal study of the development in the *same* group of children of all the ideas we have analysed in cross-sectional studies of *different* groups of children has not yet been undertaken. In some of our studies children were indeed asked to express their ideas about more than one theme, as in the case of the 'boss' of the factory and the 'head' of the school, or the origins of different goods (clothes, glasses, peaches), or ideas about different means of production (the factory, agriculture and public transport). In some of these instances response levels appeared to vary according to the specific content areas even within a single theme; identifying the owner of the countryside or the bus, for example, was more difficult than identifying the owner of the factory. Interviewing the same child about such diverse topics as the formation of prices, wealth and poverty and the owner-ship of the means of production, would certainly yield considerably less coherent results than the sequence we shall present. In the domain of economics, as in other fields (Piaget and Inhelder, 1941; Pinard and Laurendeau, 1969) the development of children's thinking is marked by various *décalages* according to the complexity of the problems posed and their relevance to the child, as well as whatever particular experience the child can bring to their solution.

The second aim of this synthesis is to elaborate, in a more organic way than was possible in the presentation of the individual studies, the connection between the development of economic conceptions and the development of children's intelligence as it appears in Piaget's work. While acknowledging that Piagetian theory is currently being significantly revised, we believe that it still constitutes an indispensable point of reference for anyone venturing into new areas of children's thinking. As Case (1985) remarks, one should not dwell too much on the differences between the trees while we are still making the first map of new sections of the forest.

6.1   Conceptions of the preoperatory period (3–6 years)

Very few studies have considered the ideas of preschoolers, though from at least the age of 3 children have some knowledge, however rudimentary, about the world of economics. At this age the majority of children know that shops are places where one can obtain things, recognise money and say that 'it's for paying', identify certain of the activities of grown-ups as 'work', know the difference between 'yours' and 'mine', and differentiate correctly between loans, presents and thefts. The capacity to establish relations between these bits of information and draw general rules from them is, however, quite limited. Not all 3 year olds, for instance, connect buying or working with payment. Between 4 and 5 years some 'scripts' about economic exchanges begin to be established, such as the sequence of actions which occurs in retail trade (asking for and getting the goods, giving and then receiving money); their fathers' jobs become the prototype of 'paid activity', a category which gradually expands to include other occupations.

Nevertheless, preschoolers' knowledge is restricted to the identification of 'regularities' within situations of which they have first-hand knowledge (such as the payment for goods or services by customers or consumers) and the acquisition of common information (such as 'grown-ups work for money'). Thus, not all goods come to be recognised as such, but only those which are suitable for incorporation into the 'shop-script'; a cow, land or a house are not things which can be bought. There may nevertheless be an owner, generally identified according to the criterion of use, which may even be transitory: a bus may belong to the passengers because they get on it, or a field might belong to some gypsies because they have camped on it. The reason why people pay for what they buy is not yet understood, it is done out of habit, or because of 'the law', or because otherwise people get taken to prison.

The relationship between work and payment also seems to owe more to convention than any notion of remuneration: 'one works *and* one gets money', rather than 'one gets money *because* one works'. Although children at this age know that not every job receives the same payment, they do not yet seem able to explain differences in remuneration. When asked to explain the sources of wealth and poverty they do not refer to the type of work a person does. Moreover, the idea that money is made through working exists side by side with other completely unreal conceptions about where money comes from: it is lavishly distributed by the banks, or else obtained through 'change', when people reacquire money at the same time and place in which they spend it. Whoever has money is thought to be 'rich', since children remain unable to quantify the value of money. Moreover, since anybody can obtain whatever money is needed from a variety of sources, being 'rich', even if only momentarily, is an experience accessible to everybody.

Children appear unable to conceive of conflicts of interest; they do not believe that people's desires would ever be so exorbitant that they could not be satisfied sooner or later. In every sense the world appears to be populated by well-intentioned people; everybody makes sure that whatever happens is for the best. For example, the dustman and the bus driver undertake their activities with the single intention of keeping the streets clean and driving around those people who do not have cars.

At this age children have practically no ideas about production. They believe that shopkeepers themselves make the goods or, more often that they get them from another shopkeeper, who gets them from another, and so on in an endless regression. Industrial and agricultural work are almost completely ignored.

The ideas which characterise this first level can be defined as 'pre-economic' since the recognition of an extra-domestic reality as the source of goods as well as of money is also associated with the conviction that money and goods are available without restrictions, except for those which people might reasonably impose on themselves.

The child's image of economic reality at this level is constituted by the identification of two types of figures: 'distributors' of goods, services and even money on the one hand, and consumers on the other. Exchanges which take place between these figures are conceived in script-like form, without the basic understanding of a correspondence in value between goods or work done and payment for them. This patchy knowledge, re-elaborated and integrated in a finalistic mentality, gives rise to an internally coherent vision of economic reality, even if it is one which is wildly at odds with the real picture.

The conceptions at this level reflect the limitations of children's thinking between 3 and 6 years. At this age they are not yet able to accomplish logical operations, as can be seen in the lack of quantification, apparent in their inability to discriminate different degrees of wealth, for example, or the belief that change given in a shop can be a source of money. Moreover, these children tend to take an 'egocentric' perspective when faced with complex questions whose constitutive elements they have not clearly grasped. It is important to recall Piaget's observation about the variety of ways in which egocentrism manifests itself. One form which he described was the tendency to consider phenomena from the point of view of the ends which they serve rather than their causes, particularly when the ends relate to the possibility of satisfying human needs. There are many points of comparison between the finalistic conceptions described by Piaget in the child's understanding of the physical world and those we have found in the economic field. The idea that it is easy to replenish supplies of money, or that services exist only because there is a need for them, reflects the vision of a well-ordered universe in which there is always some means of satisfying every need. The shopkeeper who gives change so that the customer will not run out of money, the driver who drives the bus because otherwise one could not go to Venice, act according to the same principle as the sun which sets so as to make it easier to go to sleep, or the moon which rises to make the night less dark (both of these latter examples are reported by Piaget, 1929). The same could be said of the idea that goods have always existed and that their vicissitudes can be reduced to a series of movements from one shop to another. Similar ideas have been found by Piaget and other authors in relation to a variety of things including raw materials, meteoroligical phenomena and even babies (Bernstein and Cowan, 1975). Children do not initially ask themselves about the origin of things, considering them as having always existed because they are necessary. At most they ask themselves where things come from. Only later do they formulate artificialistic theories. Therefore the idea which children develop, that shopkeepers make the goods they sell, precisely because it is incorrect appears to be the result of spontaneous elaborations on the origins of things in which children attribute the act of construction to the only economic figure of whom they have any experience in relation to goods.

6.2   Conceptions of the intuitive level (6–7 years)

A second stage can be identified when children begin to construct rules which allow them to create qualitative correspondences between the prices of objects and the amounts paid to buy them, and also between remuneration and work done. Children are now able to discriminate the values of various types of money, using as an index of their value either the size of banknotes or the number of zeros printed on them. They are also able to relate the different prices of things to their most evident characteristics, and to order things into a series from the least to the most expensive. In buying and selling each price comes to correspond to a particular banknote so that payment becomes a true exchange of equivalent values rather than merely a ritual which has something to do with money. Since this correspondence is not based on an extensive quantification (cf. Piaget, 1952, for a discussion of the operations of quantification) children are not yet able to interpret correctly the function of change which they continue to believe is a way of replenishing customers with money.

The idea that it is necessary to work to make money begins to be added to the notion that it is possible to make a profit from change. Moreover, in some cases 'work' is no longer considered merely as going and getting money, as is going to the bank or a shop, but as an activity which is undertaken for someone's benefit and for which the consumer pays. When children are unable to identify a consumer they go back to thinking of payment as a reciprocal relation between workmates. Children still lack a clear idea of work as employment, both because of the difficulties of representing industrial and agricultural work, and because they do not understand that the means of production can belong to people other than those who directly use them; rather possession of the proper tools is one way of gaining access to a particular job. Obtaining the tools is not difficult, it is sufficient to want something, to use it, or merely to find oneself in frequent contact with it to become the owner of something. One could also buy something with money obtained through 'change' or other providential sources which, even if they no longer allow one to live without working, nevertheless come to one's aid in cases of extraordinary expenses. Some children do not even ask themselves about work tools; instead they think that to do a certain job requires only a minimum of qualifications, such as having the appropriate clothes.

The productive aims of industrial work are completely ignored, while those of agricultural work are limited to replenishing farmworkers with foodstuffs. Goods in shops have nothing whatever to do with industry, rather they are produced by the shopkeepers themselves or by artisans through the recycling of broken or worn-out things. On the whole, the idea of a free and indiscriminate access to wealth, which was one of the particular traits of the preceding level, is already on the wane. Goods as well as money have their origins in work, and only someone who does a paid job can be 'rich'. Poverty, however, remains a marginal phenomenon, since only the old, the sick and the lazy do not work and cannot therefore earn money.

The child's image of economic reality is now more complete. While the majority of children younger than 6 years are only aware of the distribution of goods, nearly every child between the ages of 6 and 7 has some idea about production, even if it is dominated by a syncretic vision of a single figure to whom they attribute both the functions of producing and of selling. Up to the age of 6 children can describe and recognise as paid occupations only a very few activities which are particularly accessible to observation and direct experience, such as the doctor, policeman or bus driver. Now, however, the range of activities known by the child is much broader and the nexus of money-work is consolidated. Goods and services supplied by the producer-distributor are paid for by consumers, while the idea of remuneration by the employers does not exist. Exchanges of goods as much as those of work are accompanied by exchanges of money. There still remains, however, a considerable range of activities which adults call 'work' but which children cannot yet understand in any specific form; this range includes industrial activities.

In Level 2 there are elements of both continuity and novelty with respect to Level 1. The continuity is assured by the persistence of egocentric tendencies evident in finalistic, artificialistic and realistic explanations. Finalism survives in ideas about change, to which children return whenever they are unable to give any other type of explanation for the source of money; similarly, the idea of poverty as a marginal phenomenon corresponds to a providential vision of reality. Artificialism can be seen in the idea that objects (and sometimes even fruit) are made out of recovered waste, or from other objects of the same type. Realistic explanations can also be seen in children at this level: prices are determined by the apparent characteristics of goods; access to work-roles occurs through the possession of the most striking and superficial requirements; ownership of the means of work is confused with the physical contact arising from the use of tools or from proximity to buildings; payment for work is made by those consumers who happen to find themselves in direct contact with the workers.

The novelties of this level can be seen in the identification of rules, however rudimentary they may be, which connect money and goods on the one hand, and money and work on the other. The price paid is made to correspond to the characteristics of the object; and money comes to be considered as the recompense for work. These rules are constructed through the cognitive abilities of the later preoperatory stage described by Piaget as that of 'intuitive thinking' (cf. Flavell, 1963). Such thinking is apparent in the establishment of qualitative correspondences as, for example, when the price to be paid for an object increases with an increase in the value attributed to it, without the child being able to identify any unit of measurement which might yield a precise quantitative relation.

6.3 Conceptions of the concrete operatory period (7–10 years)

Between 7 and 10 years (Level 3) the various kinds of 'pre-economic' ideas of the preceding levels are replaced by an ever wider and more articulated understanding of buying and selling on the one hand, and of work on the other. Buying and selling is no longer limited to the physical exchange of objects and money in shops, but is also extended to include non-transportable goods such as houses or land. The shopkeeper is differentiated from the producer (first identified as an artisan and later as an industrialist) and other intermediate commercial figures also appear, such as transporters and wholesalers.

Children do not yet understand, however, that the price of goods is based on the costs of production, including the cost of labour. The majority of children continue to view price as a characteristic of the goods themselves, related to their phenomenal attributes, thereby remaining invariant through the course of various commercial transactions. Some children, by paying attention to the work of producers and middlemen, lose sight of the value of goods and arrive at the paradoxical formulation that the cost of an object decreases as it passes from the factory to the shop, since the work of selling something is less tiring than that of making it, and is therefore less well paid.

Children's understanding of the flow of money through commercial exchanges contains many errors, even though the value and use of money in single acts of buying and selling are now completely understood. A quantitative correspondence is now recognised between the price of something and the money paid to buy it, and change is understood correctly as the difference between the value of the money offered by the buyer and the price of the goods. This level, therefore, sees the definitive elimination of the erroneous beliefs about the function of change typical of the earlier levels.

With the disappearance of these ideas and other finalistic conceptions, work comes to be seen as the sole source of money, and children are now more precise about the rules which govern the relations between the quantity of work done and its remuneration. This specification is also accompanied by a finer differentiation of economic strata. The dichotomy of wealth and poverty is elaborated by a distinction between those who work normally and those who, because they work longer hours or more intensively, are paid more. The magnitude of differences in income is better understood by middle-class children than by lower-class children, and the former are also more convinced that this distinction is fair and ought not to be abolished, a conviction which grows with age.

The most important development in the range of working activities understood by children at this level is certainly the emergence of ideas about production. Factories are no longer places in which some indeterminate activities allow people who undertake them to take money home; children now understand that factories are where various kinds of things are made. Thus, when they are asked where things in the shops come from, children now talk about the factory as the source of all kinds of goods. Nevertheless, the idea still persists that the materials necessary for production are nothing other than old or broken things, so that many children confuse making something with mending something. Fewer children recognise raw materials as natural products.

In the preceding level children considered the means of production as belonging to the workers, and the most complex organisation they could construe consisted of a group of friends who work together. Now, however, they recognise the existence of a hierarchy in which the 'boss' is also the owner of building and tools. It is this boss who pays the workers and to whom people need to apply for a job, it is no longer sufficient merely to want to do something or to dress appropriately in order to obtain a job. Children at this level, however, do not understand that the money which workers are paid is derived from the sale of the goods or services produced by their work. To explain how the boss obtains this money, children return to more primitive beliefs, such as going to the bank, or the boss's savings, or from the boss having another job.

The economic world as it is represented by children at this level consists, in fact, of two as yet uncoordinated areas. There is the area of work which comprises bosses and workers, and in which payments are made in recompense for activities undertaken. There is also the area of buying and selling composed of consumers, shopkeepers, middlemen and producers (at the moment in which they sell their goods); in this area payments are made in exchange for goods. The relations of exchange which form the connecting links within these two areas are not the same in each case (money for work in the former, money for goods in the latter), and children do not yet know how to find any common denominator.

Compared to the preceding level, this image of economic reality is certainly more complex and differentiated, reflecting the development of concrete operatory thinking which appears around the ages of 7 to 8 years. One aspect of this development is the overcoming of egocentrism, which leads to the abandonment, by and large, of the 'pre-economic' ideas of the earlier levels. Finalistic conceptions of the source of money disappear, while artificialism and realism decline and a more adequate vision of social roles emerges. The capacity to distinguish their own thoughts and wishes from those of others allows children to conceive of relationships based on authority, and thus to be able to represent the boss who is in control and command of various working situations. Their own social position becomes less of a paradigm than it was for children at the earlier levels. The status of their own family is assumed to be one of 'normality', but in relation to this children are now able to distinguish wealthier classes, and not just those who are visibly above an extreme level of poverty. From another point of view the acquisition of the idea of the 'boss' and an economic stratification which includes the rich, the poor and the 'normal', can be seen as an attempt to organise a wider and more complex grasp of economic reality through the introduction of asymmetric relationships. A similar effort at organisation can also be seen in the systematic way children at this level establish correspondences between the quantity of work and its remuneration, or the equivalence between withdrawals and deposits in the bank. Children at this level, then, apply the operations of seriation and establish correspondences in a much more systematic and extensive way than at preceding levels.

Nevertheless, children at the third level do not yet possess the cognitive instruments which would enable them to resolve all the questions we put to them which involved a verbal type of reasoning. Their solution only becomes possible with the later development of formal operatory thinking. The only problem, which is in fact fully resolved around 7 years, is that of the use and value of money, which is a concrete problem. At this age children are able to calculate change when they simulate retail buying and selling. The discrepancy between the type of problem presented to them and the cognitive instruments of children at the third level can be seen in the approximate, rather rough and ready character of some of their conceptions. For example, in establishing a correspondence between work and remuneration children only take account of the effort or time expended, and ignore less visible factors which actually determine the remuneration paid for different jobs. Children use an extremely small number of elements to construct the seriations which underly their recognition of power relationships and economic stratification: only two elements for the former, and three for the latter.

But the most conspicuous limit of concrete operatory thinking is its failure to connect separate areas of experience. The most typical characteristic of this level can be considered the incapacity to relate the areas of 'work' and 'buying and selling'. This difficulty can be seen in two specific conceptions: the idea that the boss needs to have access to sources external to the factory in order to pay the workers, and the idea that prices remain the same or decrease in the transition from production to consumption. In fact the 'system of work' and the 'system of buying and selling' each include beliefs which originate from distinct problems and experiences; for the former these are the problem of the source of money and verbal information about work and its remuneration, for the latter the problem of the origin of goods and the direct experience of buying things. So long as these two areas of experience remain heterogenous, children remain unable to coordinate the beliefs which they articulate about them; they are constrained to search for 'makeshift' solutions. To explain how workers come to be paid, for instance, they return to new versions of older ideas about sources of money, while to balance shopkeepers' accounts they commit errors of quantification.

Another example of children's difficulties in going beyond their circum-scribed experiences can be seen in their ideas about the bank. At first they say that the bank is only for looking after money, later that the bank also lends it. In each case they establish a precise correspondence between deposits and withdrawals, or between loans and repayments, but without ever finding a connection between deposits and loans. Children imagine that money deposited in a bank is locked in a safe or a strongroom until the moment of withdrawal, and that the bank provides loans with money obtained from external sources (the council, the state, other banks). Thus children do not construct any synthesis between these two functions of the bank, which they probably get to know at different times and in different ways.

6.4 Conceptions of the formal operatory period (11–14 years)

After the age of 10 (Level 4) children begin to coordinate in a single frame-work of exchanges the various economic roles which they know, now more numerous and more clearly delineated than at the preceding level. They say that the owner pays the workers with money received from the sale of the factory's products and, correspondingly, they consider the price of goods to be the result of the costs of materials, labour, commercial intermediaries and the industrialist's profit margin. The idea of a hierarchical organisation of work is also extended to include sectors such as urban transport and agriculture which, because of the way in which children experience these activities, are more easily conceived as forms of self-employed work. The industrial world becomes further stratified. For at least some children the worker and the boss are no longer the only recognisable figures in the factory; now the figure of the owner is added, a person with a more abstract and indirect relationship to the means of production.

The child's vision of economic stratification also broadens through the idea of differing degrees of wealth and poverty. The different rates of payment for different types of jobs are no longer related only to the time and effort expended or their social utility, as was the case at the preceding level; the 'prestige' of different occupations and, more generally, the existence of classes in society are also taken into account. Differences in opinion appear: some children oppose social stratification, others accept and justify it on the basis of a principle of equity. These opinions do not in fact necessarily coincide, as one might have expected, with the class membership of the children, perhaps because some of them, particularly those from working-class backgrounds, appear to have rather vague ideas about the life styles of the more prosperous classes and how they differ from their own way of life.

On the one hand, then, these conceptions indicate an enrichment of, and finer distinctions within, the human panorama of the world of work and of economic exchanges in general. On the other hand, these conceptions also contribute towards a clearer distinction between the order of reality consti-tuted by human activities, and the order of natural processes. Indeed notions of production as the recycling or repair of old or worn out things disappear, to be replaced by assertions that all types of goods, industrial and agricultural, are the result of actions undertaken to transform natural resources.

At this level children are also able to represent more correctly the functions of various institutions. In regard to the bank, for instance, they say that the money for loans comes from deposits, and they also understand that interest from loans constitutes the source of income from which the bank obtains the money to pay interest on deposits. The understanding of public institutions is also clarified at this level. At earlier levels the words 'council', 'government' or 'state' were either void of meaning or else assimilated to a very general idea of someone who commands or provides for other people; now they are taken as denoting institutions which provide collective services.

In the ideas about economic reality that emerge at this level two new figures can be seen: the owner of the means of production, who is distinguished from the 'boss'; and public institutions, which are distinguished from private owners. The area of exchanges constituted by acts of buying and selling and that constituted by work relationships, which remained uncoordinated at the preceding level, now become merged into a single homogenous system. The money with which the worker is paid comes from the sale of products, and retail prices include the costs of labour necessary to produce and distribute the goods. Thus the main limits of the preceding level are overcome; children now represent the different economic exchanges within a single reality.

We noted previously that the beliefs of children younger than 7 had a unitary quality, even if their sketchy and incomplete image of economic reality was unified on the basis of such subjective and egocentric principles as finalism and realism. The emergence of concrete operatory thinking while enabling the 7–10 year olds to leave behind 'pre-economic' conceptions do not suffice to allow them to synthesise a coherent image. Thus we have noted the ways in which children at this age turn back towards earlier ideas when they reach the limits of their understanding, as well as the gaps at significant points in the representation of the economic world at Level 3. Now, however, not only can the exchanges represented by children be truly described as economic, but they are also coordinated in a single system, a *structure d'ensemble*, such that, no matter at what point in the system one starts, it is always possible to arrive at any other point.

The realisation of this progress is the consequence of the child's ability at Level 4 to locate on the same level heterogenous bits of information obtained through a variety of experiences. Children no longer remain tied to the marginal aspects of these experiences, but are able to grasp what is essential to them. They are able to consider money as pure quantity independently of the operations undertaken with it or the people who perform them. Savers, for instance, who deposit their money in the bank for a variety of reasons, are a source of cash flowing into the bank, and this income corresponds to the flow which leaves the bank through the various loans which it makes. The homogenisation of the money-work nexus with the money-goods nexus is also derived from the separation of children's conception of them from the concrete fields of experience in which the individual representations emerged. The ability to construct ever broader connections is shown by those responses in which children talk simultaneously about different exchanges and different processes: '*the boss sells the products and pays the workers*', '*the bank is somewhere to put money and somewhere to get loans from*', '*the comic costs 500 lire because the publisher checks how much he's paid for the paper, the ink, the people who work there*'.

The extension of the domains to which the operations of classification, seriation or correspondence can be applied, which constitutes one of the first acquisitions of the period of formal operatory thinking, enables children at this level to use these operations in a wider and more systematic way than in the preceding level, where their use was very limited and rudimentary. Seriations of three terms or more, involving concrete material, are easily accomplished by children even at the intuitive level. If it is not until about the age of 12 that children begin to be able to comprehend a simple hierarchy of three terms, such as worker-boss-owner, this delay is due to the fact that such series consist of terms which have to be represented mentally and coordinated with one another without any perceptual support. Classification is also an operation which children acquire before they are 10 years old, but when the things to be classified are abstract notions rather than concrete, visible objects or things which can be represented in mental images, then again it is not until the onset of formal operatory thinking that children become able to perform such operations. It is only at Level 4, for instance, that children are able to organise into a single set, which we can describe as the 'class of costs', the different factors which contribute to the formation of prices. The same could also be said of the ability to construct correspondences, which can be handled on a concrete level from about the age of 6. Children at Level 3 are able to construct such correspondences when the degree of abstraction is not too great as, for instance, in the case of the correspondence between deposits and withdrawals, or between loans and repayments. However, when the elements to be placed in correspondence are more empirically distant (deposits and loans, for instance), or are themselves the products of other operations (interest on deposits and interest on loans) then children only begin to succeed with the emergence of formal thinking.

7 Cultural, social and educational influences on the development of children's economic conceptions

7.1 Cross-cultural validity of developmental sequences of economic concepts

Cross-sectional studies, such as those reported in Chapters 2–5, do not permit definite conclusions to be drawn about the stage character of any of the sequences identified; such studies, undertaken with children from a particular culture, need to be complemented by longitudinal and cross-cultural studies. To say that a concept develops through a sequence of stages is, in fact, to say that this sequence describes the actual developmental progression through which every child passes in constructing the concept. Apart from our own research on the use of money noted in Chapter 3, there have been no other longitudinal studies of economic concepts. Some cross-cultural comparisons explicitly concerned with economic concepts, however, have recently been reported.

Hong Kwan and Stacey (1981) examined conceptions of buying and selling, work, gambling, the bank, wealth and poverty, and the origin of goods in a group of 6–15-year-old Malaysian Chinese children. Their aim was to compare the conceptions of this group with those found in Western countries. Even though the scoring and analysis of the data were quite different, they obtained results largely in line with those reported here in previous chapters. In fact, in every area covered by their interview the responses reflected a progression from a fragmentary reproduction of observational data integrated through imaginative elaborations, to the identification of relationships between pairs of people and their integration into functional systems. The developmental progression which Hong Kwan and Stacey report for buying and selling (the only theme for which they give detailed interview information) corresponds precisely to that reported by other authors. They also suggest that differences with Western samples might be found in relation to gambling, about which their Chinese subjects appeared to have quite a thorough understanding. Additionally, Chinese children seem to be less inclined than Westerners to invoke imaginary sources of money, and show a stronger tendency to refer to parents or work as a source of money. Finally, the idea that to make a profit the shopkeeper needs to increase the price of goods is already present in the Chinese subjects from the age of 9, which is younger than the age of 11 reported by both Furth and Jahoda, but roughly equal to the results of our own studies with Italian children, where this notion was generally present from the age of 9 or 10.

The idea of profit from trading has also been studied by Jahoda (1983) among a group of Zimbabwean children (aged 9 to 11) who lived in an environment characterised by small-scale trading and agriculture, with the direct sale of products by the farmers. The children were divided into three groups according to their familiarity with buying and selling: firstly the children of retail traders; secondly the children of farmers (who sold their own produce retail); and thirdly those children whose parents had nothing to do with commerce. As a whole this group of children were developmentally more advanced than the Glaswegian children of Jahoda's (1979) previous study, or Furth's (1980) English sample, or a group of Dutch children.[1] Indeed at every age there was a notable proportion of African children who said that shopkeepers had to sell the goods at a higher price than they had paid for them. Jahoda argues that this result does not agree with the picture drawn from the numerous cross-cultural studies of Piagetian tasks (cf. Dasen and Heron, 1981) where children from nonindustrial countries generally appear to be delayed in their cognitive development in comparison with their Western peers, when not actually incapable of reaching higher developmental levels in the understanding of particular concepts. This Zimbabwean study suggests that one should not jump too quickly to conclusions about retardations or lower levels of cognitive development *in general*, since these children appeared more advanced when interviewed on themes other than those studied by Piaget.

How should these differences be explained? One could say that the superiority (of children from industrialised societies on the Piagetian tasks, or of the Zimbabwean children in relation to buying and selling) reflects a greater familiarity with the subject of the interview. Indeed, among the African sample, the most advanced answers were given by children whose parents participated in commerce, and especially those children who actively helped them. All the same, this explanation is not sufficient; when those children with greater familiarity with buying and selling are left to one side, the African sample loses some but not all of its superiority over the European sample. Jahoda (1983) suggests that neither the parental model, nor even selling as such, is sufficient to account for the relative African advantage. Other factors, which he suggests might exert an influence, include communi-

---

[1] The data on the Dutch children were taken from the preliminary phase of the study on the understanding of the functions of the bank (Jahoda, 1983) undertaken with working-class children aged 11 to 16. Only 5 of the 16 eleven-year-old subjects showed a full understanding of the notion of profit.

cation between peers and a social environment in which the activities of buying and sellng have a particular importance.

To those specifically cross-cultural studies can be added comparisons of data from studies of similar themes undertaken at different times in different environments. We have already emphasised the congruence of results from the various studies on buying and selling by Strauss (1952) and Burris (1983) in the United States, Danziger (1958) in Australia, and Furth (1980) and Jahoda (1979) in Great Britain. Our own research undertaken with Italian children (Chapter 4) also led to similar results. On the basis of this widespread agreement it is possible to assert that the developmental sequence of ideas about buying and selling and about profit have a cross-cultural generality; the same sequence can be observed in different environments and different countries; the only differences concern the velocity with which children pass through the various stages.

Another issue which has been the focus for cross-cultural comparisons is that of banking, which Jahoda has studied among both Scottish (Jahoda, 1981) and Dutch (Jahoda and Woerdenbagch, 1982) children, and which Ng (1983) has studied among Hong Kong children. From these comparisons as well, it seems that ideas about the bank develop through the same sequence in different countries, even if at different rhythms. The Dutch and Hong Kong children appeared to be more advanced than the Scottish sample in recognising the existence of bank loans and interest. These differences might be due to the greater importance or availability of information about banking in the Netherlands (Jahoda and Woerdenbagch, 1982), and to the business ethos characteristic of Hong Kong society being reflected in a higher degree of economic socialisation (Hong Kwan & Stacey, 1982).[2]

The most interesting consequence of this cross-cultural research has been the demonstration that in different countries and in different socio-economic environments, children's ideas about various aspects of economic reality develop through the same sequence, a result which strongly supports the hypothesis that such development proceeds by stages. On the other hand, both the data and interpretations concerning the different rates with which children from different countries pass through this sequence seem to us much weaker.

Above all we think that such small samples as those employed in these studies (about a hundred subjects in each one) provide an inadequate basis for conclusions to be drawn about whole nations, let alone entire continents

---

[2] Albertini *et al.* (1983) have also undertaken a cross-cultural study of social representations of the economic system in 11–16 years olds from Belgium, France, West Germany and Great Britain. This study did not, however, examine the developmental sequences relating to specific notions and so has not been reviewed here. The interested reader can either consult the original text of Albertini *et al.* or the more succinct exposition of this study given by Ryba (1984).

(Jahoda, for example, speaks of a European 'lag' in relation to Africa, even though his data actually only compare British and Dutch children with a Zimbabwean sample). The differences between the Italian children we interviewed and the British and North Europeans interviewed by Furth and Jahoda (and considered as a sample of 'Western' children) are greater than the differences reported between North European children and those from Africa and Asia.

It also seems to us that cross-cultural research has not, so far, been able to identify those environmental factors which influence the rate at which children develop economic concepts. The societies which have been studied and compared differ in many aspects, and it has not been possible to establish which aspects exert significant influences. It would be necessary to undertake comparisons between children belonging to the most similar socio-cultural environments which differed only with respect to some dimension considered pertinent to a specific conceptual development. If, for instance, one wanted to examine the hypothesis that variations in the accessibility of information about buying and selling exercise some influence on the development of ideas about profit, one would need to compare children from the same country who had different opportunities to participate in retail trade.

To examine the effect of the availability of specific information on the development of children's economic concepts, we have replicated some of our own studies in environments where relevant experiences were particularly accessible to children. Thus we have examined ideas about the source of money among children whose parents undertake activities involving different forms of payment. We have also studied ideas about the origins of goods among children from a mountain community in which they could observe the entire production cycle for wood products.

7.2 The source of money according to the children of workers and merchants

The children whose ideas we examined about the source of money in Chapter 3 all came from the middle class. In varying degrees, all of these children up to the age of 7–8 years expressed the idea of easy and ready access to money. It was just such an idea that we defined as 'finalistic', thereby connecting it with an attitude peculiar to the child's mentality. However, might not such an idea simply be the fruits of their social conditions? The relatively well-off environment of these children might have generated the attitude of confident expectation, which would thus be more the expression of a contingent circumstance than a tendency of children's thinking.

However, similar responses have been reported by other authors from studies undertaken in different social environments. Furth (1980), whose sample included both working-class and middle-class subjects, provides some extracts from interviews in which children assert that money is distributed by the bank, or the government, or even directly from God. Burris (1983), who also studied a mixed sample, demonstrated that very few preschoolers connect work and money, and that they consider shops and banks as the places where adults obtain money. Neither of these authors, however, analysed their data for variations in finalistic conceptions as a function of social class. Not even Connell (1977) mentions any differences in the frequency of primitive ideas about the origins of wealth (such as becoming wealthy by finding gold in the basement) among the upper, middle- and lower-class children of his sample. Goldstein and Oldham (1979) did find that among their subjects it was the working-class children who more frequently spoke about work as a source of money, although they (and especially the youngest ones) frequently added other sources such as banks and shops; Goldstein and Oldham do not report any differences for these other sources. Jahoda (1979), finally, examined a homogenous sample drawn from children from a poor locality, in many cases the children of unemployed parents who received financial support from public sources. He frequently found the idea that shopkeepers received money from social security, even if they also made money from the sale of goods. Jahoda suggests that such ideas derive from a generalisation of the child's own familial experiences. The conception that there are other sources of money aside from work might, therefore, reflect both a situation of wellbeing, as well as the familial experiences of poorer children of receiving money without having had to work for it.

In order to see how far the idea of ready access to money does indeed reflect the availability of money within the family, we replicated our own study on the source of money (Chapter 3) among a group of children from lower-income families, whose parents were factory workers and housewives living in a suburb of Turin. Turin is the home of Fiat, the most important Italian manufacturer of cars, and all the fathers of these subjects worked in the local Fiat factory.[3]

The interviews began with a question about the source of their father's money ('How does your father come to have money?'), and this was extended to three other work activities, those of the farmer, shopkeeper and bus driver. In this phase we sought first of all to see if these activities were recognised, then if they were considered as a source for earning money; finally, the mode of payment described for these three activities was compared with that which emerged regarding their father's work.

The results were similar to those obtained from the earlier study of middle-class children in Padova, and were categorised according to the same sequence of levels (described in Chapter 3). The distribution of subjects across

---

[3] The sample consisted of 15 kindergarten children (4–5 years old) and an equal number of second-grade children (7–8 years old). The data were collected by Angela Fiora.

these categories was also similar in the two studies, a chi-square showed no significant difference in these distributions. If these responses are examined in greater detail, however, some interesting peculiarities emerge among the Turin children. Among the younger children, 4 had not yet established any connection between money and work (Level 1), 8 said that not only their fathers, but also farmers, shopkeepers and bus drivers 'worked at Fiat' (Level 2), and only 3 said that some other activities besides their fathers' jobs could be considered as work and hence be paid (Level 3). The majority of the 7–8 year olds gave Level 3 responses (n = 9), while the remainder (n = 6) recognised all of these occupations as paid work (Level 4). Particularly interesting is the concentration of responses at Level 2 ('working' means going to Fiat), where 7 out of a group of 8 children see this Turin industry not as an enterprise in which one may be engaged, work and receive payment, but rather as a sort of charitable institution, very like the bank or the council to which the middle-class children interviewed in Padova usually referred.[4]

M. CRISTINA (4:6) – Do you know what your daddy does to get money? – *No.* – What does your daddy do to get money to buy food? – *He goes to Fiat.* – Why does he go there? – *... He works.* – At Fiat is there someone who gives him money or does he get it by himself? – *By himself.* – Where? – *... – At Fiat.* – Do you know how come the money is there? – *... I don't know.* – Can he take as much money as he wants or not? – *... No.* – Why not? – *I don't know.* – (...) – At Fiat do they give your daddy money every day or not? – *Yes, every day.* – Why? – *Because if not we couldn't live.* – (...) – Have you seen the man who drives the bus? – *Yes.* – Does he work? – *... Yes.* – And what does he do while he works? – *... I don't know.* – And he has money? – *Yes.* – What did he do to get it? – *He went to get it at Fiat.* – Can everybody go and get money at Fiat? – *Yes.* – Why? – *... I don't know.*

DANIELA (4:6) – Do you know what a farmer does? – *... Makes milk ... –* When he does that is he working? – *Yes.* – Does he have money? – *Yes.* – What did he do to get it? – *He went to work.* – What does he do when he goes to work? – *He works.* – What work does he do? – *Near the machines.* The shopkeeper, too, according to Daniela, has money because he got it – *By working.* – What does he do when he works? – *... The machines.* Finally, the bus driver also gets his money *by working the machines.*[5]

---

[4] Translator's note: In point of fact, Fiat's domination of the local Turin economy is so great that such responses are perhaps not altogether inaccurate. The conglomerate is owned by the Agnelli family whose scions are among the best known Italian industrialists and who figure prominently as personalities in the media (indeed Gianni Agnelli, the chairman, is frequently referred to by just the title *l'avvocato* – the lawyer). Agnelli and Fiat are practically synonymous, and together with their ownership of other enterprises the Agnelli family appear to have a visible presence in every street and square in the city. Turin, in short, appears as a vast company town.

[5] Translator's note: Daniela always spoke about *macchine*, which is ambiguous in this context: in Italian this is not only the word for 'machines' in general, but also the everyday word for 'car' or 'automobile'.

FABIO (4:6) provides some hints for understanding what happens when one 'works at Fiat' and 'gets money' – Do you know how your daddy comes to have money? – ... *By working* ... – And is there someone there who gives it to him, or does he just get it by himself? – ... *By himself* ... – How come? – *Well ... at Fiat ... Fiat isn't just a job ... there's also money.* – How come there's money there? – ... *There's a 'radio' ... money ... my daddy takes the 'radio' and puts in 10 lire, pushes a button and paper money comes out ... lots ...* – Why? – *Because if you put 10 lire in you get lots of money.* – Do you just have to put 10 lire in? – ... *Yes, you put it in and then press the button.* – Are there any other ways of getting money? – *No.* – Does everybody do that to get money, or not? – *Yes ... everybody does so.* – If I want to get some money what do I have to do? – ... *Go to Fiat ... then take the 'radio' ...* – And if you want to get some money? – *I have to have 10 lire to put in* ... .

One can see from these examples how a familiarity with the existence of something called Fiat where the child's father goes every day and from which he derives money, does not itself allow any clarification of the connection between work and receiving money. On the contrary, the dominant factor is the mentality of the children, which enables them to assimilate even elements which are obscure for them into that vision of the world which is characteristic of their age. These data seem, then, to indicate that the belief in 'charitable institutions' is not so much the reflection of a more or less wealthy way of life, as an indication of the way in which children resolve, with the cognitive instruments at their disposal, the problem of the source of money.

Another aspect of the environment which could influence children's conceptions of the source of money is the possibility of observing both work being done and the act of payment for it. This aspect was examined by interviewing a group of children whose parents were engaged in local businesses. The children were able to observe the relationships between their parents and their parents' customers or clients. The inquiry was undertaken in the Val di Pejo, a small mountain community frequented by tourists.[6]

The number of subjects younger than six was too small to allow any detailed comparisons or definitive conclusions. Nevertheless, it is interesting to note that:

1. in spite of the visibility of their parents receiving money from clients some subjects did refer to the bank as a source of income, and extended this modality to the other occupational activities about which they were questioned (factory worker and farm worker);
2. already by 5–6 years there were children who had achieved an under-

---

[6] The sample consisted of 40 children, the entire population of this region whose parents were either artisans, merchants or small hotel keepers (there were 7 children aged 4–6 years, 16 aged 6–8 years, and 17 aged 8–10 years). The data were collected by Maria Migazzi.

standing that their parents were paid by the people who bought goods from them, and there was tendency to attribute the same mode of remuneration to the other occupational activities;

3. the better understanding of their parents' activity, itself undoubtedly favoured by their experience, is reflected in the greater caution with which the children considered the other occupational activities; in addition to the responses which assimilated factory workers and farmworkers to tradesmen there were also quite a few 'don't knows', as if to indicate a less fantastic vision of the world of work.

7.3 The source of goods according to children able to observe an entire production cycle

The interview about the source of goods from Chapter 4 was repeated among a sample of 80 children living in an Alpine village in the Val di Fiemme, where it is possible to observe the entire cycle of the production of wooden objects.[7] The Val di Fiemme is, in fact, rich in forests whose wood is processed in the valley itself in large sawmills, and some of this wood is then worked in small local carpentry shops. Questions about a chair were added to the original questions about peaches, glasses and clothes.

A first point to note about the results of this replication is the emergence of the same types of responses as those found among the urban children. This was the case for both the source and the production of goods, and once again response levels were highly correlated with age (cf. Table 7.1).

Nevertheless some differences do emerge when the numbers of children responding at each level in the two localities are compared. For the source of goods the chi-square values are 3.12 (n.s.) for the clothes, 8.65 (df = 3, $p < .05$) for the glasses, and 23.00 (df = 2, $p < .001$) for the peach. Table 7.2 shows the distributions of these responses.

As one can see from the table, the children from the mountains tend to give lower responses than the urban children regarding glasses, while for the peaches they give both more primitive responses (Levels 1 & 2) as well as more advanced responses (Level 4). For the chair, the most frequent responses were at Level 3 (n = 48), followed by Level 4 (n = 19). Thus a knowledge of the work of woodcutters, sawmen, hauliers, or artisans is not in itself sufficient to generate a clear concept of the production chain. Rather, children focus on a single figure, the carpenter, who makes and sells wooden objects (Level 3).

In the data on production, a significant difference was found between the distributions of the two groups with respect to glasses (chi-square = 31.3;

[7] All the subjects were grouped into the same age levels as in the earlier study (4–5 years, 6–7 years, 8–9 years, and 10–11 years). Their fathers were either general workers or labourers employed in working with wood. The data were collected by Isanna Wohlgemut.

Table 7.1 *Rank order correlations between age group and response levels for the Val di Fiemme sample*

	Clothes	Glasses	Peaches	Chair
Source	.48	.66	.56	.43
Production	.51	.56	.39*	.48

In each case p < .001

Note:
* For this distribution the existence of a large number of empty cells mitigated against the use of a Spearman correlation; the figure quoted is a point-biserial correlation.

Table 7.2 *Distributions of children from Padova (PD) and Val di Fiemme (VF) for the source of goods*

	Clothes		Glasses*		Peaches	
	PD	VF	PD	VF	PD	VF
1. Don't know, or at home	4	10	1	7	2	12
2. In a shop	12	11	10	18	7	9
3. The shopkeeper makes them	24	25	25	14	43	16
4. The shopkeeper buys them from a producer	40	34	44	41	28	43
Total	80	80	80	80	80	80

Note:
* For the glasses Levels 1 and 2 were combined in order to make the chi-square calculation possible.

df = 3; p < .001). A particular difference was the greater number of subjects classified at Level 1 in the Val di Fiemme sample, that is, children whose interviews did not proceed beyond the first part because they did not identify any producer, but only spoke about the shopkeeper or even failed to identify any economic figure. However, no significant differences were found for either the clothes (chi-square = 6.5; df = 3) or the peaches (chi-square = 0.71; df = 2). Table 7.3 shows the response distributions for the two groups.

The vast majority of responses about the production of chairs were classified at level 4 (n = 60); of the remaining subjects, only 1 mentioned recycling as the source of the materials, while the other 19 were more or less equally divided between Levels 1 and 2.

The clearest difference between the data from the urban and mountain samples is the reduction of Level 3 responses among the Val di Fiemme children, that is responses in which the production of goods is explained through the recycling of broken or worn-out objects and in which no mention is made of raw materials. Of those subjects who did speak about production

Table 7.3 *Distributions of children from Padova (PD) and Val di Fiemme (VF) for the production of goods*

	Clothes		Glasses		Peaches*	
	PD	VF	PD	VF	PD	VF
1. No production	13	13	9	24	7	15
2. No comprehension	18	23	12	29	2	1
3. Recycled materials	20	8	37	9	7	0
4. Natural origin of						
raw materials	29	36	22	18	64	64
Total	80	80	80	80	80	80

Note:
* For the peaches Levels 2 and 3 were combined in order to make the chi-square calculation possible.

(i.e. excluding children classified at Level 1) Level 3 conceptions accounted for 14 per cent of the Val di Fiemme subjects for the clothes, as against 30 per cent of the Padova sample; for the glasses the figures are 14 per cent in Val di Fiemme and 52 per cent in Padova; while no such responses were given in Val di Fiemme about the peaches, and only 9 per cent in Padova. The majority of the mountain children preferred to say 'don't know' when they were unable to identify any raw material or natural process as the source of goods.

It seems, therefore, more appropriate to talk of qualitative differences rather than any differences in developmental tempi between the samples. The possibility of knowing the source of a raw material such as wood seems to have had the effect of limiting young children's 'imaginative elaborations': they knew that they did not know. The children did not mention a shopkeeper-producer as a source of goods except in relation to craft or artisan production (clothes, chair); nor did they refer to recycling when talking about production, being well aware of the natural sources of the materials used in the construction of goods with which they were familiar, such as the chair.

7.4 The effect of different environments on children's economic concepts

Given that the studies undertaken so far have been limited to a few themes investigated with small groups of subjects it is more appropriate to ask how these data might be interpreted rather than draw firm conclusions from them.

Comparisons of children from different countries or continents, or from different environments in the same country have yielded similarities as well as differences. The similarities seem clear enough, with the same types of responses being observed in children from different environments, even if there are differences in the rhythm and frequency with which they appear. These similarities can be related to a multiplicity of factors. Some characteristics of economic processes are essentially the same even when they occur in different cultures (the use of money, for instance, or retail buying and selling). Even when more specific characteristics are considered, where one might expect to find cross-cultural differences, the diffusion of information through the mass media suggests that even if children lack access to direct observation, they are in touch with similar verbal or imaginative data (what Connell described as the 'free-floating information' which passes through the child's immediate environment). This ensures that even in different parts of the world there are certain invariant elements in the information available to children.

A different argument needs to be advanced concerning those recurring responses which emerge in contrast to relatively accessible information, such as, for instance, the belief that money can be easily obtained from banks even when children see customers paying their parents every day; or children's inability to trace the source of goods back to raw materials even though they live in a region whose economic activities are dominated by the collection and transformation of some raw material (wood). Such examples illustrate the existence of a tendency in children's thinking towards conceptions which are only loosely connected to the available information.

More radically, our data also suggest the need for rethinking the concept of an environment. The possibility of observing a phenomenon does not, *ipso facto*, imply that its true significance will be grasped, much less that it will be applied to analogous phenomena. The fact that a phenomenon is accessible to direct observation does not mean that children (particularly youngest) will understand it, perhaps because it is not important to them or perhaps they do not possess any framework within which to organise the data in a meaningful way. For example, the child might simply view the chain of production and distribution, which runs from the cutting of the tree, through the working of the wood, to the sale of the finished object, as 'many jobs' unconnected to one another.

All the same, in some cases the information is not only accessible but even particularly significant. Such is the case, for instance, for the dependence of the Turin workers on Fiat. Not only do they work in the Fiat factory, but they also live close by in the so-called 'Fiat houses' rented out by the factory owners themselves. In this case the information gathered by the child (work = Fiat, money = Fiat) may become a nodal point to which other aspects of economic life become attached, even if this occurs through erroneous generalisations (e.g. everyone who works obtains money from Fiat). A child might also, however, come to understand an economic process and be unable to extend this notion to different cases, leaving them secure only in the knowledge of not knowing what happens in these other instances. This is what seems to have happened with the children of small businessmen (Val di Pejo) who said they did not know where employees obtained money, even though they knew one form of payment for work through direct experience in their own family (when their parents sell something they are paid by the customers). The same could also be said of the many Val di Fiemme children who replied 'don't know' to our questions about the origins of clothes and glasses, even though they also knew that one needs wood to make a table and that fruit grows on trees. It is these salient aspects of the environment, above all when they are presented to the child in pervasive and congruent ways (cf. Emler and Dickinson, 1985) which determine the differences between groups which we have noted above, in the sense of the greater or lesser frequency of certain types of responses (cf. the research in the Val di Fiemme), as much as the elaboration of 'particular versions' of concepts also found elsewhere (e.g. Fiat as a source of money for everybody), or accelerated developmental rhythms (as reported by Jahoda, 1983, or Hong Kwan and Stacey, 1982).

It is, however, extremely difficult to predict what the effect of a particular environment will be on children's economic conceptions given that it is not always possible to anticipate which features of the environment will appear significant in the child's eyes. One part of any such prediction would have to be our knowledge of general cognitive development, given that the cognitive structures present at each age level will contribute to the degree to which children are able to relate pertinent information.

7.5   Educational research on the acquisition of economic concepts

So far we have considered environmental effects in terms of the knowledge which children are able to extract through direct observation or from occasional verbal information (such as that supplied by the mass media or conversations between adults). Another fundamental source of economic understanding for the child is formal instruction both by parents and school, although economics seems to be largely absent from explicitly pedagogic situations.

Some information about parents' intentional efforts to teach their children about economic concepts is available from collateral research undertaken in association with two of our studies reported earlier; the study of the source of money (undertaken with the Turin sample), and the study of the ownership of the means of production.[8] In both cases parents reported having tried to communicate with their children through speech adapted to their particular

---

[8] The first of these studies consists of interviews, the second of questionnaires distributed through school. In both cases the parents of children interviewed as part of our research samples were asked what they had told their children about their own jobs and about their domestic organisation. The second study also asked what parents had told their children about the ownership of their house. The interviews were undertaken by Angela Fiora (unpublished doctoral dissertation, University of Padova), while the questionnaires formed part of a study undertaken in collaboration with another researcher (Berti, Bombi and Lis, 1982).

age, which took into account, fairly realistically, their children's cognitive capacities without, however, any attempt at conveying complete information to the children nor at taking the children beyond their actual developmental level.

The teaching of economics in school occurs only in some countries and in certain types of school, though never, or only marginally, does it occur before the age of 14 (Whitehead, 1985, gives a description of the situation in England).[9] In the new syllabus for Italian elementary schools a brief account of economics appears for the first time, as an aspect of 'social studies' and closely connected with history. As part of the preparation for these 'social studies', the *Università Scuola* research group and one of the present authors undertook a longitudinal study of the teaching of basic economic concepts from the third to the fifth grades (i.e. with children aged 8–11 years; Ajello *et. al.*, 1986, 1987a, and 1987b). The basic hypothesis for this study was that the 'spontaneous' levels of development which children expressed in the various cross-sectional studies do not correspond to the highest level which they might be able to reach. Rather, these spontaneous expressions were considered as reflections of what children have acquired 'against the current', as it were, in unfavourable conditions. The children had to put together uncoordinated pieces of information obtained from overhearing adult conversations or via the mass media, with very limited opportunity for direct observation; and, apart from the very few cases of working children, it was only in relation to retail trade that children could learn through practice about the rules which govern the interactions between participants in economic exchanges. Thus it was hypothesised that a teaching programme which aimed to make pertinent information available to children in a clear and organic way would stimulate their thinking and lead to the early acquisition of some fundamental economic concepts.

Three curricula were prepared, one for each of the third, fourth and fifth grades. Each course consisted of a minimum of 6 and a maximum of 9 instruction units which could be presented in the space of one month at the rate of two mornings a week. These curricula were used for three successive years with the same five classes (each of which retained the same teacher for the whole of the three years). The classes were located in three different Roman schools, two from the central zone of the city frequented by middle and upper-middle-class families, and the other from a lower-middle-class suburb.

From a methodological point of view these curricula have two main characteristics:

---

[9] In Italy economics is only taught in some 'vocational' schools; it is not included in the syllabus for the high schools which prepare students for university, even though there are important degree courses in economics and commerce.

1. a minimal use of teacher-led lessons, relying rather on active work by the children including research and the interpretation of data (along predefined lines) as well as group discussions;
2. the use of visual as well as verbal information (including field trips, the presentation in class of slides, or drawings to be placed in order, commented on or interpreted in various ways) so that economic concepts could be anchored gradually in the 'social scenes' (recurrent and observable situations) in which the relevant transactions took place.

The content of the three curricula progressed through the secondary, primary and tertiary economic sectors in the course of the three school years. The third grade began with aspects of economic life familiar to city children: work and goods. Children learned first to distinguish between self-employment and employment by others on the basis of ownership of the means of production; they then visited a small clothes factory to see how the production cycle operated and to interview the owner about costs and sale prices. Later, in a class discussion, they had to confront the problem of the difference in price between goods in the factory and in the shops. The explanation offered by the teacher was that, as a general rule, the price reflects the quantity of work necessary to produce the goods, and that, therefore, the price of something rises as it passes through the successive phases of production and distribution.

In the fourth grade attention turned to the primary sector. This curriculum had three aims. First, we tried to extend the application of the 'price rule' to agriculture, a type of production less familiar to these city subjects (this was presented to them through slides in class). Secondly children had to reorder a series of drawings so as to reconstruct the chain of distribution for agricultural products, and thus to extend the 'price rule' by adding the costs of distribution to those of production. Thirdly children were introduced to variations in prices by examining price fluctuations at the fresh food warehouses during the course of the day. In fact, the objective reasons determining the necessity of quick sales at reduced prices were particularly evident for primary products.

The fifth-grade course dealt with the service sector, and focused on the analysis of commercial services as a way of re-examining some concepts which had not been clearly assimilated by the end of the preceding curricula, particularly explanations for variations in prices. The course began with the analysis of the functioning of large shops (undertaken through a field trip to a department store and an interview with the manager), with a particular emphasis on administrative costs and the procurement and sale of goods. The children then discussed the problem of why prices in large shops are generally lower than those in small shops; the explanations proposed by the teacher touched on the lower overheads for large shops. Finally the phenomena of clearance sales were examined to show how they allowed excess stock to be eliminated by being sold at reduced prices, though not, as a rule, at a price lower than their cost.

The efficacy of this programme was investigated through wide-ranging individual interviews on the themes of the curricula with the pupils of the five classes (about 130 children in all), both before and after each of the three teaching phases. The responses for each theme were ordered in a sequence of levels which permitted each child's response to be awarded a score. Pre- and post-teaching scores were then compared through a repeated measures analysis of variance. Each of the three curricula were shown to have resulted in significant progress for the main themes of the programme. In addition, this quantitative analysis was followed by a qualitative analysis of the distributions of the responses with particular regard to modalities of transition between levels. It is not possible to report all the results of these analyses in detail, though some idea can be seen in the following examples.

Prior to the third-grade curriculum, children (aged 8–9 years) had similar ideas about retail trade as the children of the same age we had already interviewed in other Italian cities. Shopkeepers, according to these children, set prices completely arbitrarily, or following some guidelines from the authorities, or on the basis of the quality of the goods. In each case, however, no account was taken of wholesale prices and the question of profit. When the issue of profit was approached in a different way, by asking what the shopkeepers did with the money received from sales, it gave rise to one or other of the following responses: either the child said that shopkeepers used the money to maintain their family, or that they used it to buy other goods. A month later, at the end of the teaching programme, the majority of subjects said that shopkeepers had to take account of wholesale prices in deciding retail prices, even if not all the children were certain that retail prices had to be higher than wholesale prices. The majority of children could now also coordinate the notions of the shopkeeper's personal expenditure with the requirements of running their shop.

This latter problem was re-examined a year later in relation to agricultural production, and prior to the course many fourth-grade subjects (9–10 years) did not generalise to the farmer what they had learnt about the shopkeeper the previous year. After the course, however, the majority of children said that farmers devoted a part of the money they received from the sale of their products to maintaining themselves and their families, and a part to the acquisition of seeds, fertilizers and tools. This fourth-grade course also enabled children to realise some progress in relation to distribution. Prior to the course they identified only the points of departure and arrival of goods; afterwards they also identified various intermediaries (wholesalers, transporters). The most difficult question for the fourth-grade children remained that of price fluctuations, for which no significant progress occurred.

Even at the beginning of the fifth grade, children (10–11 years) continued to give erroneous explanations for the reduction in prices during sales and for the lower costs of goods for the larger stores than for small shops. They believed that shopkeepers arranged sales as a gesture of goodwill towards their customers, or simply in order to follow a current trend. Many children believed that as a rule sale prices were lower than wholesale prices. The majority of children also believed that the big stores 'could sell for less because they sell a lot' and that 'they sell a lot because they sell for less', without being able to explain how this was possible. After the course children understood that one of the reasons for clearance sales was the necessity for disposing of excess stock before taking in fresh supplies, and that the lower prices did not, as a rule, fall below cost. A large proportion of the subjects had also understood that the lower prices charged by large stores depended on the lower wholesale costs of goods bought in great quantities directly from the factory, and on lower overheads.

As well as confirming the possibility of teaching basic economic concepts to children as young as 8–10 years old, these results also indicate a fundamental validity for these particular didactic strategies. The conclusion which could be drawn about the reasons for any of these observed developments was, however, limited by the absence of any control group in this study.[10] This was particularly problematic for those themes for which there did not exist any cross-sectional data, such as the question of price fluctuations. In some cases, therefore, it was not possible to establish whether the particular efficacy of this teaching programme was linked to its implementation at a particularly favourable developmental moment (in other words to the concomitant development of general abilities such as the interpretation of information or drawing inferences). The qualitative analysis of transitions between levels did, however, produce some interesting points for future research. We have been able to observe, for instance, that not all the levels identified through cross-sectional studies had the same degree of 'psychological reality'. Some beliefs, such as the idea that price depends on the quality of goods or that low prices in some shops reflect their ability to 'sell a lot', are very resistant. Not only did several children maintain these beliefs in spite of the instruction, but there were also children who *acquired* these beliefs during the course; these data also provide reinforcement for the arguments in favour of construing the development of economic understanding in terms of stages. Other children

[10] From the second year of this teaching programme the children were no longer comparable with their contemporaries who had received no instruction in economics. Thus the only way of establishing control groups would have been to have started with a larger number of classes so as to have been able to reduce the number of classes participating in the teaching programme in each successive year. Such a strategy was not feasible for two reasons. First it would have involved greatly increased research costs. Secondly, and more importantly, unacceptable discriminations would have had to have been made between teachers taking part in the study thereby creating a situation not at all conducive to the aims of a project involving the application of curricula by teachers themselves.

passed directly from primitive beliefs to correct ideas between pre- and post-teaching interviews. It is not possible to establish if these children passed through the intermediate levels in the two months which elapsed between the interviews, or if, more simply, the teaching programmes enabled children to acquire the more developed conceptions through different cognitive routes than those identified from the sequences described in the cross-sectional studies.

Another point which emerged from this study was the coexistence in children at a given age of beliefs of different levels in relation to similar problems, though applied to different contents. The testing of third-grade children, for instance, showed that the majority was able to generalise to a hairdresser the idea, which they had been taught in relation to the shopkeeper, that earnings contributed both towards living expenses as well as enabling their work to continue. These children were not able, however, to generalise this idea to the farmer. This again confirms the hypothesis we have put forward many times that 'economic thought' does not exist as a general notion which develops globally from one age to the next, but that it consists, rather, in a series of distinct economic notions which develop relatively independently for each child according to their experience and their individual capacity.

7.6   Developmental transitions in the construction of economic understanding

Research like the curricular study reported in the previous section shows that children can learn economic notions through educational interventions. Such research does not, however, identify which of the various activities included within the curricula are effective, nor which processes associated with children modifying their ideas or acquiring new ones. To understand the processes through which children's economic concepts become modified one needs to turn to research which has examined this specific issue. Unfortunately, the literature on this point is particularly scarce, and consists more of speculations than hard evidence in favour of one or another hypothesis.

The first hypotheses about developmental processes in the formation of economic concepts were those formulated by Furth (1980) and Jahoda (1979) in response to some aspects of the data produced in their research. Both authors noted that some children appeared to construct their responses in the course of the interview rather than expressing already formulated concepts. Sometimes these children arrived at the correct solution to a question they had been asked after a silent pause and then a sudden illumination typical of a new insight; at other times they were able to give correct responses at the end of the interview thereby contradicting their own earlier erroneous statements. An example of the first type is a child interviewed by Jahoda (1979) about the way in which a shopowner obtains the money to pay the shop assistant. Only after a pause and a sudden illumination did the child exclaim 'from the till!' with the tone of someone who had just made a discovery. In his research on banking Jahoda (1981) records various examples of the second type. In order to assess the impact of the study itself on the level of children's thinking Jahoda asked the question about the bank's source of money twice, once at the beginning of the interview and once at the end after the child had also been asked about deposits and loans. A significant number of subjects reached the correct solution to the problem only when it was asked for the second time; it was only at this point that they were able to say that people who borrowed money from the bank had to repay a little more than they had borrowed. Jahoda drew the following conclusions:

> When speculating about the factors prompting the transitions from one level to the next, Piaget's concept of equilibrium is relevant. He would maintain that two elements of knowledge continue to co-exist in isolation until there is some tension or conflict, in which an external source is always in some way involved; this then leads to a restructuring, bringing the elements into a relationship. In the present study it was apparent that the stimulus was often the interview itself. (Jahoda, 1979, p. 125)

According to Jahoda, then, for the restructuration which leads to the acquisition of more advanced levels of thinking to occur, children need to be already in possession of some items of correct knowledge, which only need to be integrated with each other. Moreover, for this integration to take place, the children need to have reached a level of cognitive development which makes them aware of contradictions and provides them with the operations required for integrating separate pieces of information. In his study on the bank Jahoda (1981) added some clarifications to this argument. He emphasised there that children made progress through the course of the interview only if their initial conceptions permitted them to experience a degree of uncertainty when faced with the interviewer's questions, since it was this uncertainty which constituted the stimulus to search for correct solutions. Thus, for example, children who were convinced that the bank obtained money from the government could not ask themselves any questions about the source of a bank's profits; the same could be said of those children who believed that banks merely look after money deposited in them. Another obstacle to full understanding is the persistence of interpersonal norms of equality and reciprocity. Children who are convinced that it is not fair to ask for more money to be repaid than was lent will not be able to answer questions about the bank's source of money, even if they understand the problem.

As we noted in Chapter 1, Furth also stresses the importance of conflict and the process of equilibration. Indeed each of the stages in his proposed sequence is characterised by a different degree of awareness of contradiction and the ability to construct ever more equilibrated conceptual systems. As has already been noted, Furth (1980) argues that those children classified in stages 1 and 2 have only a very limited need for logical coherence, and it is therefore difficult for them to grasp the contradictions in their own ideas or to be sensitive to conflict. At subsequent levels the construction of coherent economic concepts takes place according to the same scheme suggested by Jahoda. This is not to say, however, that Furth considers young children entirely insensitive to contradictions and unable to put into effect any active force for changing and enlarging their understanding. As well as producing playful types of ideas, or just passively accepting reality as it appears to them, young children, too, ask themselves some questions and try to find answers for them. While this may give rise to mistaken conceptions (such as the idea that adults get pocket money in the same way as do children), it nevertheless demonstrates young children's capacity to go beyond direct experience and to infer events which they cannot see.

> a more detailed consideration is in order of those situations that indicate spontaneous thinking and especially expanding progress in societal understanding (developmental experiences). The children on their own ask questions that reveal an internal conflict and come up with a relevant answer (at least to them); they express discontent about their own opinions and correct themselves or hesitate in an otherwise fairly fluent conversation: they expressly volunteer their gap in understanding and get excited as they discover a new insight. These are some occasions when the process of equilibration is particularly active in the children. In response to an internal disturbance they reach out toward a new balance. (Furth, 1980, p. 91.)

Thus both Furth and Jahoda depict the child as the principal protagonist of the developmental process; the role of adults is that of offering support, which means sometimes giving answers to questions which children themselves have posed, at other times stimulating children's reflections.

This hypothesis has recently been taken up by Sik Hung Ng (1983) in a study which replicated, with some modifications, Jahoda's (1981) research on the bank. Ng's aims included testing the hypothesis that conflicts between the responses expressed by children through the course of an interview might lead to an understanding of how the bank makes a profit. He was also interested in finding out if the notion of profit, once it had been understood in relation to the bank would be generalised to retail trade, and if the lack of any understanding of the notion of profit could be the result of the absence of a differentiation between the socio-economic and physical domains. In the physical domain the principle of conservation holds that a certain quantity remains invariant if nothing is added to it nor subtracted from it. According to Ng:

> Mastery of the conservation principle, however, does not automatically lend help to the understanding of profit, for the very nature of profit implies that goods, money and values are there to be changed and manipulated economically. In the absence of a differentiation between the socio-economic and the physical domains, the conservation principle would actually handicap the understanding of profit. (Ng, 1983, p. 271.)

Only by differentiating the physical domain from that of economic relations can the child understand that a given sum deposited in a bank will have increased a year later. In our view, however, Ng formulates this problem inaccurately. The conservation principle is just as valid for money as it is for any other object. What is crucial here is that money does not remain unused in a bank, but is employed in economic activities that yield profits; it is precisely for this reason that money deposited in a bank accumulates in value, which does not contradict the conservation principle.

A fourth aim of Ng's study was to see if children differentiated the sphere of interpersonal relationships (such as friendship) from that of societal relationships, and if any such differentiation helped them to distinguish the norms which regulate the lending of things between friends from those which regulate bank loans.

Ng's interviews on buying and selling and on the bank were based on those undertaken by Jahoda (1979, 1981). His subjects were 100 Hong Kong children aged 6 to 13 years. Half of the subjects were also asked questions intended to promote an understanding of the functioning of the bank, at least among those children who had already differentiated between societal, interpersonal and physical domains. These questions were asked at the beginning of the interview. The first concerned the amount of money a child might find in their piggy bank a year after having saved $50. The second question asked how much money a child would have to give back to a friend from whom they had borrowed $5. The hypothesis underlying this procedure was that children who had already differentiated the societal domain from the physical would feel dissatisfied with the idea that money deposited in a bank would remain unchanged in the same way as money kept in the piggy bank; something similar was expected to occur for those children who already had a knowledge of the difference between relations among friends and relations with an institution such as the bank. Both of these comparisons were expected to provide an intellectual stimulus toward a more mature reconstruction of the profit relationship between interest on loans and interest on deposits. But in fact this hypothesis was not confirmed by the results of the study.

The results did, however, support the hypothesis that the conflict arising from different responses given at different points during the interview would lead children toward an understanding of how the bank makes a profit. The conflict was provoked in the same way as in Jahoda's (1981) study, and Ng's finding of significant progress agrees with those results. Progress was most noticeable among children whose conceptions were initially at an intermediate level. Finally, the results for the hypothesis that a notion of profit in a bank would generalise to buying and selling were rather uncertain and difficult to interpret.

These studies by Jahoda (1981) and Ng (1983) lead to the conclusion that intrapersonal conflict between different bits of knowledge possessed by children may engender developments in the notion of profit. However it is not clear from these studies how effective or durable any such progress may be, since the comparisons they report were separated by only a few minutes in time. Both the idea of equilibration and these kind of learning studies based on conflict are derived from Piagetian theory which would suggest that the evaluation of a training procedure requires the retesting of children after a period of several weeks. If they have indeed formed a firm grasp of a concept it will also be apparent in the later post-tests (cf. Inhelder, Sinclair and Bovet, 1975). Moreover, since learning through conflict was not compared with any other procedure, these studies do not indicate if conflict is really the most relevant process in the development of children's economic understanding (as Jahoda, Furth and Ng have all argued).

Another approach to the study of cognitive development, also based on Piagetian theory, emphasises interpersonal rather than intrapersonal conflict. According to this approach children reconstruct and coordinate their understanding when they have to coordinate their own actions and their own ideas with those of other people who hold a different perspective (Doise and Mugny, 1984). The influence of interpersonal conflict on the development of economic concepts has recently been examined by Gerardo Echeita (1985) in a study of the acquisition of the understanding of shopkeepers' profit among a sample of Spanish children aged 6–9 years. All the children were individually pre-tested in an interview which examined their understanding of buying and selling and of profit. The children were then combined in groups of three for a buying and selling game. Two of the children took on the roles of shopkeepers, the joint owners of the same shop, while the third child played the role of the customer. The experimenter took on the role of the supplier from whom the shopkeepers had to obtain the goods. Once this had been done the two shopkeepers had to decide together on the price to charge for the goods. At the end of the game the experimenter asked what they had based their price on, if they had made a profit and, if so, how much. Three different experimental conditions were established by varying the combinations of children participating as shopkeepers in each game according to their performance on the pre-test. In each case one of the children was convinced that retail prices should be equal to wholesale prices. In one condition their partner also believed that the shopkeeper would sell goods for the same as their cost price; in this situation there was, therefore, only a minimal possibility of children experiencing an interpersonal conflict whose resolution might lead to the change in their understanding. In the second condition, however, the partner was a child who believed that shopkeepers fix prices arbitrarily; they might, then, mention an increase in retail over wholesale prices but without understanding the necessity for any such increase. This condition could, therefore, generate interpersonal conflict, and one could expect, therefore, that it would lead to change and development in children's ideas. The third condition presented a partner who understood clearly the notion of profit. Echeita expected this situation to produce the most dramatic developments since the conflict of ideas between the children was at its highest. Finally the children who took on the role of the customer constituted a fourth experimental group. These children were able to witness the discussions of the 'shopkeepers' without having to be a party to their decision and without having to express their own point of view. The members of this group could, then, also experience a conflict by noticing that their friends expressed ideas different from their own. In this case, however, the conflict would be attenuated because the children of this group did not themselves participate in the interpersonal interactions. Changes in children's understanding were examined in individual post-tests carried out 4–6 weeks after the game, and the four experimental groups were compared with a control group who were given pre- and post-tests but did not participate in any of the game sessions.

As expected, the children who participated in the situation of greatest conflict (condition 3) showed the most progress. In the other two conditions where children were exposed to a partner with more advanced conceptions than their own (conditions 2 and 4) subjects also showed some progress, even if it was generally less than in condition 3. No progress was apparent, however, in children who participated in condition 1 where they interacted with another child who shared their conviction that retail and wholesale prices were the same. Another interesting aspect of these results was that it was among the older children (8–9 years) that most progress was observed. This suggests that there are cognitive prerequisites without which children are unable to take advantage of experiences of interpersonal conflict or exposure to points of view different from their own.

Various conclusions can be drawn from this study. First, situations of conflict can stimulate children to take account of the existence of other points of view and to modify their own. In this study the conflict was determined by children having to reach agreement on a decision with a partner who held a different point of view. The fact that the most progress was recorded among children who interacted with partners who already understood profit correctly could be due, as Echeita suggests, to the fact that in this case the conflict was at its strongest, though it might equally well arise because in this case children were confronted with a correct understanding rather than having to discover it for themselves. The progress made by those children who participated only as customers indicates that mere exposure to different points of view can lead to progress even without any active participation in the interaction leading to a decision. According to Echeita children in this condition made only slight progress, and the results did not reach a conventional level of significance. However this group also included children who had witnessed discussions between two 'shopkeepers' who were both convinced that retail prices were equal to wholesale prices. Echeita does not record whether the 'customers' who witnessed interactions between two shopkeepers who disagreed showed a different degree of progress than that of their friends who took an active part in the discussions. Thus, this research does not establish whether children's progress is due to the interpersonal conflict engendered by the necessity of having to reach a decision in common with a companion who held a different point of view, or the simple fact of coming to recognise the existence of ideas distinct from their own.

7.7   Necessary prerequisites for acquiring the notion of profit

Is conflict, whether inter- or intra-personal, a necessary condition for progress in children's economic understanding? The research reviewed in the preceding section does not lead to such a strong conclusion, nor even to a weaker version which suggests that some form of conflict, and the self-constructive processes which it engenders, increases the opportunities for children to realise some progress. Evidence for either version of the hypothesis requires comparison between a situation of conflict with a second situation in which children are explicitly given the correct information without having to reconstruct it or discover it for themselves. The efficacy of this type of 'tutorial' intervention, in which an adult directly tells the child the information or rule, has been documented in various fields (Brainerd, 1978). We have also participated in a study which examined the effectiveness of this procedure for economic concepts (Berti, Bombi and De Beni, 1986).

This latter study attempted to encourage the acquisition of an understanding of shopkeeper's profits among children aged 8–9 years attending the third grade of elementary school. A 'tutorial' type of intervention was compared with a 'conflict inducing' situation derived from the procedures used by Inhelder, Sinclair and Bovet (1975). The two training procedures were given to different groups of children, each of whom had already been interviewed in a pre-test which examined their understanding of buying and selling, of how shopkeepers fix their prices and what they do with the money received from customers. Children who said that shopkeepers sell goods which they had themselves bought were also tested to see if they already understood the notion of profit. The interviewer showed them a handkerchief and said she had bought it that morning for 1,000 Lire; she then asked the child how much the shopkeeper must have had to pay to have bought it. The pre-test thus served to exclude children who already understood profit. In addition children who were convinced that shopkeepers themselves made the goods they sold, or that they obtained them from a friend were also excluded since their ideas were too undeveloped to participate in the study. Following the pre-test, children were randomly assigned to one of three groups, each of which comprised 16 subjects. The first of these was a control group which was not exposed to either of the training procedures, while the children in the other two groups received either the tutorial or conflict-inducing training.

The aim of the conflict-inducing procedure was to provoke a conflict between the child's expectation that shopkeepers made a profit by selling goods at the same (or even a lower) price than they had paid for them, and a recognition that in this way shopkeepers would neither be able to earn a living nor replenish their shops. A buying and selling game was used in the attempt to generate this conflict. The child took the role of the customer, while two experimenters played the shopkeeper (who sold handkerchiefs) and her supplier. The children were encouraged to discover for themselves, or with the help of the experimenters when necessary, that the shopkeeper had to charge a higher price than she had paid, if she was to be able to meet both kinds of expenses, personal and business. The procedure can be seen in greater detail in the extracts from the protocols given below.

The tutorial training also used a buying and selling game, though in this case the experimenter explained that the shopkeepers increased the retail price so as to receive more money than they had paid for the goods, and that some of their earnings was spent on buying new goods and some on personal expenses.

Children's comprehension was evaluated immediately after the training phase by asking them how shopkeepers made money, and also a month later by repeating the pre-test interview on buying and selling, though with the question about the price of a handkerchief replaced by a question about the price of a pen.

Analysis of the comprehension tests showed no significant differences between the two groups; for both types of training a little more than half the children said that the shopkeepers increase their prices. In both groups there were qualitative differences in children's responses. Some children simply described the whole game they played, including the price increase, while others focused their answers more clearly on the central point saying that 'shopkeepers raise the price', or even explaining that this is necessary in order to make money. The remaining children did not acquire anything at all from the training, and simply said that 'shopkeepers sell', or described the game without mentioning the price increase. The post-test results also made clear the similarities between the two experimental groups, both of whom performed better than the control group on the questions about how shopkeepers fix their prices. The children who had undergone the conflict-inducing training did not perform significantly better than those exposed to the tutorial training. Moreover, although the progress recorded was sufficient to reach a statistical level of significance, it was generally not very dramatic. Only 13 out of 32 children reached a more or less complete understanding of the question of profit.

A first conclusion to be drawn from these results is that the mode of intervention chosen by the adult – giving information or inducing conflict in the child – is not the decisive variable in engendering development in the understanding of profit. Indeed both types of intervention were shown to be effective to a similar degree. There are other important influences at work, and one needs to ask why so many children were not even able to repeat immediately after the training that shopkeepers increase their prices, and also why these procedures did not lead to any stable understanding of profit for a large number of subjects. The behaviour of children during the conflict-inducing training revealed various difficulties which obstructed their ability to arrive at a correct notion of profit by themselves. It seems likely that these difficulties were similar to those which prevented children from understanding profit on the basis of information given by the experimenter during the tutorial training. Many of these problems can be seen in the following training-phase interview.

CRISTIAN (8:7) has several 500 Lire and 1,000 Lire notes available to him; the shopkeeper has only ten 1,000 Lire notes which she counts out with the child so as to draw his attention to how many she has. The shopkeeper then turns to the supplier and buys ten handkerchiefs at 1,000 Lire each, so spending all her money. Then she has to decide the selling price for the handkerchiefs according to whatever ideas the child has previously expressed. Cristian had said that the selling price should be equal to the price paid to the supplier. The child is then allowed to buy handkerchiefs until all ten have been sold. The shopkeeper then begins the following conversation – *Did I make any money? – Yes. – Do I have more money now than I had before, or less, or the same amount? – (Cristian counts the number of handkerchiefs* he has bought) *You sold me 10 handkerchiefs, now you have ten 1,000 Lire notes.* – Is that more, or less, or the same as I had before? – *The same.* – I made money even though I have the same amount of money as before? – *Yes.* – With this money I have to buy myself something to eat, some clothes and some more handkerchiefs, otherwise I'll have to close the shop. Do you think there's enough? – *Yes.* – Are you sure? – *Yes, you just need 4 notes to buy something to eat, and with the other 6 you can buy 6 handkerchiefs.* – Let's see. We'll put these 4 notes over here and pretend that they aren't mine anymore because I used them to buy something to eat. With the other notes I'll buy the handkerchiefs. The experimenter does this, and sells handkerchiefs to the boy until she has none left. Then she asks him again – Did I make any money? – *Yes.* – How much? – *6,000 Lire.* – Now I have to spend money again just like the last time. If I put 4 of these 1,000 Lire notes over there I'll have only 2 left to buy handkerchiefs. Do you think that would be all right? – *No.* – What could I do then? – *Buy the handkerchiefs and then sell them.* – (the shopkeeper buys two handkerchiefs from the supplier and then sells them to the boy) And now? – *2,000 Lire . . . you always have 2,000 Lire left.* – But I also have to buy myself something to eat! How am I going to manage? What do shopkeepers usually do? – *When they've finished the money and they don't have enough things, they go and get some more money.* – Where? – *I think they go and ask their husbands.* – But if he gives it to me and I carry on as I have been doing, it will all end up just as it is now. – *. . . then the shopkeeper changes the price.* – How? – *Take away the first price they put, put another and throw the first one away.* – What price should I put? – *2,000.* The experimenter does just this and then shows the boy that in this way she ends up with more money than she had had initially to buy the 10 handkerchiefs. She is then able to divide the money she has into two piles, one for buying another 10 handkerchiefs, and the other for buying the things she needs to live.

Even though he himself had suggested that the shopkeeper increase her price at the end of the training session, a month later in the post-test Cristian said that shopkeepers usually sell goods at the same price they had paid for them 'because that seems fair to them', though sometimes shopkeepers did sell at a slightly higher price 'to make more money'. He continues to say that even by selling at the same price shopkeepers would have enough money to replenish their stocks as well as taking care of their personal needs. In the pre-test Cristian did not mention any increase between wholesale and retail price. The training has, therefore, modified his conceptions, but only in a limited and superficial way. Indeed Cristian demonstrates that he has not understood that an increase in price is necessary since he speaks about it only as an occasional event and is unable to produce the actual reasons why it occurs. He has not acquired the notion of profit.

What prevented Cristian acquiring a stable understanding of profit? An examination of his behaviour during the training session provides some answers to this question, even if they are only partial and tentative. First of all Cristian was not immediately aware that, by selling the handkerchiefs at the same price she had paid for them, the shopkeeper would only receive the same amount of money as she had paid. Indeed Cristian only reached the correct solution after counting the handkerchiefs and calculating how much money she had made. This behaviour might be the result of the child forgetting how the price of handkerchiefs was fixed; or it might signify that he lacked the general understanding that if goods are sold at the same price for which they were bought, then costs and income will be equal; finally it could be that although Cristian did possess such an understanding he was unable to access it easily. The data from this study do not allow us to choose between these alternative explanations. They do, however, suggest a hypothesis: children do not grasp the necessity of increasing prices because they lack the understanding that if goods are sold at the same price for which they were bought, shopkeepers will *always* end up with the same amount of money as that with which they began. Only 10 of the 16 children who participated in the conflict-inducing training understood immediately the equivalence between money spent and money received. The others had to compare the two quantities, and in some cases they were able to do so only through the experimenter's suggestions.

Cristian's later responses, however, showed that understanding the equality of costs and income is not enough to realise that the shopkeeper still does not have sufficient money for both the shop and her personal expenses. Even while believing in the equality of retail and wholesale prices Cristian continued to say that the shopkeeper's income could be divided in two parts, one to be used for restocking the shop and the other for personal expenses. During the training, 10 of the 16 children expressed the same idea, and it was necessary to act out this procedure in order to show them that the shopkeeper would eventually run out of money. The other 6 children understood by themselves that the shopkeeper would not have enough money. However not even this understanding, whether they reached it themselves or with the help of the experimenter, was sufficient for the child to understand the necessity for the shopkeeper to raise the retail price. As we saw, Cristian at this point turned back to suggesting a source of money external to buying and selling, the shopkeeper's husband. In all, 11 children proposed erroneous solutions. Some suggested turning to the bank, or to friends, or charitable people.

GIANFRANCO (8:11), for instance, said at the beginning of the session that the shopkeeper received more money than she had started with – More? How much did I have before? – *10 . . . oh, no, no, it was right the way it was before.* – So did I make any money? – *No, because you have the same price you had when you had the other money. You haven't made any money at all.* – What can I do with this money? – *You can either get something to eat or get some more handkerchiefs. If you had some more money you could buy something to eat and some more handkerchiefs, so that you could sell them and then get some more money.* – How do shopkeepers manage to avoid this situation? – *They go to the bank and ask for a loan.* – Could they do it in any other way? – *No ... they could ask for charity.* Gianfranco could not suggest any other solutions, and so the experimenter had to suggest that the shopkeeper could raise the price. In the post-test Gianfranco repeated what he had said in the pre-test: shopkeepers sell things at the same price they had paid for them, otherwise their customers would think they were thieves, and that this arrangement also produces enough money for them.

Both Gianfranco and Cristian spoke about sources of money external to retail trade. Other children suggested different solutions, such as reducing money spent on personal expenses, or buying fewer handkerchiefs. Others even suggested a temporary closure of the shop or the suspension of payments to the supplier when the shopkeeper had to support personal expenses. All of these ideas were contradicted by the experimenter.

By the end of their training sessions 10 children had themselves suggested increasing the price. Others, like Gianfranco, could not come up with any solution to the problem of the shopkeeper's accounts. In these cases it was the experimenter who explained the solution to them. There was however no difference on the post-test between those children who had reached the solution for themselves and those to whom it had had to be explained. Among the other responses given during the training sessions, only the immediate understanding of the equivalence between costs and earnings was correlated with success on the post-test. Whether or not children produced wrong answers did not influence their post-test performance.

On the whole, the results of this study suggest that, from the point of view of understanding profit, it does not matter if children receive correct information from adults of if they are able by themselves to reorganise their ideas after discovering some internal contradiction. What does seem to be important is whether or not children possess the prerequisites which enable them to understand fully the significance of pertinent information. Only when these prerequisites have been acquired are children capable of a stable understanding of profit, whether it is an adult who gives them information, or whether they work out the solution for themselves. One prerequisite suggested by this study is the necessity for children to understand that if shopkeepers sell goods at the same price they buy them then their income and expenditure will *always* be equal.

If this conclusion is correct, then future research on the development of economic concepts needs to address itself to the identification of those notions and abilities which constitute the prerequisites for the acquisition of specific economic ideas, rather than trying to clarify the effects of a general process as difficult to operationalise as equilibration. Until recently this issue has received little attention. Some research has sought to identify the relations between economic concepts and general logico-mathematical abilities as measured by Piagetian tasks, or between economic notions and conceptions of interpersonal relations. Jahoda (1984b) found no evidence of any sharp distinction separating economic from logico-mathematical thinking; the correlation obtained between these two sets of measures was of much the same magnitude as those reported for interrelationships among sets of logico-mathematical and physical problems. Maria Wong (1985) found that the notion of reciprocity appeared earlier in conceptions of friendship than it did in conceptions relating active and passive interest in banking. The two notions of reciprocity were not correlated, however, when the effect for age was partialled out. This suggest that these two notions develop along different paths rather than the one being a prerequisite for the other.

Both Jahoda and Wong found only a weak link between economic thinking and thinking in other fields, a fact which we would argue arises because the notions compared were not really pertinent to one another. The Piagetian tasks used by Jahoda had no precise link with the economic notions examined; and it is not clear in Wong's study why an idea of friendship as a relation based on reciprocal help and cooperation should be considered as a prerequisite for understanding that the bank can pay interest only because it earns profits from deposits.

A first exploration of the specific abilities necessary for an understanding of profit has been made in a recent study (Berti and De Beni, 1986) which examined how children at different ages made the comparisons between costs and income. This study also sought to establish if an immediate understanding that costs and income will be equal if shopkeepers sell at the same price they buy constitutes a prerequisite for understanding the idea of shopkeepers' profit. 59 children aged between 7–8 and 9–10 years were interviewed using a procedure similar to that described in the preceding study (Berti, Bombi and De Beni, 1986). To examine how children made the comparison between costs and income they were given an illustrated book which showed a greengrocer who bought baskets of strawberries which he then sold at the same price. The transactions made by various customers were shown as were the amounts of money they paid. At the end the greengrocer had no strawberries left. At this point the child had to say if the greengrocer had received more, or less, or the same amount of money as he had spent. The responses showed that there were four different ways of making the comparison between costs and income, and that they could be ordered in a sequence of levels.

At the first level children do not apply arithmetical rules or carry out any arithmetical operations; they say that the shopkeeper has got more money because 'so many people came to buy', or that he has the same amount as before because 'he had a lot and now he still has a lot'. At the second level children try to add together the sums paid by each customer in order to calculate how much money the shopkeeper has made. Although surprised to discover that he received as much as he had paid originally, they cannot give any justification for this result. A correct explanation for this fact comes from children at the third level who say that it is because the shopkeeper sold the strawberries at the same price he had paid for them. At Level three, then, children show that they have a grasp of the general rule even if they had not applied it immediately. Only at Level four do children use this rule instantly and say straightaway that costs and income will be the same, without making any calculation. They are also able to give a correct explanation as to why this should be so.

The performance of children in making the comparison between costs and income was related to the level of their understanding of profit, even when the effect for age was partialled out. Moreover only one of the children who understood the notion of profit was unable to give an explanation for the equivalence of costs and income. On the other hand some children who performed at Levels 3 and 4 in making the comparison did not yet have an understanding of profit. It seems, therefore, that the ability to make the comparison between costs and income is a prerequisite for an understanding of profit.

7.8 Epilogue

As a finale to this review of research into children's economic thinking, it is appropriate to give a brief evaluation of the results and to offer a reflection on what remains to be done. As we have seen, the majority of studies undertaken have sought to identify and describe children's economic conceptions. Rather fewer studies have sought to identify the mechanisms through which these conceptions are transformed in the course of the child's development.

Even if descriptive studies have been more common, the picture of children's economic ideas is still incomplete. These studies have examined how children represent various economic roles and connect them with one another in relations of exchange, or order them according to their perceived income. On the whole these studies have shown how children come to recognise and relate these roles firstly in pairs, and later in a wider framework. However, all of these conceptions, including even the most developed ones, remain at some distance from the real world of economics in which the most prominent phenomena result from the cumulative effects of the decisions and actions of innumerable economic subjects (Leiser, 1983). How do children come to perceive such phenomena and to understand that a complex of individual decisions can produce effects which appear to have an impersonal force? This is a theme which has yet to be tackled.

This is one direction which we think future research ought to take by studying older subjects than those who have been considered up to now. Such research would necessarily be different from the kind of work presented in this book. The questions posed to subjects would have to have a hypothetical nature; it is indeed through hypothetico-deductive thinking that questions about the dynamics of economics can be considered (what, for instance, can the producers of a certain type of goods do if the price drops?). Moreover, as they get older, children come into contact with increasingly differentiated sources of economic information, so that in research with older subjects it would be necessary to know something about these sources. In Italy, for example, the new syllabus for secondary schools (which cover the ages of 11 to 14 years) presents economic information in the context of history and geography. Not all teachers give the same time and space to these topics and, in addition, the textbooks they use also vary in the type of information they provide, its quantity and quality. One can, therefore, assume that there are also considerable differences in the concepts which children develop. These differences will increase over the coming years as children have the opportunity to choose between different kinds of schools, only some of which will include economics studies.

Another direction which we think research should follow concerns the processes through which economic concepts develop. Existing experimental studies in this field have considered only concepts of profit for shopkeepers and for the bank. Their main concern has been to examine the role of conflict in cognitive development. Studies of the transformations of other economic notions need to be undertaken, as well as more research on the contribution which 'tutorial' interventions might make to such changes. The difference between economic understanding and the kind of logico-mathematical concepts studied by Piaget is that economic concepts are constructed largely on the basis of information derived from adults and the mass-media, rather than the child's own active exploration of the world. If one wants research to assist in the creation of suitable instruments, through which children might come to an understanding of economic events, then it is necessary to move away from emphasising the child's spontaneous and self-constructing activities towards finding the most efficient way of presenting educational interventions. Two distinct and parallel types of study are required in order to reach this objective: one is the examination in greater depth of the prerequisites necessary for understanding particular economic notions; the other is curricula studies which examine the impact of broader interventions. Though distinct, these two types of study are interrelated insofar as each needs to take into account the results obtained by the other.

The research we have reviewed here illustrates the long and complex road children travel in order to connect various aspects of the social world in which they live and to construct a realistic, even if simplified, image of it. Even those children who have reached the highest levels in the various sequences we have described still have a long way to go before they will understand the effective functioning of the economy. In fact the majority of adults who are not themselves economists remain far from any such understanding. More generally a complete understanding of those institutions (social, economic, political, juridical) which determine the life and destiny of individuals within a society is quite rare, and at least in Italy has never been the object of any adequate instruction. We hope that, in the years to come, research on children's understanding of economic reality, and society in general, will move from a description of what children come to understand when left to their own devices, to the construction of forms of educational intervention capable of leading children as well as adults towards a wider understanding of the complex world in which they live.

References

Adelson, J. and O'Neil, R.P., 1966, Growth of political ideas in adolescence: the sense of community. *Journal of Personality and Social Psychology*, 4, 295–306.

Ajello, A.M., Bombi, A.S., Pontecorvo, C. and Zuccchermaglio, C., 1986, Understanding agriculture as an economic activity: the role of figurative information. *European Journal of Psychology of Education*, 1, 67–80.

Ajello, A.M., Bombi, A.S., Pontecorvo, C. and Zuccchermaglio, C., 1987a, Teaching economics in the primary school: the concepts of work and profit. *International Journal of Behavioural Development*, 10, 51–69.

Ajello, A.M., Bombi, A.S., Pontecorvo, C. and Zuccchermaglio, C., 1987b, Prezzi alti, prezzi bassi: dove, quando e perchè? Risultati di un curricolo di economia in quinta elementare. (High prices, low prices: where, when and why? Results of an economics curriculum in fifth grade elementary schools). Unpublished manuscript.

Albertini, J.M. Leclercq, D., Silem, A., Koppen, E., and Ryba, R.H., 1983. *Enquete sur les Représentations des Jeunes Consumatores dans Quatre Pays de la Communauté Economique. Européene*. Lyons, France: CNRS, IRPEACS.

Asch, S., 1952, *Social Psychology*. Englewood Cliffs, N.J.: Prentice-Hall.

Baldus, B. and Tribe, V., 1978, The development of perception and evaluation of social inequality among public school children. *Canadian Review of Sociology and Anthropology*, 15, 50–60.

Bernstein, A.C. and Cowan, P.A., 1975, Children's concepts of how people get babies. *Child Development*, 46, 77–91.

Berti, A.E. and Bombi, A.S., 1981, The development of the concept of money and its value: a longitudinal study. *Child Development*, 52, 1179–82.

Berti, A.E. and Bombi, A.S. and De Beni, R., 1986a, Acquiring economic notions: profit. *International Journal of Behavioural Development*, 9, 15–29.

Berti, A.E. and Bombi, A.S. and De Beni, R., 1986b, The development of economic notions: single sequence or separate acquisition? *Journal of Economic Psychology*, 7, 415–24.

Berti, A.E. and Bombi, A.S. and Lis, A., 1982, The child's conceptions about means of production and their owner. *European Journal of Social Psychology*, 12, 221–39.

Berti, A.E. and De Beni, R., 1986, Logical and mnemonic prerequisites for the concept of profit. Paper presented to the Second European Conference on Developmental Psychology, Rome, Italy.

Brainerd, C.J., 1978, Learning research and Piagetian theory. In L.S. Siegal and C.J. Brainerd (eds): *Alternatives to Piaget*. New York: Academic Press.

Burris, V.L. 1983, Stages in the development of economic concepts. *Human Development*, 36, 791–812.

Case, R. 1985 *Intellectual Development from Birth to Adulthood*. New York: Academic Press.

Connell, R.W., 1971, *The Child's Construction of Politics*. Carlton, Vic.: Melbourne University Press.

Connell, R.W., 1977, *Ruling Class, Ruling Culture*. Melbourne: Cambridge University Press.

Cummings, S. and Taebel, D., 1978, The economic socialization of children: A neo-Marxist analysis. *Social Problems*, 26, 198–210.

Damon, W., 1977, *The Social World of the Child*. San Francisco: Jossey-Bass.

Danziger, K., 1957, The child's understanding of kinship terms: a study in the development of relational concepts. *Journal of Genetic Psychology*, 91, 213–32.

Danziger, K., 1958. Children's earliest conceptions of economic relations (Australia). *Journal of Social Psychology*, 47, 231–40.

Dasen, P. and Heron, A. 1981. Cross-cultural tests of Piaget's theory. In H.C. Triandis and A. Heron (eds): *Handbook of Cross-cultural Psychology*, 4. Boston: Allyn & Bacon.

Dickinson, J., 1984, Social representations of socio-economic structure. Paper presented to the London Conference of the British Psychological Society.

Doise, W. and Mugny, G., 1984, *The Social Development of the Intellect*. Oxford: Pergamon Press. (*Le Développement social de l'intelligence*. Paris: Inter-Editions, 1981.)

Duveen, G. and Shields, M., 1983, Young children's understanding of money and banks. Unpublished paper, University of London Institute of Education.

Duveen, G. and Shields, M., 1984, The influence of gender on the development of young children's representations of work roles. Paper presented to the First European Conference on Developmental Psychology, Groningen, The Netherlands.

Echeita, G., 1985, El mundo adulto en la mente de los ninos. La comprension infantil de las relaciones de intercambio y el efecto de la interaccion social sobre su desarollo. (The adult world in children's minds. Children's comprehension of exchange relations and the effect of social interaction on their development.) Unpublished doctoral thesis, University of Madrid.

Emiliani, F. and Carugati, F., 1985, *Il Mondo Sociale dei Bambini*. (*The Social World of Children*) Bologna: Il Mulino.

Emler, N, and Dickinson, J., 1985, Children's representations of economic inequalities: the effect of social class. *British Journal of Developmental Psychology*, 3, 191–8.

Flavell, J.H., 1963, *The Developmental Psychology of Jean Piaget*. Princeton, N.J.: D. Van Nostrand & Co. Inc.

Flavell, J.H. and Ross, L. (eds), 1981, *Social Cognitive Development*. Cambridge: Cambridge University Press.

Furby, L., 1978a, Possession in humans: an exploratory study of its meaning motivation. *Social Behaviour and Personality*, 6, 49–65.

Furby, L., 1978b, Possessions: toward a theory of their meaning and function throughout the life cycle. In P.B. Baltes (ed): *Life Span Development and Behaviour*, 1, New York: Academic Press.

Furby, L., 1979, Inequalities in personal possession: explanations for and judgements about unequal distribution. *Human Development*, 22, 180–202.

Furnham, A., 1982, The perception of poverty among adolescents. *Journal of Adolescence*, 5, 135–47.

Furth, H.G. 1979. How the child understands social institutions. In F. Murray (ed): *The Impact of Piagetian Theory*. Baltimore: University Park Press.

Furth, H.G. 1980. *The World of Grown-ups*. New York: Elsevier.

Furth, H.G., Baur, M. and Smith, J.E. (1976) Children's conceptions of social institutions: a Piagetian framework. *Human Development*, 19, 351–74.

Goldstein, B. and Oldham, J., 1979, *Children and Work: A Study of Socialization*. New Brunswick, N.J.: Transaction Books.

Greenstein, F.I., 1969, *Children and Politics*. New Haven: Yale University Press.

Heider, F., 1958, *The Psychology of Interpersonal Relations*. New York: Wiley & Sons.

Hong Kwan, T. and Stacey, B., 1981. The understanding of socio-economic concepts in Malaysian Chinese school children. *Child Study Journal*, 11, 33–49.

Inhelder, B. and Piaget, J., 1958, *The Growth of Logical Thinking from Childhood to Adolescence*. London: Routledge & Kegan Paul. (*De la Logique de l'enfant à la logique de l'adolescent*. Paris: P.U.F., 1955.)

Inhelder, B., Sinclair, H. and Bovet, M., 1975, *Learning and the Development of Cognition*. London: Routledge & Kegan Paul. (*Apprentissage et structures de la conaissance*. Paris: P.U.F., 1974.)

Jahoda, G., 1959, Development of the perception of social differences in children from six to ten. *British Journal of Psychology*, 50, 158–96.

Jahoda, G., 1979, The construction of reality by some Glaswegian children. *European Journal of Social Psychology*, 9, 115–27.

Jahoda, G., 1981, The development of thinking about economic institutions: the bank. *Cahiers de Psychologie Cognitive*, 1, 55–73.

Jahoda, G., 1983. European 'lag' in the development of an economic concept: a study in Zimbabwe. *British Journal of Developmental Psychology*, 1, 113–20.

Jahoda, G., 1984a, The development of thinking about socio-economic systems. In H. Tajfel (ed): *The Social Dimension*. Cambridge: Cambridge University Press.

Jahoda, G., 1984b, Levels of social and logico-mathematical thinking: their nature and inter-relations. In W. Doise and A. Palmonari (eds): *Social Interaction in Individual Development*. Cambridge: Cambridge University Press.

Jahoda, G. and Woerdenbagch, A., 1982. The development of ideas about an economic institution: a cross-national replication. *British Journal of Social Psychology*, 21, 337–8.

Kohlberg, L., 1963, The development of children's orientations toward a moral order: 1. Sequence in the development of moral thought. *Vita Humana*, 6, 11–33.

Kohlberg, L., 1969, Stage and sequence: the cognitive-developmental approach. In D.A. Goslin (ed): *Handbook of Socialization Theory and Research*. Chicago: Rand McNally.

Kourilsky, M., 1974, *Beyond Simulation: The Mind-society Approach to Instruction in*

Economics and Other Social Sciences. Los Angeles, Calif.: Educational Resource Association.

Kourilsky, M., 1981. Economic socialization of children: Attitude toward the distribution of rewards. *Journal of Social Psychology*, 115, 45–57.

Lea, S.E.G., Tarpy, R.M. and Webley, P., 1987, *The Individual in the Economy*. Cambridge: Cambridge University Press.

Leahy, R.L. 1981, The development of the conception of economic inequality: descriptions and comparisons of rich and poor people. *Child Development*, 52, 523–32.

Leahy, R.L. 1983, Development of the conception of economic inequality: II. Explanations, justifications and concepts of social mobility and change. *Developmental Psychology*, 19, 111–25.

Leiser, D., 1983, Children's conceptions of economics. The constitution of a cognitive domain. *Journal of Economic Psychology*, 4, 297–317.

Lewin, K., 1935, *A Dynamic Theory of Personality. Selected Papers*. New York: McGraw-Hill.

Lickona, T., 1976, (ed): *Moral Development and Behaviour*. New York: Holt, Rinehart and Winston.

Livesley, W.J. and Bromley, D.B., 1973. *Person Perception in Childhood and Adolescence*. London: Wiley.

Marx, K., 1966, Economic and philosophic manuscripts. In E. Fromm (ed): *Marx's Concept of Man*. New York: Unger.

Mead, G.H., 1934, *Mind, Self and Society*. Chicago: University of Chicago Press.

Miller, G.A. and Johnson-Laird, P., 1976, *Language and Perception*. Cambridge, Mass.: The Belknap Press of Harvard University.

Mookherjee, H.N. and Hogan, H.W., 1981, Class consciousness among young rural children. *Journal of Social Psychology*, 114, 91–8.

Moscovici, S., 1976, *La Psychanalyse, son image et son public. (Psychoanalysis, its Image and its Public.)* Paris: P.U.F.

Moscovici, S., 1984, On social representations. In R. Farr and S. Moscovici (eds): *Social Representations*. Cambridge University Press.

Nelson, K., 1981, Social cognition in a script framework. In J.H. Flavell and L. Ross (eds): *Social Cognitive Development*. Cambridge: Cambridge University Press.

Ng, S.H., 1982, Children's ideas about the bank and shop profit: developmental stages and influences of cognitive contrast and conflict. *Journal of Economic Psychology*, 4, 209–21.

Overton, W.F. (ed), 1983, *The Relationship Between Social and Cognitive Development*. Willsdale, N.J.: Erlbaum.

Parsons, T., 1960, *The Social System*. Glencoe, Ill.: The Free Press.

Petrillo, G. and Serion, C., 1983, *Bambini Che Lavorano. (Children Who Work.)* Milan: Angeli.

Piaget, J., 1926, *The Language and Thought of the Child*. London: Routledge & Kegan Paul. (*Le Langage et la pensée chez l'enfant*. Neuchatel: Delachaux et Niestle, 1923.)

Piaget, J., 1928. *Judgement and Reasoning in the Child*. London: Routledge & Kegan Paul. (*Le Jugement et le raisonnement chez l'enfant*. Neuchatel: Delachaux et Niestle, 1924.)

Piaget, J., 1929. *The Child's Conception of the World*. London: Routledge & Kegan Paul. (*La Representation du monde chez l'enfant*. Paris: P.U.F., 1926.)

Piaget, J., 1930, *The Child's Conception of Physical Causality*. London: Routledge & Kegan Paul. (*La Causalité physique chez l'enfant*. Paris: Alcan, 1927.)

Piaget, J., 1932, *The Moral Judgement of the Child*. London: Routledge & Kegan Paul. (*La Jugement morale chez l'enfant*. Paris: Alcan, 1932.)

Piaget, J., 1952, *The Child's Conception of Number*. London: Routledge & Kegan Paul. (*La Genèse du nombre chez l'enfant*. Neuchatel: Delachaux et Niestle, 1941.)

Piaget, J., 1969, *The Child's Conception of Time*. London: Routledge & Kegan Paul. (*Le Développement de la notion du temps chez l'enfant*. Paris: Alcan, 1946.)

Piaget, J., 1970, *The Child's Conception of Movement and Speed*. London: Routledge & Kegan Paul. (*Les Notions de movement et de vitesse chez l'enfant*. Paris: P.U.F., 1946.)

Piaget, J. and Inhelder, B., 1974, *The Child's Construction of Quantities*. London: Routledge & Kegan Paul. (*Le Développement des quantites physiques chez l'enfant*. Neuchatel: Delachaux et Niestle, 1941.)

Piaget, J. and Weil, A.M., 1951, The development in children of the idea of homeland, and of relations with other countries. *International Social Science Bulletin*, 3, 561–78.

Pinard, A. and Laurendeau, M., 1969, 'Stage' in Piaget's cognitive-developmental theory: exegesis of a concept. In D. Elkind and J.H. Flavell (eds): *Studies in cognitive development*. Oxford: Oxford University Press.

Pryor, J. and Day, J. (eds)., 1985, *The Development of Social Cognition*. New York: Springer Verlag.

Renshon, S.A., 1977, *Handbook of Political Socialization*. Glencoe, Ill.: The Free Press.

Rest, J., 1983, Morality. In P.H. Mussen (ed): *Handbook of Child Psychology*, 3, New York: Wiley.

Ryba, R., 1985, Some aspects of children's ecnomic thinking in the 11–16 age group. In D. Whitehead (ed): *Economics Education: Research and Development Issues*. London: Longman.

Searle, J.R., 1969, *Speech Acts*. Cambridge: Cambridge University Press.

Selman, R., 1976, A guide to educational and clinical practice. In T. Lickona (ed): *Moral Development and Behaviour*. New York: Holt, Rinehart & Winston.

Selman, R., 1980, *The Growth of Interpersonal Understanding: Developmental and Clinical Analysis*. New York: Academic Press.

Shantz, C.U., 1975, The development of social cognition. In E.M. Hetherington (ed): *Review of Child Development Theory and Research*, 5, Chicago: University of Chicago Press.

Shantz, C.U., 1983, Social cognition. In P.H. Mussen (ed): *Handbook of Child Psychology*, 3, New York: Wiley.

Siegal, M., 1981, Children's perceptions of adult economic needs. *Child Development*, 52, 379–82.

Siegler, R.S., 1981, Developmental sequences within and between concepts. *Monographs of the Society for Research in Child Development*, 47.

Stacey, B., 1978, *Political Socialization in Western Society*. London: Edward Arnold.

Stacey, B., 1982, Economic socialization in the pre-adult years. *British Journal of Social Psychology*, *21*, 159–73.

Stacey, B., 1985, Political socialization. *Annual Review of Political Science*. Norwood, N.J.: Ablex.

Stendler, C., 1949, *Children of Brasstown*. Urbana, Ill.: Bur. Res. and Serv. (University of Illinois).

Strauss, A., 1952, The development and transformation of monetary meaning in the child. *American Sociological Review*, *17*, 275–86.

Strauss, A., 1954, The development of conceptions of rules in children. *Child Development*, *25*, 193–208.

Sutton, R.S., 1962, Behavior in the attainment of economic concepts. *Journal of Psychology*, *5*, 37–46.

Turiel E., 1983, *The Development of Social Knowledge*. Cambridge: Cambridge University Press.

Vygotsky, L.S., 1986, *Thought and Language*. Cambridge, Mass.: MIT Press (originally published in 1934).

Ward, S., Wackman, D.B. and Wartella, E., 1977, *How Children Learn to Buy*. London: Sage.

Werner, H., 1948, *Comparative Psychology of Mental Development*. Chicago: Folet.

Whitehead, D. (ed), 1985, *Economics Education: Research and Development Issues*. London: Longman.

Wong, M.N., 1985, Children's construction of economic and social reality: development of understanding of banking operations and social relationships. Paper presented at the Eighth Biennial Meeting of the International Society for the Study of Behavioural Development, University of Tours, France.

Index

abstract, 9, 14–15, 18, 23, 53, 85,
    109, 129, 136, 170, 172, 185
action, 5–6, 19, 66, 113, 137, 175,
    206, 216
addition, 99, 120
Adelson, J., 135
adolescence, 13, 16, 18, 20, 22, 76,
    136, 164
adult, 2, 5–6, 10, 14–15, 17–18,
    25, 52, 58, 60, 76, 108, 110,
    132–3, 135, 137, 163–4,
    197–8, 204, 208, 210, 213,
    216–17
Africa, 187–8
age, 1–2, 12–13, 20–2, 27, 29n,
    41n, 54n, 60n, 67n, 68n, 78n,
    90n, 94, 99, 108, 114n, 125,
    130, 135n, 137n, 151, 168,
    174, 180, 190n, 192n, 193,
    198, 208
Agnelli, G., 191n
agriculture, 26, 27, 42, 46, 72, 90,
    168, 174, 176, 178, 183, 187,
    199
agricultural land, 162, 167, 170–1
agricultural production, 49, 51,
    130, 151–8 passim, 171, 199,
    200
Ajello, A.M., 198
Albertini, J.M., 188n
America, 2, 3, 54n, 188
animals, 45, 139, 157
Andreotti, G., 161n
anthropomorphism, 89
apple, 114–18, 120–5
arithmetic, 99, 107–8, 128, 214–15
artificialism, 52, 89, 94, 130, 134,
    141–3, 151, 160, 172, 177,
    179, 181
artisan, 92, 127, 130, 151, 178,
    180, 192n, 193, 195

Asch, S., 4
assimilation, 22, 39, 86–7, 92,
    192–3
association, 38, 163
asymmetric pairs, 51
asymmetric relations, 54, 137, 181
attitude, 2, 7, 71
Australia, 13, 22, 163, 188
authority, 35–6, 41, 53–8 passim,
    136, 181

Baldus, B., 11
Balestrazzi, C., 42n
bank, 10–11, 27, 30–6, 40,
    59–60, 62–3, 66–70, 75,
    78–87 passim, 114, 124,
    130–1, 146, 165, 168, 176,
    178, 181–8, 190–2, 196,
    203–6, 212–14, 216
banknote, 82, 100–1, 103, 107,
    177
Baur, M., 7, 10, 15, 88, 98, 124,
    130, 134
beauty, 109, 111
beliefs 21, 40, 84, 99, 105, 119,
    127–8, 202
Benetton, R., 54n
Beolchi, D., 41n
Bernstein, A.C., 94, 177
Berti, A.E., 7, 107, 197n, 208,
    214
Bombi, A.S., 7, 107, 197n, 208,
    214
book, 18, 52, 62, 109, 111, 147
Bordet, E., 133n
borrow, 79, 82, 84, 203
boss, 10–11, 19, 28–30, 33, 35–7,
    39, 43–5, 47, 51, 53–9, 65,
    67, 72, 83, 87, 116, 122,
    127–8, 130–1, 139, 142–5,
    147, 151–2, 153, 155,

158–60, 162–4, 168–74,
181–5
owner, 48, 54–8 *passim*, 139,
142, 145, 166, 168, 172
Bovet, M., 206, 209
bracelet, 109–11
Brainerd, C.J., 208
bricklayer, 30–1, 33, 47
Britain, 54n, 188, 189
Bromley, D.B., 4, 12
build, 31, 46, 48, 52–3, 56, 64,
112, 141, 148, 154
Burris, V.L., 10, 13–14, 40, 54n,
66, 86, 98, 112–14, 131–2,
188, 190
bus, 31, 34, 130, 138, 144, 151,
158–69 *passim*, 170–3, 175
bus driver, 29–53 *passim*, 59–63,
130–1, 158–9, 161–74, 176–8,
190–1
business, 29, 37, 39, 48, 52, 172
buy, 8, 10, 13, 18, 38–9, 46, 56,
60–2, 73, 79–80, 86, 90–2, 95,
98, 101–6, 108, 110–11, 129,
132–4, 141, 143, 152, 154–6,
166, 168, 172, 175, 177–8,
182, 191, 193, 200
buyer, 172, 180
buying and selling, 5, 8, 10, 15–19,
28, 40, 86, 88, 98–108 *passim*,
113, 115, 117–20, 122–4,
127–9, 146, 149, 151, 157,
177, 179–82, 184, 186–9,
196, 205–6, 209–15

capital, 46, 48, 143
car, 11, 72, 100, 103–4, 106,
109–13, 145, 147, 160, 165,
173, 176, 190
Carugati, F., 4
Case, R., 24, 175
centration, 77, 117–18, 127
ceramic tiles, 42, 44–5, 48–9
chair, 36, 193–5
change, 16–17, 30, 32, 34–5, 40,
60, 63–4, 66, 98, 100–2,
104–8, 115–16, 126, 131,
133, 165, 176–80, 182
characteristics of objects, 11–12, 21,
52, 58, 109–10, 112–13,
115–17, 123,179
characteristics of work, 59, 67, 126

charity, 22, 36, 98, 191–2, 212–13
Chatel, C., 68n
Chinese 186–7
chocolate, 100, 102–5
circulation of money, 26, 29, 37,
83–4, 87, 126, 128, 168, 180
city, 30, 38, 71, 118, 122, 162,
199
class,
dominant, 2
lower, 21–2, 180, 198
middle, 11, 20–1, 23, 29n, 49,
73–4, 77, 92, 99n, 126, 133n,
180, 189–91, 198
social, 1–2, 11–14, 20–3, 76–7,
118, 122, 136, 162, 190, 199
upper, 29n, 190, 198
working, 22, 54, 68–9, 108n,
126, 183, 187n, 190
classification, 7, 14, 67, 113, 185
clerk, 34, 47, 52, 76, 78n
client, 9, 67, 192
cloth, 89, 91, 95–6
clothes, 51, 63, 90–8 *passim*, 118,
145, 174, 193–5, 197, 199,
211
worker's, 43, 178
cognition, 3–6, 19, 24, 58, 96
cognitive ability, 22–3, 96, 134–5,
179, 198
cognitive construction, 76, 87, 120,
134, 136–7, 177, 202–8
passim, 217
cognitive development, 27, 171,
187, 197, 203, 206, 216
cognitive-developmental, 4–5, 14,
20–3
cognitive instruments, 76, 182, 192
cognitive operations, 16–17, 23–4,
51, 84, 107, 135, 137,
178–84, 203
cognitive prerequisites, 207–216
passim
cognitive structure, 5–6, 19, 137,
197
coins, 8–9, 99–100, 103, 116
comic, 99–100, 104, 106, 114–16,
118–20, 122–5, 127, 185
command, 135–6, 181
commerce, 10, 17, 90, 114, 115,
118, 122, 130, 139, 158, 169,
180, 183, 187

commercial exchange, 27, 86, 180
commodity, 10, 113
common sense, 25, 163
communication, 158, 187
communism, 3
compensation, 67, 105
concept,
  economic, 3, 7, 11, 14, 17, 19,
    20, 23–4, 26, 28, 163,
    174–217 *passim*
  physical, 15–19, 23–4, 137, 205,
    214
  political, 134–8 *passim*
  social, 7, 14, 19, 54
concrete, 9, 13, 18, 53, 58, 100,
  109, 170, 185
concrete operations, 15–16, 84,
  135, 137, 179–84
conflict, 17–18, 109, 172, 203–4,
  206–10, 212, 216
  interpersonal, 206–8
  intrapersonal, 208
  of interest, 9, 176
  of opinion, 136
Connell, R.W., 7, 12–13, 22, 68,
  75–7, 135–8, 163–4, 190, 196
conservation, 24, 118, 205
consumer, 2, 30, 33, 37, 113, 120,
  123, 147, 164, 168, 175–6,
  178–9, 181
consumption, 26, 108, 114, 116,
  152, 157–8, 182
contiguity, 170
contradiction, 19, 23, 118, 128,
  203–4, 213
convention, 6, 175
conversation, 4–6, 17, 54
co-operation, 214
co-ordination, 37–9, 51, 79, 82, 85,
  114, 117, 127–9, 168–9,
  182–5, 200, 206
corn, 138, 153–7
correspondence, 100–1, 104–5,
  107–8, 176–7, 179–82, 185
cost, 8, 73, 99, 104–6, 108–14,
  120–3, 126, 128, 148, 180,
  185, 199–201, 207, 212–15
cost of labour, 109, 114, 122,
  127–8, 180, 183–4
cost of materials, 109, 111, 114,
  122, 183
cost of production, 111, 113, 122,
  127–8, 149, 180, 184

council, 33, 36, 38–9, 43, 45, 47–8,
  56, 65, 79, 81–2, 114, 131,
  141–2, 144, 146, 148–50,
  155, 158–63, 165–7, 171,
  183–4, 191
councillor, 38, 74, 162n
country, 52, 75
countryside, 30, 38, 46, 122, 138,
  152–3, 164, 170–1, 174
cow, 113, 153, 175
Cowan, P.A., 94, 177
credit, 9
cross-cultural, 7, 25, 186–9, 196
cross-sectional, 26, 174, 186, 198,
  201–2
cultivation, 45, 51, 96, 122, 152–3,
  155–6, 162, 172
cultural differences, 163, 196
cultural influences, 21, 25, 186–95
  passim
Cummings, S., 2–3
curriculum, 42, 198–200, 202, 216
customer, 7–9, 14, 16–18, 30–1,
  33, 37, 39–40, 84, 98, 101–2,
  105–6, 108, 111, 114–16,
  118, 127, 175, 178, 192,
  196–7, 206–9, 213–15

Damon, W., 4, 58, 67
Danziger, K., 7, 10, 12–13, 18–20,
  23, 28–9, 40, 54, 57, 68, 75,
  86, 98, 114, 188
Dasen, P., 187
Day, J., 3–4
De Beni, R., 7, 208, 214
De Bernardi, F., 133n
debt, 87, 162
décalage, 86, 137, 174
decentration, 4–5, 76
demand, 51, 123
department store, 95, 199, 201
deposit, 11, 78–87, 182–5, 203,
  205–6, 214
desire, 58, 176
development, 2, 4, 6–7, 14–15,
  17–20, 23, 26, 28, 54, 57, 67,
  76, 86, 88, 94–5, 98, 99, 126,
  128, 169–73 *passim*, 174–5,
  182, 186–7, 195, 197, 201,
  203, 206, 210, 214–16
developmental processes, 24, 76,
  202, 204, 216
developmental progress, 207–8

developmental sequence, 6–7, 9–10,
  14–15, 19, 22, 25, 27, 77,
  125, 130, 151, 169, 174,
  186–9, 202, 214, 217
developmental stage, 7–9, 13–14,
  17–19, 23–4, 132, 135, 137,
  186, 188, 201, 204
developmental transition 7, 25–6,
  119, 200–8 *passim*
Dickinson, J., 7, 12, 20–3, 76–7,
  197
differentiation, 12–14, 16–17, 19,
  21, 38–9, 51, 56, 58, 67, 92,
  103, 124, 134, 136, 140, 143,
  151, 158–9, 168–9, 175,
  179–81, 205, 216
dimensions, 104
discrimination, 12, 104
distribution, 127, 196, 199, 200
distribution of goods, 90–4 *passim*,
  158, 176, 178, 184
distribution of money, 11, 176
distribution of services, 26–7, 176
doctor, 12, 29–53 *passim*, 178
Doise, W., 206
domain, 6, 24, 205
dramatic contrast, 13, 22, 75
driver, 12, 96, 117–19
  bus, 29–53 *passim*, 59–63, 130–1,
    158–9, 161–74, 176–8, 190–1
  train, 60, 62–3, 133
dustman, 60–1, 63–4, 176
Duveen, G., 7, 12, 28, 40, 65–6,
  75n

earn, 73, 84, 98, 148, 214
earnings, 73–4, 76, 146, 202, 209,
  213
eat, 63, 69–71, 111, 118, 156–7,
  164, 211, 213
Echeita, G., 7, 206–8
economic activities, 2, 94, 156, 160,
  205
economic actors, 1, 120, 122, 124,
  128
economic chain, 114, 196
economic concepts, 3, 7, 11, 14, 19,
  20, 23–4, 26, 28, 163,
  174–217 *passim*
economic exchanges, 10, 28, 37–9,
  88, 94, 164, 175, 183–4, 198
economic figures, 38, 90–1, 94,
  176–7, 194

economic reality, 25–6, 36, 39, 169,
  176, 178
economic relations, 6, 9–10, 17–18,
  23, 30, 33, 37, 54, 106,
  126–7, 134, 205
economic roles, 7, 10, 14, 25, 88,
  168, 215
economic sectors, 26, 29–30, 41n,
  130, 199
economic stratification, 7, 73,
  180–3
economic subject, 2, 20, 134, 215
economic system, 17, 20, 88, 168
economic understanding, 2, 7,
  14–15, 23–4, 26, 67, 88,
  202–8 *passim*
economics, 198
education, 12
educational influence, 186
educational intervention, 25, 202,
  216–17
educational research, 197–202
effort, 182–3
egalitarianism, 22
egocentrism, 4, 67, 76, 152, 164,
  177, 179, 181, 184
election, 47–8, 53, 131, 135–6,
  144, 158, 160–4
Emiliani, F., 4
Emler, N., 7, 12, 20–3, 76–7, 197
employee, 8–9, 32–3, 35–7, 39–40,
  47, 61, 65, 145, 147, 152,
  164, 196
employer, 8, 32, 36, 179
employment, 28, 38, 41–5, 178,
  199
  self–, 41, 42, 45, 183, 199
enrolment tax, 34, 45
environment, 3, 5, 20–1, 76–7,
  135, 188–9, 192, 195–7
epistemic, 24
equality, 203, 212
equilibration, 16–17, 23, 204, 206,
  214
equity, 20
equivalence, 118, 182
Europe, 189
exchange, 7, 10, 23, 25, 28, 33, 62,
  67, 80, 85, 88, 94, 102, 106,
  115, 120, 127, 143, 147–8,
  164, 175–7, 179, 181, 183–5,
  198, 215
  commercial, 27, 86, 180

exchange (*cont.*)
  monetary, 7–8, 28, 30–3, 37, 39,
    116, 126, 179
  network of, 2, 7, 23, 113, 127
expenditure, 127, 149, 200, 213
expenses, 209, 212, 213
experience, 5–6, 11, 17–18, 25, 54,
    57, 60, 71, 77, 86–7, 94, 100,
    126, 128–9, 167–8, 170–2,
    177–8, 182–5, 190, 193,
    196–8, 202, 204
explanation, 13, 19–22, 24, 76, 94,
    98, 106, 108–10, 112, 128,
    134, 143, 147, 159, 172, 179,
    199, 201, 212, 215

factory, 10, 17, 36–37, 42–58
    passim, 64, 69, 72, 74, 92, 96,
    116, 119–20, 122, 127–8,
    130, 138–51 *passim*, 157, 160,
    162, 164, 167, 169–72, 174,
    180, 182, 199, 201
factory owner, 7, 38, 42–3, 46–9,
    52, 54–8 *passim*, 139–51
    passim, 160, 172, 174, 183,
    196
factory worker, 29–53 *passim*, 76,
    78n, 139, 190, 192–3
fair, 87, 123–4, 180
fair price, 117, 126
family, 4, 11–12, 17, 21, 29n,
    68–71, 74, 76–7, 135, 181,
    190, 197, 200
farmer, 117–18, 121–3, 128, 138,
    151–8 *passim*, 162, 164, 168,
    170–1, 187, 190–1, 200, 202
farmland, 151–8 *passim*, 162
farm worker, 29–53 *passim*, 63, 76,
    92, 94, 96, 152–6, 171, 178,
    192–3
father's work, 54–8 *passim*, 60–2,
    67, 71, 126, 138–40, 171,
    175, 190
fatigue, 74, 76–7
Fiat, 190–2, 196–7
field, 32, 138, 151–7, 162, 170–2,
    175
finalism, 64–7, 78, 89, 126–7, 156,
    177, 179–81, 184, 189–90
Fincato, S., 90n
Fiora, A., 190n, 197n
Flavell, J., 3, 179

food, 36, 72, 111, 118, 141, 154,
    156, 178, 191
formal operations, 5, 14, 16, 18, 85,
    129, 136, 182–5 *passim*
fraud, 9, 70
Frezzato, A., 133n
friend, 4, 17, 30, 32–3, 36, 39, 47,
    87, 116, 139–41, 144, 152,
    160, 181, 207–9, 212
friendship, 205, 214
fruit, 37, 92, 96, 116, 118, 122,
    152, 154, 156, 197
Furby, L., 7, 14, 77, 131–2
Furnham, A., 7, 20
furniture, 80, 144, 150
Furth, H.G., 7, 10–11, 14–19, 23,
    26, 41, 86, 88, 98, 114,
    124–5, 130, 134, 138, 187–9,
    202, 204, 206

generalisation, 35–7, 39, 67, 86,
    126, 171, 190, 200, 202,
    204
gift, 17, 70, 132–3
Glasgow, 126, 187
glass, 89–97 *passim*, 149, 174,
    193–5, 197
God, 52, 134, 190
gold, 13, 109–12, 190
Goldstein, B., 1, 12, 20, 22, 28–9,
    41, 54, 58, 67–8, 75, 88–9,
    92, 190
goods, 1, 8, 10, 16, 26, 39, 69, 86,
    88–131 *passim*, 168, 175–9,
    182–3, 193, 199–201, 205–6,
    216
  characteristics of, 115, 179, 180
  distribution of, 90–4 *passim*, 158,
    176, 178, 184
  exchange of, 7, 179
  payment for, 16, 18, 88, 98, 99,
    101–8, 115–21, 127, 147–8,
    169, 175, 177, 180–1, 209–15
  price of, 9, 16, 25, 88, 149, 180,
    183, 186
  sale of, 8, 10–11, 13, 16, 29–31,
    33, 37–8, 88–90, 127–8, 146,
    181, 187, 190, 200, 207, 209
  source of, 27, 88–98 *passim*, 116,
    126–7, 130, 151, 174, 176,
    180, 186, 189, 193–6
government, 10, 39, 74, 79, 87,

134–5, 144, 160, 162, 168, 184, 190, 203
grain, 46, 157
grapes, 31, 153–4, 156–7
greengrocer, 33, 92, 96, 114–17, 121, 157–8, 214
Greenstein, F.I., 134
groupings, 137
grow, 63, 123, 153, 155–7

hairdresser, 30, 34, 202
handkerchief, 209–13
harvest, 31, 96, 158
headteacher, 18, 37–8, 54–6, 174
Heider, F., 4
Heron, A., 187
hierarchical relations, 33–7, 39, 52
hierarchy, 25, 57–8, 130, 136–7, 181, 183, 185
Hogan, H.W., 7, 11
home, 34–6, 44, 46, 62, 71, 81, 83, 90–1, 93–4, 136, 140–1, 146, 171, 180
Hong Kong, 188, 205
Hong Kwan, T. 7, 186, 188, 197
house, 11, 31–2, 36, 45–6, 52, 56, 64, 66, 70, 72, 79–80, 91, 112, 142, 154–6, 160, 175, 179
household 82–3
human activity, 68, 89–90, 98, 118
hypothetico-deductive, 16, 216

ideology, 136–7
illegality, 70, 73–4
income, 2, 12, 21, 68, 116, 149, 165, 184, 192, 212, 214–15
levels of, 59, 71, 76, 180, 190
industrial, 27, 53, 150, 160, 168, 176, 178–9, 183
industrialist, 20, 36, 76, 127–8, 130, 180, 183
industry, 26, 49, 51, 118, 130, 143, 172
influence, 1, 4
cultural, 25, 186–95 *passim*
educational 186
environmental, 20, 189, 195–7
social, 21, 186
information, 25, 76, 128–9, 134–5, 182, 196–7, 199, 208, 210
free-floating, 76–7, 196

Inhelder, B., 15, 24, 129, 174, 206, 209
inherit, 13, 74
institution, 54, 56, 78, 114, 131, 160, 163, 184
charitable, 191–2
political, 23, 131, 134, 136, 144, 162, 217
public, 38, 117, 121, 123, 158–9, 184, 217
social, 6, 15, 127, 138
instruction, 197, 201
integration, 127–9, 136–7, 168, 176, 186, 203
intelligence, 6, 14–15, 20, 76
interaction, 3, 5–6, 25
interest, 11, 78–80, 83–7, 184–5, 188, 206, 214
intermediate figure, 9, 90, 114–16, 120, 124, 126, 180, 183, 200
interpersonal, 16, 206
conflict, 206–8
interaction, 25
norms, 17, 203
relations, 5, 87, 205, 214
intervention, 25, 202, 208, 216–17
interview, 7, 10, 22, 26–7, 29, 42, 54, 60, 65, 68, 78, 90, 99–100, 108, 114, 133, 135, 138, 190, 197n, 202
intrapersonal, 206, 208
intuitive, 177–9
invariance, 115, 117, 180, 205
Israel, 14
Italian, language, 31n, 36n, 37n, 42n, 45n, 48n, 84n, 90n, 133n, 191n
Italy, 29n, 54n, 74n, 78n, 91n, 131n, 161n, 162n, 164, 188–9, 198, 216

Jahoda, G., 7, 10–11, 14–17, 26, 28–9, 40, 78, 85–6, 88, 98, 114, 124–5, 127, 187–90, 197, 202–6, 214
job, 12, 29–30, 33, 35–6, 38, 41–53 *passim*, 60, 64, 67, 71–5, 77, 122, 127, 134, 166, 173, 175, 181
Johnson-Laird, P., 132–3, 169
judgement, 3–4, 21, 76, 85, 100, 109

justice, 76
justification, 13–14, 20, 64, 86,
    102, 108, 110, 112, 117, 126,
    134, 143, 152, 172, 215

knowledge, 5, 15, 21, 23, 171
Kohlberg, L., 4

labour,
    cost of, 109, 114, 122, 127–8,
        180, 183–4
    division of, 26, 40, 51
    supply of, 51
labourer, 46, 51, 73–4, 92, 143
land, 45–6, 51–2, 112, 152, 154–7,
    162, 167, 175, 179
Laurendeau, M., 5n, 174
law, 2, 64, 124, 134, 136, 161,
    175
Lea, S.G., 1–2
Leahy, R.L., 7, 12–13, 20, 22, 76–7
Leiser, D., 10–11, 19–20, 23, 88,
    215
lend, 79, 81–5, 182, 203, 205
Leone, G., 74n
lettuce, 30, 109, 153–4
Lewin, K., 4
Lickona, T., 4
linguistic, 24, 29, 65
Lis, A., 197n
Livesley, W.J., 4, 12
loan, 133
    bank, 35, 78–87, 175, 182–85,
        188, 205–6, 213
logic, 18, 20, 204
logical abilities, 26
logical development, 67
logical multiplication, 135
logical operations, 107, 176
logical relations, 129
logico-mathematical, 214, 216
longitudinal, 107, 174, 186, 198
lorry, 64, 92, 95–6, 112, 117–19,
    133
Lo Scalzo, M., 108n

machine, 43, 48–9, 56, 95–6,
    111–12, 114, 141–4, 147,
    172, 191
management, 9, 53, 171
manufacturer, 8–9, 14, 89, 94
Marghera, 138, 158–60, 166, 171

market, 123, 158
mass-media, 5–6, 17, 196–8, 216
Marx, K. (also marxist), 2, 13, 20
materials, 89–90, 143, 156
    cost of, 109, 111, 114, 122, 183
    raw, 9, 90, 94–8, 111, 114, 172,
        177, 180, 194–6
    recycled, 95–8, 195
mayor, 41–53 *passim*, 135–6, 160–2
Mead, G.H., 4
means of communication, 158
means of production, 5, 25, 27,
    130–74 *passim*, 178, 181,
    183–4, 197, 199
means of work, 133, 179
mediation, 38, 168
merchant, 130, 189–93 *passim*
Mestre, 160
Mezzogiorno, 45n
middle-class, 11–12, 20–1, 23, 29n,
    49, 73–4, 77, 92, 99n, 126,
    133n, 180, 189–91, 198
middleman, 180–1
Migazzi, M., 192n
Milan, 161
Miller, G.A., 132–3, 169
minister, 74, 123–4, 135–6, 160–1,
    163–4
monetary exchange, 7–8, 28, 30–3,
    37, 39, 116, 126, 179
monetary meaning, 7, 9
money, 8–11, 13, 16–18, 29–40
    passim, 41, 45–6, 49, 59–87
    passim, 130–1, 133–4, 139–40,
    144, 146–51, 155, 157,
    164–9, 173, 175–86, 196,
    200, 203, 205, 209–15
    availability of, 9, 23, 68, 76
    circulation of, 26, 29, 37, 83–4,
        87, 126, 128, 168, 180
    goods and, 88–129 *passim*, 179,
        200
    in buying and selling, 9, 88,
        98–108 *passim*, 174, 176, 180,
        182
    source of, 13, 27, 33, 39, 59–67
        passim, 70, 78–9, 81–2, 84–5,
        87, 124, 126–8, 131, 145–6,
        167, 176, 178–83, 186,
        189–93 *passim*, 197, 203,
        212–13
Montedison, 140, 142–3, 146–9

Mookherjee, H.N. 7, 11
morality, 4, 9, 19, 64, 66, 117, 123
Moscovici, S. 21
Mugny, G., 206
Murano, 141

Naples, 1
natural resources, 98, 183
natural phenomena, 52, 65, 89, 95,
     177
needs, 69, 98, 131–2, 177
Nelson, K., 66
Netherlands, 187–9
network,
     monetary, 9
network of exchanges, 2, 7, 23, 113,
     127
network of relations, 10, 14, 168
Ng, S.H., 7, 188, 204–6
normal, 75, 181
norms, 6, 87, 113, 203, 205
number, 99, 103–4, 107, 137
nursery, 6, 26, 54

object, 8
     characteristics of, 11–12, 21, 52,
        58, 109–10, 113, 115–17,
        123, 179
     concrete, 58
     manufactured, 89–90, 96
     physical, 15, 25
obligation, 64, 102, 165
     reciprocal, 102, 132
occupation, 1, 13, 21, 28, 36, 40,
        42–3, 45, 49, 51, 60–1, 130,
        183, 191–3
     parental, 21, 30, 60
office, 30–1, 43, 62–3, 66, 73
old, 70, 72, 178
Oldham, J., 1, 12, 20–2, 28–9, 41,
        54, 58, 67–8, 75, 88–9, 92,
        190
O'Neil, R.P., 135
operations, 16–17, 23–4, 51, 84,
        107, 135, 137, 178–84, 203
     arithmetical, 99, 107, 215
     classification, 7, 14, 67, 113, 185
     concrete, 15–16, 84, 135, 137,
        179–84
     compensatory, 67
     correspondence, 100–1, 104–5,
        107–8, 176–7, 179–82, 185

formal, 5, 14, 16, 18, 85, 129,
        136, 182–5 *passim*
     logical, 107, 176
     seriation, 7, 12, 58, 108, 182,
        185
opinions, 136–7, 183
orders, 54–5, 57, 148
origins, 52–3, 65, 78, 89–91, 94–8
        passim, 114, 128, 130, 174,
        177, 182, 186, 189, 195, 197
overheads, 199, 201
Overton, W.F., 4
owner, 11, 51–5, 58, 116, 133–4,
        138, 169, 171–5, 178, 181,
        184–5, 206
     factory, 7, 38, 42–3, 46–9, 52,
        54–8 *passim*, 139–51 *passim*,
        160, 172, 174, 183, 196
     private, 39, 158, 162, 184
owner-boss, 48, 54–8 *passim*, 139,
        142, 145, 166, 168, 172
owner-builder, 47–8
ownership, 27, 73, 84n, 131–4
        passim, 169–73 *passim*, 179
     of agricultural land 138, 151–8
        passim
     of buses, 130, 138, 144, 158–64
        passim
     of factories, 138–51 *passim*
     of means of production, 130–74
        passim, 197, 199

Padova, 54n, 60n, 78n, 90, 114n,
        190–1, 194–5, 197n
paired comparisons, 7, 12, 75n,
        109, 112
paper, 97, 103, 118–19, 122, 185
parallelism, 24, 162
parents, 1, 12, 52, 54, 60–1, 66,
        94, 186–7, 189–90, 192–3,
        196–7
Parsons, T., 20
passenger, 131, 158, 162, 164–5,
        167, 170, 175
pay, 21–2, 28, 39, 72, 82, 86–7,
        183
payment, 8–10, 12, 16, 38, 43, 48,
        51, 78–9, 130, 143, 155,
        165–8, 175, 177–9, 189,
        196–7
     as an obligation, 64, 102
     for goods, 16, 18, 88, 98, 99,

payment (*cont.*)
   101–8, 115–21, 127, 147–8,
      169, 175, 177, 180–1,
      209–15
   for services, 9, 23, 175
   for work, 9–10, 21–2, 26–8,
      29–40 *passim*, 49, 51, 59–67,
      72, 74, 77, 87, 92, 112, 117,
      124, 126–8, 131, 144,
      147–50, 168–9, 172, 175–7,
      179–80, 182–5, 190–2, 197,
      203
peach, 90–8 *passim*, 157, 174,
   193–5
personalistic, 13, 17
Petrillo, G., 1
physical domain, 15–19, 23–4, 137,
   205, 214
Piaget, J. (also Piagetian), 4, 5,
   14–16, 18–19, 22–7, 41, 51–2,
   58, 65, 85, 89–90, 94,
   99–100, 129, 133, 135, 137,
   174–5, 177–9, 187, 206, 214,
   216
Pinard, A., 5n, 174
plant, 153, 155–6
plastic bags, 148–9
play, 111, 152–3
police, 12, 40, 63–4, 73, 105, 165,
   178
political concepts, 134–8
political institutions, 23, 131, 134,
   136, 144, 162, 217
political roles, 134–6
politics, 4–5, 74, 135, 163
poor, 11–13, 20–3, 35–6, 67–77
   passim, 111, 181, 190
posession, 13, 58, 66, 132–3, 143,
   169–70, 178
   personal, 14, 132
posession of goods, 9, 69, 169
poverty, 10, 12–13, 19–20, 22, 27,
   59, 67–77 *passim*, 126, 174,
   176, 178–81, 183, 186
power, 4, 58, 136, 144, 160, 182
pre-economic, 179, 181, 184
preoperatory, 15, 22, 51, 175–7,
   179
prerequisites, 207–16 *passim*
preschoolers, 41, 74–5, 175, 190
president, 135–6, 161n, 162n
prestige, 12, 183
price, 9, 17, 27, 38, 99–101, 104,
   107–8, 177, 179–80, 182,
      199–200, 206–7
   fair, 117
   formation of 9, 28, 114–29
      passim, 168–9, 174, 179, 185,
      200, 207, 209–16
   of goods, 9, 16, 25, 88, 149, 180,
      183, 186
   retail, 15, 184, 200–1, 207–9,
      212
   variations of 88, 107–14 *passim*,
      177, 199–201
   wholesale, 15, 200–1, 207–8,
      212
price-rule, 199
prison, 98, 102, 105, 175
private economic sector, 29, 38, 134
private ownership, 39, 158, 162,
   184
private property, 3, 134
privilege, 20, 71
producer, 2, 89–90, 92–3, 95–6,
   114–18, 120–1, 124–8, 130,
   168, 179–81, 194–5, 216
   shopkeeper, 91–2, 94
product, 16, 96, 141, 143, 146–7,
   164, 168–9, 172, 180, 183–5,
   187
production, 26, 28, 30, 88–9, 91–2,
   94, 108–9, 111, 113–14, 116,
   118, 120–2, 127–32, 146,
   150–1, 176, 180, 182–4,
   193–4, 196, 199
   agricultural, 49, 51, 130, 138,
      151–8 *passim*, 171, 178, 200
   cost of, 111, 113, 122, 127–8,
      149, 180, 184
   industrial, 49, 51, 118, 130, 138
   means of, 5, 25, 27, 130–74
      passim, 178, 181, 183–4, 197,
      199
production cycle, 189, 193–5, 199
progress, 207–8
profit, 9, 11, 16, 85–6, 88, 114,
   120, 122, 124, 127, 130, 178,
   183, 186–9, 200, 203–16
property, 3, 21, 132, 158
proximity, 133–4, 145, 152, 154,
   156, 170–2, 179
Pryor, J., 3, 4
public economic sector, 29, 38, 134
public institution, 38, 117, 121,
   123, 158–9, 184, 217

public ownership, 144, 158
public transport, 27, 158, 174

qualification, 74, 178
qualitative, 14, 25, 177, 179, 195,
    200–1, 210
quality, 110, 118, 120–2, 126,
    200–1, 216
quantification, 118, 128, 176, 178,
    182
quantitative, 104, 179–80, 200
quantity, 115, 118, 149, 157,
    180–1, 184, 205, 216
Queen, 134–6, 163

raw materials, 9, 90, 94–8, 111,
    114, 172, 177, 180, 194–6
realism, 13, 41, 51, 172, 179, 181,
    184
reciprocity, 17, 19, 87, 203, 214
recycle, 95–8, 142, 178, 183, 194
regulation, 13, 17, 59, 70, 77, 87,
    113, 205
relations, 87, 130, 179, 215
    asymmetrical, 54, 137, 181
    economic 6, 9–10, 17–18, 23, 30,
        33, 37, 54, 106, 126–7, 134,
        205
    interpersonal, 5, 87, 205, 214
    logical, 129
    network of, 10, 14, 168
    power, 58, 182
    reciprocal, 178
    social, 38, 67, 76, 113, 137, 205
    symmetrical, 39
    systems of, 18–19, 23
remuneration, 13, 28, 36, 59–60,
    64, 67, 75n, 88, 175, 177,
    179–80, 182, 193
Renshon, S.A., 134
repair, 90, 141–2, 147, 181, 183
repayment, 182, 185, 203
replenish, 89, 114–15, 209, 211
representation, 8, 12–15, 19, 25–6,
    33, 37, 39–40, 49, 53–4, 58,
    60, 66, 77–8, 90, 94, 96–8,
    113, 115, 124, 128, 131, 144,
    146, 152, 154, 160, 168, 171,
    178, 181, 183–5, 215
    social, 21–2, 77, 188n
requirements, 1, 44, 51, 56, 58
research design, 26, 107, 174, 186,
    198, 201–2

Rest, J., 4
retail, 98, 113–17, 120, 122, 124,
    127, 130, 175, 187, 189, 196,
    198, 200, 204, 213
retail price, 15, 184, 200–1, 207–9,
    212
retailer, 89, 118, 121
retributive, 13, 64, 67, 76
rich, 12–13, 20–1, 23, 35, 39,
    67–77 *passim*, 87, 131, 144,
    166, 173, 176, 178, 181
rights, 132–3
risk, 72–3
road sweeper, 31, 34–5, 62–3, 133
role, 8, 10, 14, 16, 19–20, 43, 46,
    51–3, 55, 57–8, 101–2, 130,
    206
    economic, 7, 10, 14, 25, 88, 168,
        215
    political, 134–6
    social, 10, 51, 94, 181
    work, 1, 28–9, 40–53 *passim*,
        130, 134, 154, 179
role-taking, 4, 14
Ross, L., 3
rule, 4, 8, 16–17, 86, 98, 101, 177,
    179–80, 199, 208, 214
Ryba, R., 188n

safe, 79, 183
salary, 73, 83, 169
sale of goods, 8, 10–11, 13, 16, 18,
    29–31, 33, 37–8, 88–90,
    127–8, 146, 181, 187, 190,
    200, 207, 209
sale of products, 146–9, 152–4,
    156–7, 169, 183–5, 187,
    199–200
sales, 200–1
salesman, 40, 78n
save 1, 13, 73, 82
savers, 2, 79, 184
savings, 10, 31, 79, 82, 85, 181
scarcity, 109, 112
school, 4, 6, 17–18, 21, 26, 29n,
    34, 54–8 *passim*, 61, 67, 116,
    133, 135–6, 149, 160, 163,
    171, 174, 197–8, 208, 216
Scotland, 188
scripts, 19, 66–7, 106, 175–6
Searle, J.R., 6
sector,
    economic, 26, 29, 30, 130

self-employment, 41–2, 45, 183, 199
selling, 9, 11, 17, 31, 37, 74, 84n, 92, 102, 106, 113, 128–9, 132, 142–3, 148, 150, 164, 168, 177–8, 180, 197
  buying and, 5, 8, 10, 15–19, 28, 40, 86, 88, 98–108 *passim*, 113, 115, 117–20, 122–4, 127–9, 146, 149, 151, 157, 177, 179–82, 184, 186–9, 196, 205–6, 209–15
Selman, R., 5, 12
seriation, 7, 12, 58, 108, 182, 185
Serino, C. 1.
services, 9, 16, 26–7, 30–1, 33, 37, 39, 127–8, 130–1, 168, 175, 177, 179, 181, 184, 199
Shantz, C., 3–4
Shields, M., 7, 12, 28, 40, 65–6, 75n
shop, 8–10, 30, 33, 36, 60, 62–4, 66–8, 70, 81, 85–6, 90–5, 98, 100–3, 105–6, 109–10, 114–16, 120–2, 124–5, 127, 143–4, 148–50, 158, 175–80, 184, 190, 194, 199–201, 206, 211
shop assistant, 7–8, 10, 14, 16, 124, 203
shopkeeper, 7–12, 14, 16–18, 31, 36, 40, 62, 85–6, 88–94, 96–8, 100–2, 104–6, 109, 111, 115–22, 124–7, 130, 148–9, 151, 158, 176–7, 179, 181–2, 186–7, 190–1, 194–5, 200, 202, 206–16
shop owner, 8–9, 18, 41–53 *passim*, 203
shopworker, 29, 40–53 *passim*
Siegal, M., 7, 12–13
Siegler, R.S., 24
Sinclair, H., 206, 209
size, 103, 109–10, 113, 120
Smith, J.E. 7, 10, 15, 88, 98, 124, 130, 134
social, 24, 65, 75, 130, 137
social categories, 11
social class, 1–2, 11–14, 20–3, 76–7, 118, 122, 126, 136, 162, 190, 199
social cognition, 3–6, 23
social concept 7, 14, 19, 54

social groups, 76–7, 163
social influence, 21, 186
social institution, 6, 15, 138, 217
social interaction, 21, 206–8 *passim*
social knowledge, 5, 21
social life, 6, 134–5
social position, 76, 181
social relations, 38, 67, 76, 113, 137, 205
social representations, 21–2, 77, 188n
social roles, 10, 51, 94, 181
social security, 124, 126, 190
social stratification, 2, 11, 20, 22–3, 28, 67, 71, 75n, 77, 183
social world, 4, 6, 21, 75n, 135, 217
socialisation, 3, 5, 131, 134
socialism, 3
societal, 5–6, 15–18, 20, 87, 205
society, 6, 136, 183
sociocentric, 12
socioeconomic, 74, 77, 164, 188, 205
source of goods, 27, 88–98 *passim*, 116, 126–7, 130, 151, 174, 176, 180, 186, 189, 193–6
source of money, 13, 27, 33, 39, 59–67 *passim*, 70, 78–9, 81–2, 84–5, 87, 124, 126–8, 131, 145–6, 167, 176, 178–83, 186, 189–93 *passim*, 197, 203, 212–13
spend, 1, 9, 73, 110, 115, 122, 124
Stacey, B., 1, 7, 134, 186, 188, 197
stage,
  developmental 7–9, 13–14, 17–19, 23–4, 132, 135, 137, 186, 188, 201, 204
  concrete operatory, 15–16, 135, 179–83
  formal operatory, 15–16, 18, 136, 183–5
  preoperatory, 15, 22, 179
state, 36, 39, 56, 81–2, 87, 114, 131, 142, 144, 148, 150, 155, 158–62, 165, 183–4
status, 21, 53, 181
steal, 10–11, 13, 74, 81, 132
Stendler, C., 11
stock, 89–90, 114, 200–1, 211
Strauss, A. 6–7, 9–11, 14, 28–9, 40, 86, 88, 92, 97, 99, 106–7, 114, 188

strawberries, 123, 214–15
strongbox, 79, 81
structure,
    cognitive, 5–6, 19, 137, 197
structural affinities, 77
structure d'ensemble, 184
subtraction, 99, 108, 120
supervision, 53, 56
supplier, 206, 209–11, 213
supply, 91, 201
supply of labour, 51
surplus, 124
    agricultural, 152, 156–7
Sutton, R.S., 10–11
sweets, 8, 62, 99–100, 102
synchronous, 67
syncretic, 51, 58, 134, 147, 170–1,
    178
system, 13, 15, 17–19, 25, 38,
    127–9, 132, 169, 184
    economic, 17, 20, 88, 168
system of buying and selling, 127n,
    128–9, 149, 151
system of profit, 16, 127
system of relations, 18–19, 23
system of work, 16, 127–9, 151

Taebel, D., 2–3
Tarpy, R.M. 1–2
tax, 38, 40, 81–3, 160, 162, 166–7
    enrolment, 33–4, 45
teaching, 197–8, 201–2
teacher, 29–40 *passim*, 41, 55, 74,
    96, 174, 201n, 216
theft, 9, 70, 79–84, 133, 175, 213
ticket, 31, 130, 140, 164–9
tiles, 42–3, 47–8, 51
till, 81–2, 98, 118, 203
tiredness, 46, 59, 112, 118–19, 180
tools, 45–6, 156, 170–1, 178–9,
    181, 200
trade, 37, 113–17, 124, 126, 130,
    175, 187, 189, 198, 200, 204,
    213
tradesman, 39, 193
trade union, 3
train, 60, 62–3, 133
training, 206, 209–13
transaction, 8, 11, 17, 19, 27, 79,
    98, 106, 108, 115–17,
    119–20, 124, 126, 214
    commercial, 17, 115, 158, 169,
    180

transformation, 7, 134, 215–16
transition,
    developmental, 7, 25–6, 119,
    200–8 *passim*
transport, 27, 43, 130–1, 158–60,
    167, 174, 183
transporter, 115–17, 180, 200
tree, 92, 95–6, 116, 121–2, 133–4,
    155–6, 196–7
Tribe, V., 11
Turiel, E., 3–6, 24–5
Turin, 190, 191n, 196–7
tutorial, 208, 210, 216

unemployment, 44–5, 75, 125,
    190
Università Scuola, 198
use, 80, 82, 132–4, 138, 145–58,
    164–72, 175, 178–9
usefulness, 77, 109, 111, 113, 183

Val di Fiemme, 193–5, 197
Val di Pejo, 192, 196
valorisation, 76
value, 10, 99–101, 104, 107–8,
    112, 176–7, 179–80, 205
value of money, 9, 88, 98–108
    passim, 174, 176, 180, 182
vegetable, 46, 120, 152, 157, 168
Venice, 61, 160, 165–6
verbal, 5–6, 12, 15, 57, 128, 182,
    196–7, 199
visible characteristics, 11, 52
voluntaristic, 19
Vygotsky, L.S., 4

Wackman, D.B., 1
wages, 30, 49, 61, 72, 77, 174
Ward, S., 1
Wartella, E., 1
wealth, 10–14, 19–20, 22, 27, 59,
    67–77 *passim*, 126, 174, 176,
    178, 180–81, 183, 186, 190,
    192
Webley, P., 1–2
well-being, 13, 70, 77
Weil, A.M., 5
Werner, H. 4
Whitehead, D., 198
wholesale, 116, 201
    price, 15, 200–1, 207–8, 212
wholesaler, 89–90, 92, 115,
    117–18, 120–1, 123, 127,
    157, 180, 200

wine, 157, 168
withdrawl, 79, 84, 182–3, 185
Woerdenbagch, A., 7, 188
Wohlgemut, I., 193n
Wong, M.N., 7, 214
wood, 98, 189, 193, 195–6
work, 4, 10, 17–18, 20, 27–8,
    29–59 *passim*, 68–9, 71–6, 86,
    88, 92, 111–13, 116, 118,
    121, 126–7, 129–31, 139,
    141–3, 146–51, 154, 157,
    160, 164, 166, 169, 171, 173,
    175–6, 178–84, 186, 190–3,
    196, 198–9, 202
  access to, 28, 40–53 *passim*, 154,
    179
  as source of money 13, 59–67
    passim, 70, 180, 186, 190
  exchange of, 7, 179
  means of, 133, 179
  payment for, 9–10, 21–2, 26–8,
    29–40 *passim*, 49, 51, 54,
    59–67, 72, 74, 77, 87. 92,
    112, 117, 124, 126–8, 131,

    144, 147–50, 168–9, 172,
    175–7, 179–80, 182–5, 190–2,
    197, 203
  system of, 16, 127–8
work activities, 12, 41, 49, 75n
work role, 1, 28–9, 40–53 *passim*,
    130, 134, 179
worker, 37, 41–53 *passim*, 54, 59,
    64–5, 73–4, 86, 126–7, 130,
    138, 140, 142–51, 161, 164,
    168–72, 179, 181, 183, 185,
    189–93 *passim*
  factory, 29–53 *passim*, 76, 78n,
    139, 190, 192–3
  farm, 29–53, *passim*, 63, 76, 92, 94,
96, 152–6, 171, 178, 192–3
  payment to, 10–11, 29, 112,
    149–50, 182–3
  shop, 40–53 *passim*
working class, 22, 54, 68–9, 108n,
    126, 183, 187n, 190
workshop, 92

Zimbabwe, 187